WEBER PIANOLA GRAND

PIANOS

AND THEIR MAKERS

+

By Alfred Dolge

A COMPREHENSIVE HISTORY OF THE
DEVELOPMENT OF THE PIANO FROM
THE MONOCHORD TO THE CONCERT
GRAND PLAYER PIANO

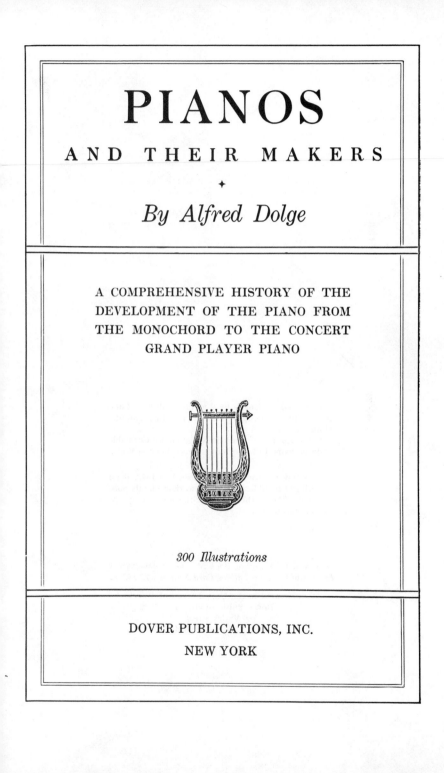

300 Illustrations

DOVER PUBLICATIONS, INC.

NEW YORK

Published in Canada by General Publishing Company, Ltd., 30 Lesmill Road, Don Mills, Toronto, Ontario.

Published in the United Kingdom by Constable and Company, Ltd., 10 Orange Street, London WC 2.

This Dover edition, first published in 1972, is an unabridged republication of the work originally published in 1911 by the Covina Publishing Company, Covina, California.

International Standard Book Number: 0-486-22856-8
Library of Congress Catalog Card Number: 72-188952

Manufactured in the United States of America
Dover Publications, Inc.
180 Varick Street
New York, N.Y. 10014

" I hold every man a debtor to his profession; from the which as men of course do seek to receive countenance and profit, so ought they of duty endeavor themselves by way of amends to be a help and ornament thereto."

FRANCIS BACON.

SEBASTIAN ERARD

After Original Oil Painting by David
Through Courtesy of Mons. A. Blondel

FOREWORD

IN describing the origin and development of the pianoforte, notice has been taken only of such efforts and inventions as lent themselves to evolution, or have stood the test of time. Therefore no mention is made of mere freak instruments, ancient or modern, nor of the many fruitless efforts of inventors whose aim seemed to be merely to produce " something different," either for commercial reasons or to satisfy the cravings of their own imagined genius.

Great pains have been taken, however, to give full credit to those who successfully developed ideas which in their original crudeness seemed impracticable. It often happens, as in the case of the " overstrung system," that an idea is born, tried, discarded, lies dormant for generations, before the genius appears who can render it adaptable for practical use.

It is to be regretted that we are still without guiding laws for the construction of the pianoforte, but the thinking piano maker of the present has the great advantage of past experiments from which to learn *what not to do* in his efforts to improve the piano.

The curiosity hunter, and student who desires more detailed information regarding past experiments in piano construction, will find entertaining and instructive reading in the various publications on the pianoforte enumerated elsewhere.

Great confusion exists among the various writers on the pianoforte regarding the names of the older keyed instruments. Clavicytherium, Clavichord, Spinet, Virginal, and Harpsichord are often confounded with one another, and some writers use " Clavier " for all these instruments.

In order to secure accuracy, I followed the development chronologically, as the most trustworthy authorities record it, aiming always to give a clear description in as few words as possible, because this work is written for those who desire to know, and who do not care merely to be entertained.

Being limited in scope to past events, the author regrets especially that no particular mention could be made of the valuable labors of Henry Ziegler, Frank J. Conover, Richard W. Gertz, Paul G. Mehlin and others, who are earnestly engaged in improving the heritage left us by the masters of the past.

In submitting this volume to the reader, the author desires to express his thanks to Messrs. Theodore C. Steinway, William E. Wheelock, Melville Clark, J. H. White, George B. Kelly, Ludwig Bösendorfer, Josef Herrburger, Jr., Siegfried Hansing, Paul de Wit and Morris Steinert, for their kind and valuable assistance, without which the work would lack much important data.

Covina, California,
April, 1911.

CONTENTS

◆

PART ONE

Technical Development of the Pianoforte

CHAPTER I

CHAPTER II

CHAPTER III

CHAPTER IV

CHAPTER V

PART TWO

Commercial Development of the Piano Industry

CHAPTER I

CHAPTER II

CHAPTER III

CHAPTER IV

CHAPTER V

PART THREE

Men Who Have Made Piano History

CHAPTER I

CHAPTER II

CHAPTER III

PART FOUR

Influence of Piano Virtuosos Upon the Industry

CHAPTER I

CHAPTER II

PART FIVE

CHAPTER I

CHAPTER II

CHAPTER III

CHAPTER IV

APPENDIX

ILLUSTRATIONS

ILLUSTRATIONS

PART ONE

Technical Development of the Pianoforte

CHAPTER I

THE MONOCHORD, Pythagoras, Guido of Arezzo, the Chinese " Ke."
THE CLAVICYTHERIUM, Italy and Germany.
THE CLAVICHORD, Daniel Faber, Bach, Mozart, Beethoven.
THE SPINET, Giovanni Spinnetti.
THE HARPSICHORD and its development.

PIANOS AND THEIR MAKERS

PART ONE

Technical Development of the Pianoforte

CHAPTER I

THE PROTOTYPE OF THE PIANOFORTE

The Monochord

T HIS instrument was used by Pythagoras (582 B. C.) for
experiments regarding the mathematical relations of
musical sounds. A single string, presumably catgut, was
strung over a wooden box. Directly underneath the string a strip
of paper was glued to the top of the box, on which the sections
and subdivisions corresponding with the intervals of the scale
were marked. Pressing the string down upon a given mark, and
then plucking it, a tone was produced, high or low, according to
the place of the scale where the string was held down with the
finger.

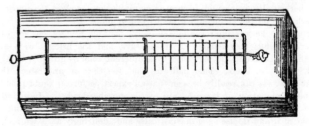

Monochord, 582 B.C.

The monochord came into universal use among the Greeks, and also in the Roman churches as an instrument to sound the keynote for chorus singing. To assure a quicker and especially more correct intonation, Guido of Arezzo (about 100 A. D.) invented the movable bridge under the string of the monochord.*

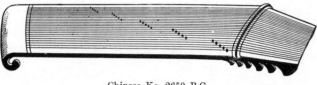

Chinese Ke, 2650 B.C.

After the invention of the movable bridge for the monochord further improvements came rapidly. The clavis (keys), which came in use on church organs shortly after the year 1000 A. D., were applied to the monochord, which then was built with more than one string. Each clavis, or key, had a tangent, or pricker. As soon as the clavis was pressed down, this tangent would prick the string on the proper division of the scale and thus assure the sounding of the correct tone required for the guidance of the singers.

The use of the clavis soon led to an increase in the number of strings and during the 12th and 13th centuries many experiments

---

* The Chinese as early as 2650 B.C. used an instrument called " ke," far superior to the monochord. The ke had fifty strings strung over a wooden box approximately five feet long. Each string was spun of eighty-one fine silk threads, and of such length that an experienced player could, by proper manipulation, produce the upper and lower fifth of each tone on the string which he pricked or plucked.

Later on the ke was improved by the use of movable bridges, one for each string; the number of strings was reduced to twenty-five, and the bridges were arranged in groups of five, each group distinguished by a different color;—group 1, blue; 2, red; 3, yellow; 4, white; 5, black. This indicates that the Chinese understood the relation of colors to tone. It can readily be seen that an expert performer could produce a great variety and combination of tones by aid of the movable bridges. Indeed the Chinese considered the ke the acme of musical instruments, and the virtuosos and masters of the ke spoke of it and its use as enthusiastically and admiringly as Bach and Beethoven spoke of the clavichord nearly 4,000 years later.

were made to construct an instrument which would give all the notes of the scale correctly.

These experiments led finally to the invention of the " clavicytherium."

The Clavicytherium

This is an instrument in which the strings were arranged in the form of a triangle (harp form). The strings were of catgut, and sounded by the pricking of a quill plectra, fastened to the end of the clavis. Fetis believes that the clavicytherium was invented in Italy about 1300 and afterwards copied and improved by the Germans. The efforts to improve the instrument finally developed the " clavichord."

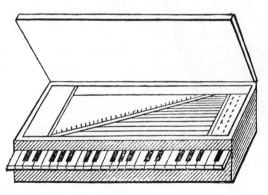

Clavicytherium, 14th Century

The Clavichord

The first clavichords, built during the 15th century, had only 20 or 22 strings of brass, which were made to vibrate, not by plucking or pricking, but by being agitated through the pressure of a tangent (a brass pin flattened on top) fastened to the clavis. The form of the clavichord was similar to the later square piano.

Toward the end of the 16th and the beginning of the 17th century, it was improved so much that it became the favorite keyed instrument of the period. It maintained its supremacy during the 18th century, long after the appearance of the pianoforte. The accompanying picture shows a clavichord with 50 keys (there are some in existence with 77 keys) and a soundboard with 5 bridges, similar to the Chinese ke. The soundboard covers only half of the instrument, the part where the keys are located being open of necessity.

Clavichord, 16th Century

The clavichord usually has more keys than strings, since the tangent, in striking, gives tone and pitch at the same time. Most clavichords have two keys to each string, some three, while on the earlier clavichords we find two tangents fastened to one key, and the performer had to manipulate the key so as to make each tangent strike at the proper place. This was rather difficult and made the execution of any but the simplest compositions almost impossible. Still, it was not until 1725 that a clavichord was constructed by Daniel Faber of Germany, which had a separate string and key for each note. To prevent vibration and consequent irritating sounding of the shorter part of the string when agitated by the tangent, a narrow strip of cloth was interlaced with the strings.

Thus the clavichord possessed four of the most vital points of the modern pianoforte: *The independent soundboard, metal strings, the percussion method of agitating the string,* the tangent touching or striking the string, instead of plucking or pricking, and lastly *the application of the damper.* The greatest improvement was the new method of tone production by which the clavichord became the first keyed instrument enabling the performer to express his individuality.

While the tone of the clavichord was very weak, it was capable of reflecting the most delicate gradation of touch of the player and permitted the execution of most exquisite crescendo and decrescendo. The *klangfarbe* (tone color) of the clavichord was of a very sympathetic, almost spiritual character. Virtuosos like Johann Sebastian Bach and Emanuel Bach produced charming and captivating effects by a trembling pressure of the finger upon the key, holding the notes, thus emphasizing the intention of the player

Clavichord, 17th Century

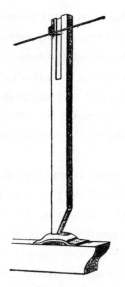

Spinet Jack

in interpreting a composition. In short, the clavichord was the first keyed instrument with a soul. It is not surprising that such masters as Bach, Mozart and even Beethoven preferred the clavichord to the more powerful harpsichord and the early pianoforte. Indeed, Mozart, while traveling about Europe as a piano virtuoso, carried a clavichord with him, for daily practice. Mozart composed his " Magic Flute " and other masterpieces on that instrument.

However, the small, weak, though sweet and musical tone of the clavichord did not satisfy many of the music lovers. They desired an instrument which would speak louder.

The Spinet

About 1503 Giovanni Spinnetti, of Venice, constructed an instrument of oblong form, with a compass of four octaves. This oblong form enabled Spinnetti to use very long strings and a larger soundboard, covering nearly the entire space, thus materially increasing the tone volume. These long strings, however, could not be agitated effectually by a striking tangent; it was neces-

Spinet of Spinnetti, 1503

sary to set the strings in motion by pricking or twanging. We, therefore, find on the clavis of the spinet, a " jack " with centered tongue on its upper end. Into this tongue a quill, fastened to a spring, is inserted, and when the key is pressed down, the point of the quill twangs the string through the upward movement of the jack. A small piece of cloth, fastened to the jack, dampens the string as soon as the jack comes down again to its natural position. This instrument was called a " spinet," after the inventor.

Although this twanging of the string produced a wiry, nasal tone, and the player could not play with any expression, as on the clavichord, the spinet became very popular, because of its greater, louder tone. Spinets were built in sizes from 3½ to 5 feet wide. The smaller instruments could be easily carried about, and were usually played upon a table, which increased the resonance. Spinnetti had placed the keyboard outside of the case, but about 1550 Rossi of Milan built spinets in which the keyboard was within the case.

In England the spinet became generally known under the name of " virginal," and many writers have fallen into the error of assuming that the virginal differs materially from the spinet.

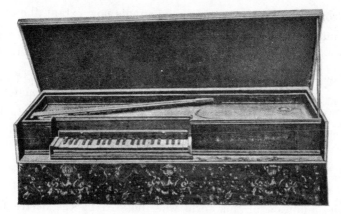

Rossi's Spinet, 1550

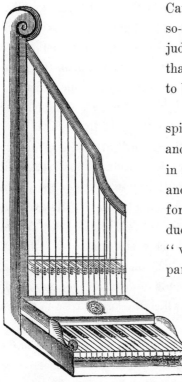

Virginal, 16th Century

Careful comparisons of spinets and so-called virginals, by competent judges, have established the fact that there is no vital difference to be found.

Naturally, the various builders of spinets in Italy, Germany, Flanders, and especially England, experimented in many ways to improve the volume and quality of tone as well as the form of the case. Rimbault reproduces a pen-and-ink-sketch of a " virginal, made harp fashion," apparently built at the end of the 16th century, which might be considered the prototype of the upright piano of the present day. If this drawing is correct, a rather complicated action must have been used to get the plectra in motion.

From specimens of spinets or virginals now extant, the conclusion may be drawn that the European continental makers gave the triangular form the preference, while English makers used the square, oblong and upright forms. The quill or wing form (German *flügel*) identical with the form of the present grand piano and later used entirely for the " harpsichord," seems to have been first used by Geronimo of Bologna (1521).

The Harpsichord

The adoption of this form was dictated by the desire for a greater volume of tone. Indeed, the early harpsichord was in all its features (except the wing form) only an enlarged spinet. The larger case, greater soundboard and greater number of much longer strings of the harpsichord opened a new field for inventive genius. While the tone produced on the longer string had a greater volume and was louder than that of the spinet, it was at the same time harsher, raw, more nasal and almost offensive to the ear. When used with the orchestra this serious fault was not so noticeable, but for solo performances the harpsichord was very unsatisfactory. To overcome, or at least mollify this harshness, many experiments were made, even to desperate attempts to attach a mechanical orchestra to it, adding devices which were to imitate the lute and flute, operated by stops; also, by means of pedals, a complete Janissary music, including snare and bass drum, cymbals, triangle, bells and other noisy instruments. In accordance with the variety of these appendages the number of pedals increased, and harpsichords with as many as 25 pedals are still to be found.

Of all those manifold experiments only four have proved of permanent value. The " forte stop," which lifted the dampers; the " soft stop," which pressed the dampers on to the strings to stop the vibration; the " buff stop," interposing soft cloth or leather between the jacks and the strings, and lastly the " shift-

Harpsichord, 1521

ing stop,'' which shifted the entire keyboard, a movement later applied to the transposing keyboard.

In the effort to produce greater volume of tone the makers continued to increase the size of the harpsichord until it had reached the extreme length of 16 feet. Very thin wire had to be used for the strings, since the frail cases would not stand the increased tension of heavier wires, nor could the flimsy quill plectra make the heavy wires vibrate well. The longer the string of thin wire, the less musical was the tone produced by twanging, and the best makers returned to the length of 8 to 10 feet, seeking to improve tone quality and volume by increasing the number of strings from one to two, three and even four, for each note.

Harpsichord with Double Keyboard, End of 16th Century

About the middle of the 17th century, harpsichords with two keyboards and three strings for each note were built. The third string, usually hitched to the soundboard bridge, was thinner and shorter than the two main strings and tuned an octave higher than the main strings. With the two keyboards the player could use the two or three strings of each note separately or together. Because of these improvements, especially the forte piano pedals, and the greater tone, musicians preferred the harpsichord to the spinet, and many compositions were written for it from Scarlatti's time (1670) to Beethoven's " Moonlight Sonata " (1802).

Toward the end of the 18th century, when the pianoforte began to take the place of the harpsichords, attempts were made to improve the tone quality of the harpsichord by using buff leather at the points of the jack, instead of quills, but evidently without

Harpsichord, Middle of 17th Century

success. The fact that the harpsichord, like the spinet, gave the player no possible opportunity to exercise any artistry, as on the clavichord or the pianoforte, sealed the doom of the instrument, and with the end of the 18th century the end of the harpsichord had come, leaving for the pianoforte maker, however, the valuable inventions of the *wing-formed case,* the use of the *two* and *three strings* for one note, and lastly the *forte piano pedal* and *shifting keyboard,* all of which are embodied in the present-day piano.

PART ONE

CHAPTER II

THE PIANOFORTE, Christofori, Marius, Schröter, Silbermann, Backers, Stein, German, Austrian and English Schools, Friederici.

THE SQUARE PIANO, Zumpe, Broadwood, Erard, Behrend, Albrecht, Crehore, Osborn, Babcock, Chickering, Steinway, Mathushek.

THE UPRIGHT PIANO, Schmidt, Hawkins, Loud, Southwell, Wornum, Pleyel.

THE GRAND PIANO, Geronimo, Still, Stodart, Broadwood, Erard, Stein, Nannette Stein-Streicher, Loud, Jardine, Chickering, Steinway, Bösendorfer, Kaps.

PART ONE

CHAPTER II

The Pianoforte

T HE desire to combine the wonderful tone sustaining capacity of the clavichord with the power of the harpsichord, was shared by musicians as well as builders. No doubt many builders attempted to put a hammer action into the harpsichord. Marius of Paris submitted (1716) three models of harpsichord hammer actions to the Academy of Sciences, but apparently no instruments have been built containing his action, probably because a hammer action, to be effective, required a different construction of the entire instrument than that of the harpsichord. It seems much more reasonable to assume that the dulcimer (the German *hackbrett*), which was played upon with hammers held in the hands of the performer, similar to the xylophone, led to the invention of the pianoforte.

It is not surprising, that, at a period when all makers of harpsichords were struggling for tone improvement, three inventors,

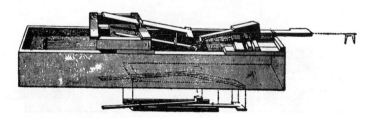

Marius' Downward Striking Hammer Action

Christoph Schröter

independent of one another, should strike the same idea at about the same time—Christofori in 1707, Marius in 1716 and Schröter in 1717. Christoph Schröter, a German organist, submitted his models of hammer actions, one with upward and one with downward movement, to the King of Saxony in 1721, claiming that these models had been finished in 1717. Schröter declared that the idea of a hammer action came to him after hearing the virtuoso, Hebenstreit, perform on his monster hackbrett (dulcimer) called "Pantaleon." Simple and crude as Schröter's action is, it must be considered the fundamental of what later on became known as the German, more particularly, "Vienna" action. The idea of having the hammer butt swing in a fork, as Schröter's model shows,

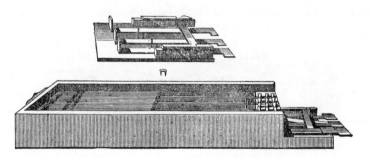

Marius' Upward Striking Hammer Action

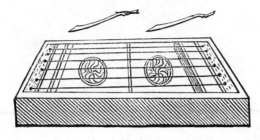

Dulcimer

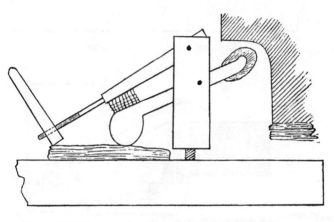

Schröter Upward Striking Hammer Action, 1717

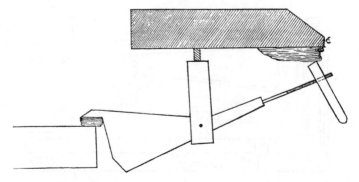

Schröter Downward Striking Hammer Action, 1717

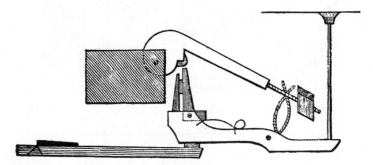

Silbermann's Hammer Action, 1728

Christofori's Hammer Action, 1707

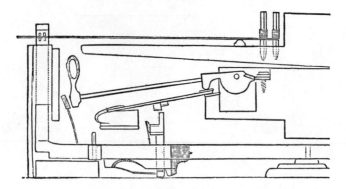

Christofori's Hammer Action, 1720

has been utilized in all later improvements of the so-called German action. Schröter was disappointed in not getting aid from his King to build his instruments, and no pianofortes of his make are known. As early as 1724, however, pianofortes containing the Schröter action were made at Dresden.

It is also of record that the great organ builder, Gottfried Silbermann, of Freiberg, Saxony, made pianofortes with Schröter actions as early as 1728. He simplified and improved the action somewhat, as illustration shows. However, the action was unreliable, the touch heavy and hard as compared to the clavichord, and the great Johann Sebastian Bach condemned the first pianoforte which Silbermann had built because it was too hard to play, although he praised the tone produced by the hammer.

Christofori's Piano e forte, 1711

It seems that Silbermann came into possession of a Christofori pianoforte, because the pianofortes built by him for Frederick the Great, about 1747, have hammer action exactly like Christofori's invention. In Silbermann's workshop originated the two schools of piano construction known as the " German school " and the " English school." There is no doubt that Silbermann used both the Schröter and the Christofori action for his pianofortes.

The invention of the pianoforte as an entire and complete instrument must be credited to Bartolomo Christofori (sometimes

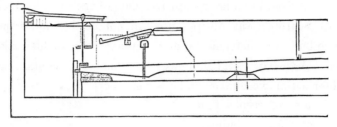

Zumpe's Hammer Action, 1760-65

called Christofali) of Padua. A publication dated 1711 contains
a drawing of Christofori's hammer action, which he had completed
in 1707, and used in his first experimental instrument which he
called " piano e forte." This instrument was exhibited in 1711.
About 1720, Christofori finished his real pianoforte. He constructed a much stronger case than had been used for harpsichords,
to withstand the increased strain of the heavier strings. The action
in this pianoforte shows important improvement over his model

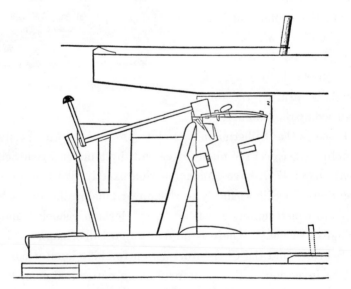

Backers' Hammer Action, 1776

Stein's Hammer Action

of 1707. He added the escapement device, a back check, regulating the fall of the hammer, and connected an individual damper for each note direct with the hammer action, thus giving the performer a mechanism with which he could, through his touch, produce a delicate pianissimo and also a strong fortissimo, impossible on either clavichord or harpsichord. Christofori died in 1731. As far as we can learn he left no pupils, unless we so consider Silbermann.

Silbermann's pupils, Johannes Zumpe and Americus Backers (Becker), went to London and introduced there a modified Christofori action, which later on, further developed by various makers, became known as the " English " action. Silbermann's most

Zumpe Square Piano, 1760-65

C. E. Friederici

talented pupil, Johann Andreas Stein of Augsburg, however, took the Schröter design as a basis for his improvement, which is known as the "Vienna" or "German" action.

The greatest activity in the development of the pianoforte took place in the periods from 1760 to 1830, and from 1855 to 1880. Modulations as well as radical departures in form were almost numberless, mainly inspired by a desire to produce an instrument which would take up less room than the long, wing-shaped grand piano. As early as 1745, C. E. Friederici of Gera, Germany, a pupil of Silbermann, constructed a vertical grand piano and about 1758 he built the first square piano in Germany. About 1760-65, Johannes Zumpe built, at London, the first English square piano.

The Square Piano

This evolved from reconstructed clavichords, retaining the clavichord form and general construction, but having a stronger frame, metal strings and the hammer action. Following Zumpe, we next learn of John Broadwood of London bringing out his square piano in 1771, and the records show that Sebastian Erard made such an instrument at Paris in 1776, copying the English model. Johann

Behrend of Philadelphia exhibited his square piano in 1775. Thus within 10 years after its first appearance, the square piano was made in Germany, England, America and France. But all the square pianos of those days were weak in tone and not to be compared to the grand (wing form) pianoforte.

It seems that the use of the Christofori action in England (as modified by Backers), having the hammer rise at the end of the key (instead of toward the center of the key as in the Stein action), suggested the idea to Broadwood of placing the wrest plank along the back of the case, instead of along the right hand side, as it had always been in the clavichord. Broadwood completed his new piano with this improvement in 1781. This epoch-making invention revolutionized the construction of the square piano, and gave the opportunity of increasing the volume of tone to an unexpected degree. As a matter of course, this invention was gradually adopted by all the leading makers. Even the German school, which had developed a square piano construction where the wrest plank was placed in the front part of the case, instead of sideways, finally accepted Broadwood's construction, together with the English action.

Not considering minor improvements, such as enlarging the scale, etc., no further development of the square piano is of record by European makers and we must look to America, where the

Friederici's Square Piano, 1758

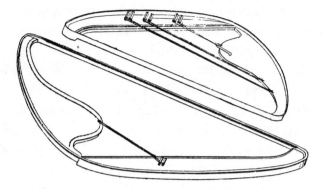

Alpheus Babcock's Full Iron Frame, 1825

square piano reigned supreme for nearly one hundred years. After Behrend we find Charles Albrecht making excellent square pianos in Philadelphia about 1789 and Benjamin Crehore founding the Boston school about 1792 at Milton, near Boston, where John Osborn and Alpheus Babcock were his most talented pupils. Indeed, Alpheus Babcock's invention of the full iron frame in 1825 was just as important an innovation and improvement as Broadwood's

Charles Albrecht's Square Piano, 1789

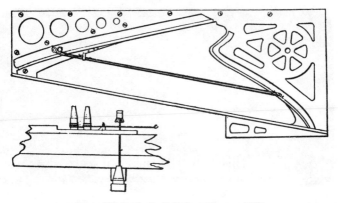

Jonas Chickering's Full Iron Frame, 1837

change of the location of the wrest plank. The never-ceasing demand for larger tone could only be answered by heavier stringing, which, however, was limited by the power of resistance of the wooden frame. Babcock's full iron frame blasted the way for further development, and Jonas Chickering improved Babcock's frame so materially in 1837 that a patent was granted to him in 1840.

Most of the Boston makers, all of whom inclined toward the English school, adopted the full iron frame, but New York makers, being more influenced by the German school, objected to the metallic tone found especially in the upper notes of pianos with iron frames, caused perhaps fully as much by the inferior composition of the castings then available as by too close connection of the strings with the iron plate or frame. All American makers of that period devoted themselves more or less to the development of the square piano, so that it soon became superior to the upright piano as that was then constructed.

At the World's Fair, in the Crystal Palace, New York, in 1855, Steinway & Sons created a sensation by exhibiting a square piano having the overstrung scale, and a full iron frame, designed on novel lines to conform with the varied and much increased strain

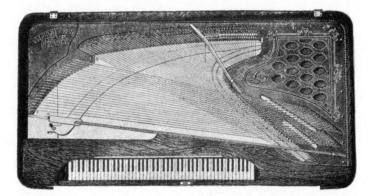

Steinway's Full Iron Frame and Overstrung Scale, 1855

of the new scale. In this instrument the Steinways had not only succeeded in producing a much greater, sonorous tone, than known heretofore, but had entirely overcome the harsh, metallic quality of tone, so objectionable in other pianos having the full iron frame. Although at first seriously objected to by many, the overstrung scale and full iron frame were soon adopted by all American makers.

With this innovation the piano industry of America had received a new impetus and it developed very rapidly from then on. Improvements were continually added, among which the linear soundboard bridge, invented by Frederick Mathushek in 1865, may be considered as the most ingenious.

After the Paris exposition of 1867, the leading American manufacturers followed the example which the European makers had set 30 years before, and began to push the upright piano to the front. For the very reason that the American square piano had been developed to a real musical instrument with a remarkable volume, sonority and clearness of tone, equal in some instances to the ordinary grand piano of the European makers, the progress of the upright piano in America was very slow, and it was not until 1880 that the making of the square piano came to an end.

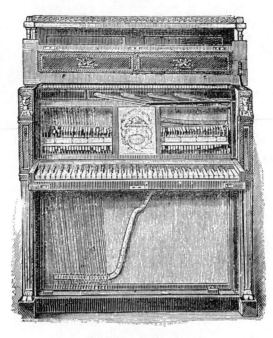

Hawkins' Upright Piano, 1800

The Upright Piano

Not considering the vertical grands of Fabrici, Stein and others of this class, history records that apparently the first upright piano was built about 1780 by Johann Schmidt of Salzburg, Austria. Twenty years later John Isaac Hawkins of Philadelphia patented an upright piano with vertical strings, full iron frame and check action. Notwithstanding its many ingenious devices, this piano was not accepted on account of its unsatisfactory tone. As A. J. Hipkins so properly says, " it was a remarkable bundle of inventions," but not a musical instrument. Hawkins was an engineer by profession.

In 1802 Thomas Loud of London patented an upright piano described as having the strings running diagonally. It is questionable whether Loud ever had any success in building such instru-

ments. None are now in existence. Loud
emigrated to New York where he built so-
called " piccolo " uprights with " overstrung " scale as early as 1830.

In 1807 William Southwell of London
came out with his " Cabinet " (upright)
piano, having a compass of 6 octaves, F to
F. In 1811 Robert Wornum of London
made his first upright with diagonally running strings.

The popularity of the upright in Europe
dates from 1826, when Wornum had developed an action for it which combined precision with durability and permitted of
repetition, responding easily to a light
touch. Ignace Pleyel of Paris adopted this
action for his upright pianos and it became known on the Continent as the
" Pleyel " action. With the exception

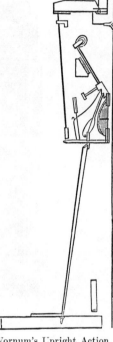

Wornum's Upright Action,
1826

of changing the dampers
from their position above
the hammers to a more
proper place below the hammers, this Wornum action is
practically used in all present-day upright pianos.

Pleyel and other Paris
firms began now to make a
specialty of upright pianos
with such success that square
pianos hardly obtained a
foothold in France.

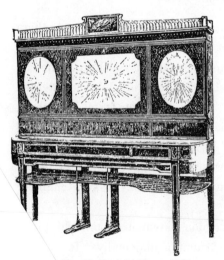

uthwell's Upright Piano, 1807

Germany began the manufacture of upright pianos in preference to the square about 1835, and discarded the square for good
about 1860. During this period the Germans, true to their national
character, built much stronger, heavier uprights, than either the
French or English, using three strings for each note and applying
iron plates for hitch-pins, also iron braces between these plates
and the wrest plank. The tone of the German uprights of those
days had greater volume than the instruments of their
contemporaries.

The later important export of, German pianos had its start at
that time because of the superior quality of tone and great durability of the instruments. When the American makers began to
pay attention again to the upright piano about 1860 they adopted

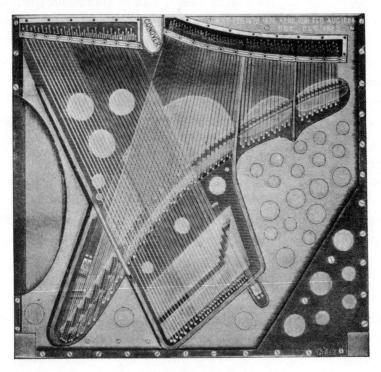

Conover Bros.' Upright Iron Frame, 1885

the now perfected system of overstrung scale and full iron frame, and thereby produced an instrument which was acceptable, although in tone and touch inferior to the best square pianos.

Germany was quick in adopting the overstrung scale and iron frame for its upright pianos and forced England to do likewise later on by capturing with their superior instruments much foreign trade formerly monopolized by England, while France, Italy and Spain came in last. By the time that the American square piano became extinct (1880) the " American System " was universally adopted for upright pianos. However, even the upright piano of to-day might still be called " a remarkable bundle of inventions." In its entirety it is an open defiance of all the laws of acoustics and of proper mechanical construction.

Because of the necessarily heavy, clumsy frame construction the soundboard is almost boxed in between back and front, so that the sound cannot develop freely and fully. Whatever tone the performer gets from the upright piano, comes straight toward him through the closed-in front, which " short-stops " the sound. The touch in the upright is tough, non-elastic, because of the necessarily short and consequently rigid, stiff keys, but mainly on account of the complicated action, which has of necessity a strip and a spring to pull and push the hammer back to its natural position after striking. In striking the string from above the hammer virtually throws the tone into the piano with no chance to escape, while in the open square or grand pianoforte it travels unhampered. The upright has always been a makeshift, a child of necessity, and for many years a total failure.

In spite of its present, so much improved form and character, the upright will never be the piano for the artist, because of its incapacity to give any satisfaction to artistic temperament, either as to tone or facility in execution.

That the upright piano is to-day, and perhaps always will be, the most popular instrument, notwithstanding its many shortcomings, can be easily explained. The growth of the cities has made land so dear that the study for architects has been how to house as many people as possible on a small piece of ground. Paris started the first so-called apartment houses in the beginning of the 19th century. Hence the Paris piano makers were compelled to develop upright pianos small enough to fit into the small rooms of the apartment house, where grand or square pianos could not possibly be placed. Germany followed French architecture next; England followed soon after; and since about 1880 we have had apartment houses in American cities, mainly with such small rooms that neither a grand nor square piano can be placed conveniently. Besides the more convenient form of the upright the lower cost, as compared to the cost of a grand piano, is a strong factor in its popularity. However, the demand for the " perfect " pianoforte is increasing so rapidly and strongly that the foremost makers all over the world have for many years, and with varied success, experimented to produce a small grand piano which in size and price would be accepted by the lover of music.

The Grand Piano or Forte Piano

As previously stated this " wing " form seems to have been used first by Geronimo (1521) and has ever since been preferred by all artistic makers in their efforts to produce a piano for the concert hall, for the artist. The square piano was born of English commercialism, the upright piano started its career of success under pressure of the apartment house, but the grand piano has ever been the love of the artistic piano maker and the musical piano player. The large size, the natural, horizontal position of the strings, the opportunity of using a forceful action, answering at the same time to the most refined pianissimo touch—an action permitting a development upon scientifically and mechanically correct lines—has ever been enticing to the inventive genius and to the thinking constructor of pianofortes. We therefore find all the early pianofortes of Christofori, Silbermann, Stein and other makers possessing this wing form.

The craze of adding all sorts of unharmonic effects to keyed instruments, as on the harpsichord, continued also for a while with the grand piano, and we hear of instruments having bell, drum, cymbal, triangle, etc., attachments. These vagaries, however, were not accepted by the true artist and soon died out. The extent to which this craze was finally carried is illustrated by the description of a grand piano built in 1796 by Still Brothers of Prague, Bohemia, for the inventor, a musician by the name of Kunz. This monstrosity had 230 strings, 360 pipes and 105 different tonal effects. It was three feet nine inches high, seven feet six inches long and three feet two inches wide, had two keyboards, one above the other, and 25 pedals. The pedals had the following functions: To lift the dampers, to produce lute effect, flute, flute traverso dulciana, salicet, viola di gamba, sifflet, open flute, hollow flute, fagott, French horn, clarinet and many others. The inventor evidently attempted to obtain, besides the ordinary piano tone, also all kinds of organ and orchestral effects, noisy additions which we find to a smaller extent with .the nickel-in-the-slot playing machines of to-day.

The perfecting of the grand piano, or forte piano (*flügel,* as it was called in Germany), depended entirely upon the development of an action capable of bringing out the greater tone of the longer strings and larger soundboard of the grand, and we find the masters of the English and German schools for many years seriously engaged in solving this problem, to be finally outclassed by Sebastian and Pierre Erard, of Paris. Backers' grand action, completed about 1776, inspired Robert Stod-

art of London to build his first concert piano which he called
" Grand Pianoforte," about 1777, and the word *grand* first applied
by Stodart was henceforth used by all English and American
makers for this instrument.

John Broadwood built his first grand in 1781. Allen and Thom
of London patented a grand piano having a complete metal framing
system in 1820, followed by the Erards in 1823, who constructed
a grand piano with six resistance iron bars, placed over the soundboard, while James Broadwood patented, in 1827, a combination
of an iron string plate (hitch plate) with resistance iron bars, thus
coming very near the full iron frame.

Meantime, Johann Andreas Stein, and his talented daughter,
Nannette Stein-Streicher, who was not only an excellent musician,
but also a thoroughly practical and scientific piano maker, had improved the Schröter action so materially that the grand pianos
made by them from 1780 on, were preferred by Mozart, Beethoven
and other masters, perhaps mainly for the reason that this action
not only had a more elastic touch than the Christofori English
action, but that it produced a more sympathetic tone, reminding
of the clavichord tone, which all the great players of that period
admired so much. This sympathetic tone could only be produced
with the Vienna action, because the hammer, when striking, would

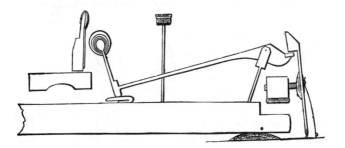

Nannette Stein-Streicher Grand Action, 1780

Erard's First Iron Bar Grand Piano, 1823

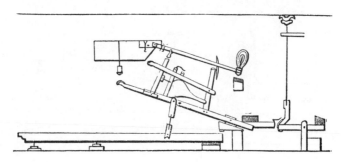

Erard Repetition Grand Action, 1821

to some extent graze or draw along the string, while the more forceful attack of the English " jack " action is a straight and direct percussion.   These two elements, the pleasant light elastic touch, and the charming musical quality of tone, assured the Vienna grand pianos (*flügel*) supremacy in Germany, Austria and Italy for many years.

Since the " Vienna school " never aimed for powerful tone, during that period, the use of metal for resistance was not developed until 1837, when Hoxa of Vienna patented a full iron frame for grand pianos.

In 1808, Sebastian Erard took out a patent for a "repetition " action for grand pianos, in which he attempted to combine the elastic touch of the Vienna action with the forcefulness of the English action, but evidently without satisfactory result, because in 1821 Pierre Erard, nephew of Sebastian Erard, obtained for the latter's invention of a " repetition or double escapement action " a patent in England.   It is this action which made the fame of the Erard grand pianos worldwide.

Among further important inventions aiding the progress of the grand piano must be mentioned Erard's agraffe, by aid of which a bearing down upon the strings was accomplished, preventing the very objectionable upward motion of the strings when struck by the hammer.   These brass agraffes, besides assuring proper counter pressure against the stroke of the hammer, also improved the tone, especially in the treble part. The idea of downward pressure of the strings near the wrest plank was followed up by other inventors in various directions and manners and finally led to the pressure bar and *capo tasto,* the latter patented by Pierre Erard, in 1838, and now used in varied forms in nearly all grand and upright pianos.

Capo Tasto

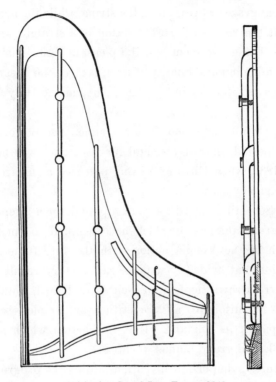

Chickering Grand Iron Frame, 1843

Turning to America, we find that Loud Brothers of Philadelphia built a grand piano of 7½-octaves about 1825, while John Jardine of New York exhibited a 7-octave grand piano in 1835. Jonas Chickering patented his full iron frame for flat scale grand pianos in 1843, a great improvement on Broadwood's combination of iron hitch plate and resisting bars, establishing the fame of the Chickering concert grand. Sixteen years later, Steinway & Sons patented their full iron frame for grand pianos with overstrung scale and disposition of the strings in the form of a fan.

After the London exhibition of 1862, the full iron frame came largely into use in Germany and Austria, while England and France retained the plain scale and bracing system for many years. At the present time all prominent makers have adopted the overstrung scale and full iron or steel frames for their grand pianos.

Noteworthy progress has also been made in the construction of the case for grand pianos. Following the harpsichord model, the original grand case was " built up " (frame and braces) by gluing boards of one to two inches in thickness together. To work out the hollow sides and rounded ends from the rough form thus con-

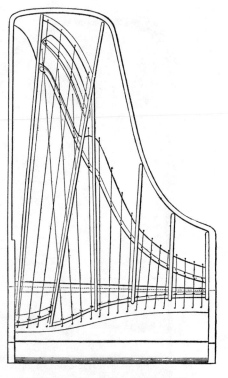

Steinway Grand Iron Frame, 1859

structed with ordinary jack plane, was a very laborious task. England, at that time the land of machinery par excellence, soon employed power machines for case making, and constructed the curved sides and back, by gluing up hardwood veneers in forms identical to the curvature of the piano case. This new process was not only more economic, but it also strengthened the case materially and was supposed to increase the acoustic properties. It was, therefore, soon generally adopted.

The concert grand piano of to-day is a model of mechanical construction with proper regard to the laws of acoustics, as we know them to-day in their relations to the pianoforte. Free from all empirical and experimental vagaries, the concert grand piano of to-day is a most noble instrument, embodying the final evolution

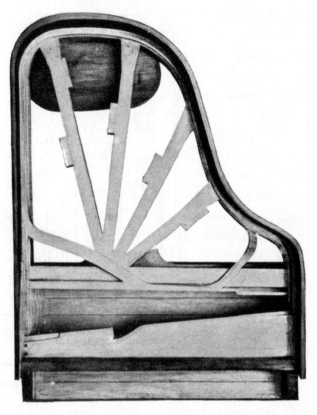

Baldwin Grand Case with Acoustic Rim

of the best thoughts of the greatest masters in the art of piano construction. The length of the modern concert grand is usually nine feet, with a compass of 7⅓ octaves. Ludwig Bösendorfer of Vienna builds a concert grand of 10 feet in length, and a compass of eight octaves. Going to the other extreme, some makers have of late years constructed a small grand as short as five feet. Ernst Kaps of Dresden was the first to build a very short grand (1865), using a double overstrung scale. Because of its novelty this instrument was for many years a commercial success. It has, however, been established as a fact that shortening the length to about five feet is the danger-line for the construction of a small grand, which is to satisfy the artist or musical amateur, as to volume and quality of tone, and especially of a well-balanced, even scale.

The short grand, baptized by Albert Weber the " baby grand," will be the instrument of the future. The clamor for an increased full round tone, elastic and easy touch, and never-failing repetition in the action of the piano, is the same to-day as it was 200 years ago, and must be satisfied. The upright piano, having evidently reached the apex of its possible development, is unsatisfactory, and hence the small grand at moderate price will find many friends among music lovers who neither require nor desire the bulky concert grand for their personal enjoyment or professional studies.

PART ONE

CHAPTER III

THE FULL IRON FRAME, Hawkins, Allen and Thom, Babcock, Chickering, Erard, Broadwood, Hoxa, Steinway.

THE KEYBOARD, Guido of Arezzo, Zarlina, Kirkman, Krause, Chromatic Keyboard, Neuhaus, Cludsam, Paul von Janko, Perzina.

THE ACTION, Schröter, Christofori, Silbermann, Stein, Streicher, Zumpe, Backers, Erard, Friederici, Wornum, Pleyel, Pape.

THE HAMMER, Christofori, Silbermann, Pape, Wilke, Kreter, Mathushek, Collins, Dolge, Ammon, Steinway.

THE SOUNDBOARD, Chladni, Tyndall, Helmholtz, Hansing, Dr. Paul, Pape, Mathushek.

CHAPTER III

THE IRON FRAME, THE KEYBOARD, ACTION, HAMMER,
SOUNDBOARD

The Iron Frame

IN the year 1808 Wachtl & Bleyer, a Vienna firm of piano makers, stated in a publication that the total tension of the strings in their grand pianos equalled 9,000 pounds. The strings in a modern grand have a total tension of 35,000 to 40,000 pounds.

The necessity of a combination of metal with wood in piano construction became apparent as soon as the perfected action permitted of the use of heavier strings. The framework had to undergo a change if further progress in tone volume was to be made. Numberless experiments were made with metal tubes and bars for braces, underneath the soundboard as well as above, without lasting result. Even the Hawkins full iron frame of 1800 was a failure, and history records many futile attempts to solve the problem.

The first acceptable system of bracing by iron tubes was invented by Allen and Thom of London in 1820. They sold their patent rights to Robert Stodart, who immediately constructed a grand pianoforte with this system, which withstood a tension of 13,000 pounds successfully. Alpheus Babcock of Boston followed in 1825 with the first full iron frame for square pianos.

With this invention the era of the full iron frame was inaugurated. That great mechanical genius, Jonas Chickering, patented in 1843 a full iron frame for flat scale grand pianos. He demonstrated the practicability of this new system, and the so-called Boston school at once followed his example, using full iron frames for grand, square and upright pianos.

In Europe, Erard experimented with iron bracing bars about 1824, putting as many as nine long bars over the sound-board of his grand pianos. Broadwood, more methodical and scientific, studied to obtain the necessary resistance with as few bars as possible, and finally combined an iron hitch-pin plate with his cross bars, which system was patented in 1827. John Broadwood & Sons are now making grand and upright pianos with " barless " steel frame, a notable accomplishment, aiding materially in producing an even scale, and also permitting the soundboard and strings to vibrate unhampered and unaffected by iron cross bars. Another important effect is that the weight of the piano is reduced in proportion. Hoxa of Vienna is on record with a patent for a full iron frame for grand pianos in 1837. No doubt the European makers of that period objected to the full iron frame because of the too metallic tone, for which reason the New York makers also were slow in following Chickering and the Boston school. The

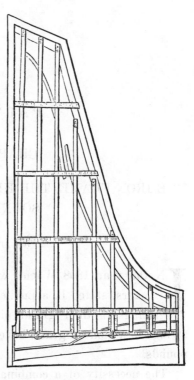

Allen and Thom's Grand Bracing
System, 1820

majority of the New Yorkers leaned toward the German school, seeking quality rather than volume of tone. When, however, Steinway & Sons demonstrated in 1855 that the overstrung system in combination with a solid iron frame, could yield the desired volume of tone of the desired musical quality, the battle for the iron frame was won.

At the London exhibition of 1862 the American pianos with full iron frames were the sensation of the entire piano exhibit. After the Paris Exposition of 1867, where the much-improved American overstrung iron frame pianos carried off the honors, the German makers capitulated and accepted the American system. England and France are following slowly, but the universal adoption of this greatest progress in piano construction is inevitable. Constant study and efforts to improve the composition of the metals for casting, together with the progress made in the methods and mechanical appliances for casting iron, have not only tended to overcome the objectionable influence of the iron frame upon the tone quality, but the modern iron frame or plate is also in form and finish pleasing even to the critical eyes of the artist.

The casting of iron plates for pianos is one of the most important auxiliary industries of the piano trade of to-day, keeping pace with the continual improvement of the piano. The average weight of plates in American pianos is as follows:

Concert Grand.... 400 pounds,   Parlor Grand..... 300 pounds,
Baby Grand...... 250 pounds,   Large Upright.... 200 pounds,
                Small Upright...... 120 pounds.

The tension these plates have to withstand averages as follows:

Concert Grand. 60,000 pounds,   Parlor Grand.. 55,000 pounds,
Baby Grand.... 50,000 pounds,   Large Upright. 38,000 pounds,
                Small Upright.... 38,000 pounds.

STEINWAY & SONS' GRAND IRON FRAME, 1875

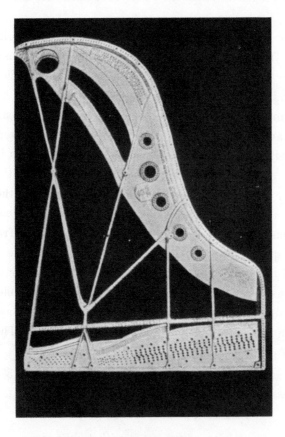

Front View

STEINWAY & SONS' GRAND IRON FRAME, 1875

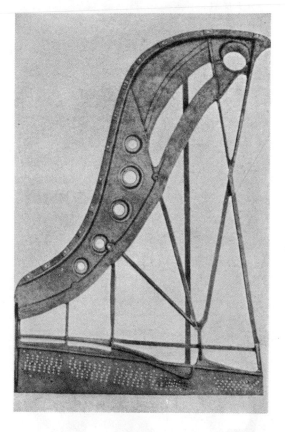

Back View
Showing "Cupola" Construction

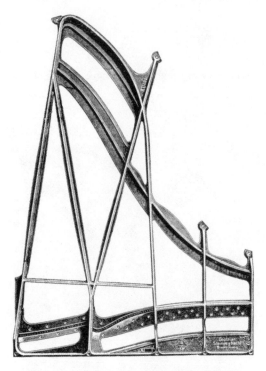

Wilhelm Grotrian's Grand Iron Frame, 1910

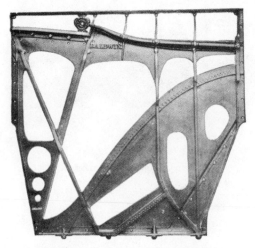

Baldwin Upright Iron Frame, 1910

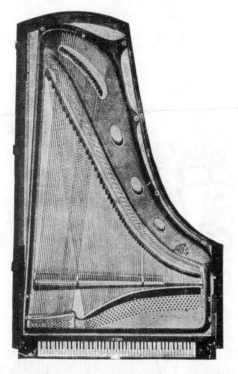

John Broadwood & Sons' Barless Grand Steel Frame, 1910

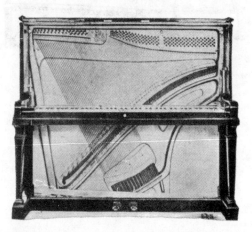

John Broadwood & Sons' Barless Upright Steel Frame, 1910

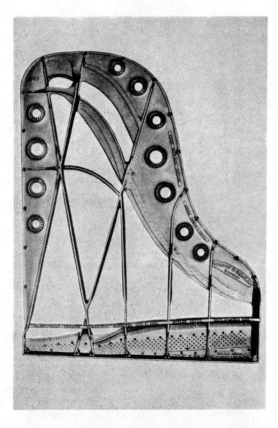

Mason & Hamlin Grand Iron Frame, 1910

The Keyboard

The origin of the keyboard for musical instruments cannot be traced with any accuracy. Old records mention a hydraulic organ invented by Ctesibius of Alexandria, in the 2d century B.C., but no reference is made to a keyboard in that organ. Vitruvius, in his work on architecture (1st century A.D.), describes an organ with balanced keys. Next we learn that Emperor Constantine sent a musical instrument having keys to King Pepin of France in 757 A.D. Whether or not that great musical genius, Guido of Arezzo, invented the keyboard for a polychord instrument or was the first one to apply it, cannot be proven, but the fact remains that the keyboard was applied to stringed instruments in his days (first part of the 11th century).

Guido's diatonic scale, eight full tones with seven intervals of which two were semitones, was used in the first clavichords, which had 20 keys. There are no reliable records in existence, as to who applied the chromatic scale first. Giuseppe Zarlino added the semitones to his instruments about 1548, but instruments of earlier date have the chromatic scale, as for instance the clavicymbala, some of which had 77 keys to a compass of four octaves. The keys in some of the early organs were three to four inches wide, and the early clavichords also had very wide keys, but with the increase of the number of strings, narrowing of the keys became a necessity.*

After the 15th century nearly all the makers of key-stringed instruments used the chromatic scale practically as we find it in the modern pianos. The semitones in most of those old instruments are elevated and of a different color than the full tones.

---

* Kirkman of London went to the extreme of building a grand piano in 1851, having a keyboard of 6¾ octaves, 2 feet 2½ inches wide, allowing only ½ inch for each key.

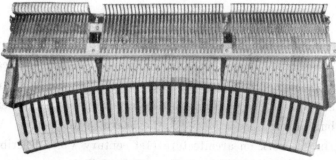

Cludsam's Concave Keyboard, 1910

Since the development of the pianoforte many experiments have been made with so-called " chromatic " keyboards, in which the semitones were on a level with the full tones. A Dr. Krause of Eisenberg constructed a keyboard in 1811, in which the semitones were not raised and all keys were of the same color. Krause maintained that with such a keyboard the performer could play in all the different keys with more ease than if the semitones were elevated. Although this innovation was generally rejected, various attempts have been made of late to revive this idea, but without any result.

About 1780, Neuhaus, a piano maker of Vienna, constructed a concave-formed keyboard for his pianos. He aimed to follow the inclination of the human arm to move in a semicircle. Curious to relate, this same idea has lately been resuscitated by Cludsam of Germany, who obtained patents on such a keyboard and is seriously attempting its introduction.

The most ingenious and really meritorious invention, revolutionary in its character, is the keyboard patented in 1882 by Paul von Janko of Austria. Moved by the desire to enable the amateur to execute the brilliant, but technically exceedingly difficult, essays of our modern composers, Janko constructed a keyboard of six tiers, one above the other, similar to the organ keyboard. On this keyboard tenths, and twelfths, can easily be produced by reach-

Janko-Perzina Keyboard, 1910

ing a finger to the keyboard above or below that on which the hand is traveling. Arpeggios through the whole compass of the keyboard can be executed with a sweep of the wrist, which on the ordinary keyboard would hardly cover two octaves. Indeed, with the Janko keyboard, the hand and arm of the player can always remain in their natural position, because to sound an octave requires only the stretch of the hand equal to the sounding of the sixth on the ordinary keyboard.

It is difficult to realize the manifold possibilities which this keyboard opens up for the composer and performer. Entirely new music can be written by composers, containing chords, runs and arpeggios, utterly impossible to execute on the ordinary keyboard, and thus does the Janko keyboard make the piano, what it has often been called, a veritable " house orchestra." It is not nearly so difficult for the student to master the technic of the Janko, as to become efficient on the present keyboard. This keyboard can be readily adjusted to any piano having the ordinary action.

Like all epoch-marking innovations, this great invention is treated with indifference and open opposition. That poetic performer on the piano, Chopin, refused to play on the Erard grand pianos containing the celebrated repetition action, because his fingers were used to the stiff percussion of the English action. To-day, however, English makers of concert grand pianos use the Erard action which Chopin disdained!

The piano virtuosos and teachers of the present day are opposing the Janko keyboard because its universal adoption would mean for them to forget the old and learn the new. The music publishers object to it, because their stock on hand would depreciate in value, as the Janko keyboard naturally requires different fingering than that now printed with the published compositions. For many years the professional piano players could rightfully object to the somewhat unelastic touch of the Janko keyboard. This objection has been completely overcome by an ingenious improvement accomplished by Paul Perzina of Schwerin, who changed the double leverage of the key successfully to a single

Paul d. Janko

movement as shown in illustration, assuring the desired elastic touch. In order to facilitate the attachment of the Janko keyboard, Perzina has invented a reversible double key-bottom, so that the Janko as well as the old style keyboard can be used on the same piano.

Although the Janko keyboard, in its present form, is thoroughly practical, and destined to inaugurate a new era for the piano industry, its universal success and adoption seem to be im-

Perzina's Key for Janko Keyboard, 1910

paired by the appearance of the player piano, which enables the musical amateur to enjoy his own performance of the most difficult compositions with hardly any exertion on his part. It remains for a coming Titan of the pianoforte to lift the Janko keyboard out of its obscurity and give it its deserved place in the concert hall, there to show to the executing amateur its wonderful possibilities.

Perzina's Reversible Key-bottom for Two Keyboards

Perzina's Action for Practice Clavier for Janko Keyboard

Perzina's Practice Clavier with Janko Keyboard

Paul von Janko, noble of Enyed, was born June 2, 1856, at Totis, Hungary. After finishing his preparatory studies, he entered both the Polytechnicum and the Conservatory of Music, in Vienna. It is quite characteristic of the dual nature of the virtuoso-inventor that he left both institutions with the highest prizes they offer.

He continued his musico-mathematical studies at the Berlin University under Helmholtz. The immediate result of these researches was the keyboard which bears his name. From 1882 to 1884 he experimented on an ordinary parlor organ; in 1885 the first Janko grand piano was built; and on March 25, 1886, he gave his first concert thereon in Vienna.

Paul Perzina of Schwerin, who is a firm believer in the future of the Janko keyboard, has constructed a very ingenious practice clavier for students. As shown by illustrations, the clavier has the full keyboard and a tone-producing hammer action. The hammer strikes a brass reed, producing a tone similar to the harp and zither, sufficiently loud for the player, but not offensive to suffering neighbors. The action is so constructed as to require the touch of the regular piano action. This practice clavier will no doubt aid greatly in introducing the Janko keyboard.

The Development of the Piano Action

No part of the piano has given the inventor more food for thought and opportunity for display of genius than the action. The experiments made are almost numberless and it may be said that every thinking piano maker has at one time or another fallen victim to the lure of " inventing a new action." Even the author, in his early days, sent his hard-earned dollars to Washington to pay the fees for a patent for an " improved upright action." Fortunately no piano maker ever embodied this " important invention " in his instruments.

The action being the motive power of the piano, so to speak, gave the restless empiric full reign for the most fantastic experiments. That a large number of the ablest piano makers of their day should, for instance, struggle with the problem of a downward striking action for grand pianos seems remarkable, but that a genius like Henri Pape should expend a fortune in money and many years of unceasing labor on the same problem, after such masters as Stein, Loud, Sackmeister, Hildebrand, Streicher and many more had given up the struggle as hopeless, seems inexplicable.*

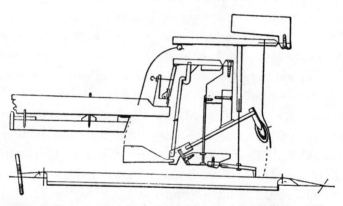

Loud's Downward Striking Action for Square or Grand Pianos, 1827

Although the very principle of the downward striking of the hammer is of itself contrary to the law of gravitation, and as a mechanical proposition ridiculous, Pape not only persisted in his own efforts but transmitted his faith in this action even to his

* While employed by Fred Mathushek (1867-69) the writer was instructed to try and put 12 square pianos, having a downward striking action, in salable condition. These instruments had been built by Mathushek and for years rested peacefully in the attic of the factory building. After wrestling with them for about one week all hope of success was abandoned and the suggestion made to Mathushek that the furnace of the steam boilers in the factory was the most economic place for those pianos. The suggestion was adopted.

pupils, such as Mathushek, Stöcker of Berlin and others, who continued the hopeless efforts for the solution of an impossible proposition. No doubt the ambition to invent something strikingly novel, and thus earn fame as one of the great inventors of the industry, prompted these men to waste their talents and time, as many others have done. In looking at the various models of these downward striking actions, we have only to regret that so much ingenuity was so hopelessly thrown away.

Even to the present day the minds of constructive piano makers are mainly busy with action improvements. While it is true that since the simplification of the Erard action by Henry Herz no radical changes of merit can be recorded, many detail changes and improvements have been made in the mechanism, which are in the line of progress and permit of a more subtle manipulation of the keyboard and pedals than would be possible without them.

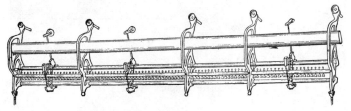

Steinway Tubular Metallic Action Frame, 1866

Rather important improvements have been made to protect the action against atmospheric influences, and to assure greater durability in general, such as the metal flanges in upright actions, the metal tubes for the protection of the wooden rails, and many others.

The evolution of the piano action has passed so regularly and correctly from stage to stage that a Darwin would enjoy the study thereof. Schröter's hammer action of 1717 is a model of inno-

cent simplicity. Even he had the notion of striking the string from
above as well as below. The drawing for his down striking action
shows, however, no possibility for lifting the hammer away from
the string after striking. It appears that Schröter depended entirely upon the counterweight of what might be called the hammer
butt. Naturally, such a clumsy device made the touch hard and
tough, and we need not wonder that Bach and other clavichord
virtuosos of that time would have none of it.

Johann Andreas Stein's Action, 1780

Christofori showed in his first model (1707) real mechanical
genius. His jack permitted an escapement, although faulty. Furthermore, the silken cord, interlocked crosswise to catch the hammer shank in its fall after striking, was undoubtedly designed to
facilitate repetition. In his model of 1720 he succeeded in devising
a positive acting escapement and substituted for the unreliable
silk cords a rigid back check for catching the hammer. Indeed,
Christofori laid down all the laws for the requirements of a
pianoforte action in his model, which all the later inventors had
to observe in their improvements.

Gottfried Silbermann improved the Schröter action by doing away with the special escapement lever. He extended the hammer butt beyond the axis, using this extension for escapement. About 1780 Johann Andreas Stein of Augsburg added to this the "hopper," by aid of which the annoying "blocking" of the hammer was overcome, at the same time improving the touch so much that most virtuosos preferred the Schröter-Stein action to the English.

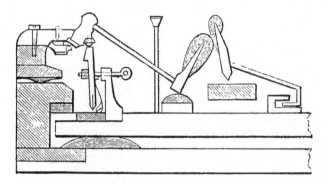

Johann Baptist Streicher's Action, 1824

The almost final development of this action we find in the model of a grand action patented 1824 by Johann Baptist Streicher (a grandson of Stein). This action found much favor with German makers and in modified forms is still used by some Vienna makers. In spite of the fact that masters like Mozart and Beethoven preferred the Schröter-Stein action, it had to give way finally to the Christofori-Backers action. Zumpe's attempt (1776) to simplify the Christofori cannot be considered a success. It seems that he merely tried to produce an action of less cost than the complicated Christofori. Americus Backers, however, invented in the same year an action on the Christofori principle which combined simplicity with all the good points of the Christofori action. The Backers invention has to this day remained the fundamental model for the English action in its various modifications, as illustrated in Broadwood's grand action of 1884.

That independent thinker and mechanical genius, Sebastian Erard, departed from both Schröter and Christofori, when he

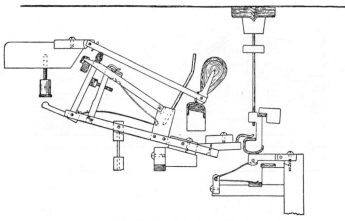

Erard's Grand Action, 1821

constructed his double escapement and repetition grand action, patented in 1821. This action is a most ingenious combination of the light elastic touch, characteristic of the Vienna action, with the powerful stroke of the English action. It is so reliable and precise in its movements that it is undisputedly the action *par excellence* for grand pianos. With more or less modifications, the Erard grand action is now used by all leading makers of grand pianos, except, perhaps, Bösendorfer of Vienna, who still prefers the English action for his excellent grand pianos.

To what extent thinking piano makers, and the modern specialists, the action makers, have endeavored to improve the original
Erard repetition action, is shown by the following illustrations,
comprising the leading models at present in use.

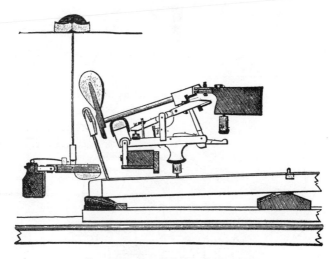

Erard-Herz Grand Action, Paris, 1850

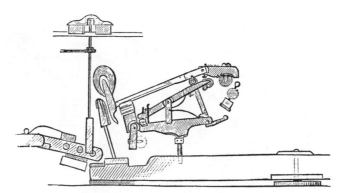

Steinway Grand Action, New York, 1884

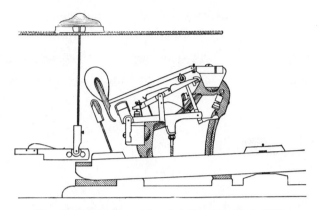

Wessell, Nickel & Gross' Grand Action, New York, 1890

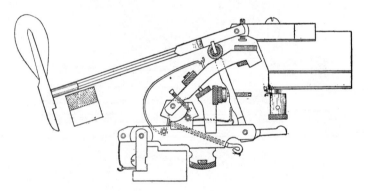

Langer Grand Action, Berlin, 1909

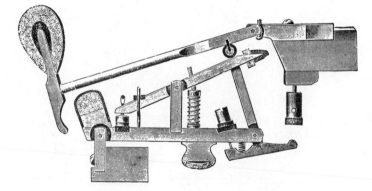

Keller's Grand Action, Stuttgart, 1909

Herrburger-Schwander Grand Action, Paris

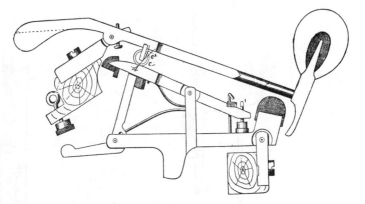

Siegfried Hansing's Grand Action, New York, 1898

Following the development of the action for the upright piano, we observe a similar evolution from the crudest device to the most complicated mechanism. The upright action of Friederici (1745) reminds one, as Hipkins so truly says, of an old German clock movement, and it is quite possible that Friederici copied it from a clock. After Friederici we find nothing of importance until the English " sticker " action appeared, a device which had nothing else in its favor than its cheapness. This unsatisfactory action was no doubt, to a large extent, responsible for the unpopularity of the early upright piano.

Robert Wornum of London accomplished for the upright piano what Sebastian Erard five years earlier had done for the grand piano. It was in 1826 when Wornum patented his " piccolo " upright action, which has remained the prototype of all upright actions used at the present time. The Wornum action made the upright piano a practical instrument. Active minds among the

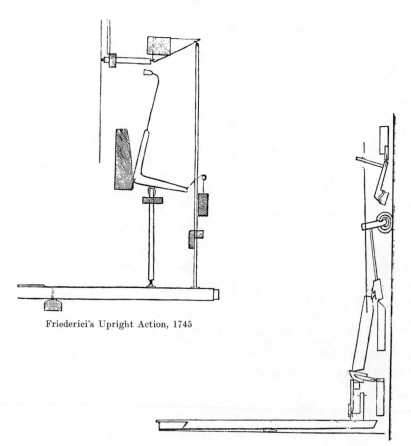

Friederici's Upright Action, 1745

English Sticker Upright Action, 1820

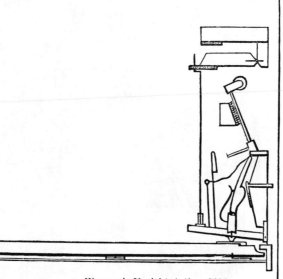

Wornum's Upright Action, 1826

piano makers set to work at once to improve this epoch-making invention. Ignace Pleyel and Henri Pape of Paris met with such notable results in their efforts in this direction that the Wornum action is to this day misnamed by most piano makers the " French " action. Perhaps it was called thus also for the reason that Paris was first in having establishments that made a specialty of producing actions for the piano trade. Their product was of such excellent quality that it was soon exported to Germany, Italy, Spain, Scandinavia, etc., and the piano manufacturers advertised that they had " French," that is, Paris made, actions in their pianos.

The extent to which the Wornum action has been developed and improved at the present day can be observed by the following illustrations:

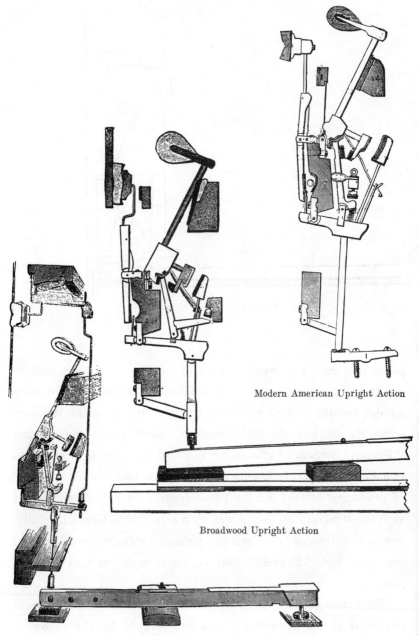

Modern American Upright Action

Broadwood Upright Action

Brinsmead Upright Action

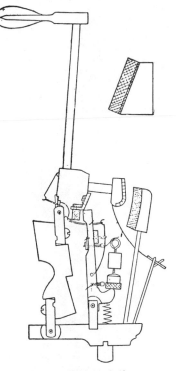

Langer Upright Action

Herrburger-Schwander Upright Action

Seaverns Upright Action
Showing Metal Flange

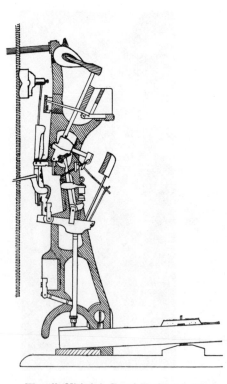

Wessell, Nickel & Gross' Upright Action

Development of the Piano Hammer

The hammer used by Christofori, Silbermann and other early makers consisted of a small wooden block covered with soft leather. With the increase of tone volume the hammer had to undergo changes and we soon find hammers having instead of the block form a longer wedge form, tapering toward the top. To assure firmness, this wedge-like molding was first covered with a piece of firm sole leather, over which a soft piece of sheepskin was glued. Next we find larger hammers in which the foundation

Christofori Hammer

Hammers Covered with Leather

over the wooden molding was a piece of very hard sole leather a quarter of an inch thick, followed by a medium firm elkskin covering and topped off with a covering of very soft, specially prepared deer or buckskin.

The art in hammer making has ever been to obtain a solid, firm foundation, graduating in softness and elasticity toward the top surface, which latter has to be silky and elastic in order to produce a mild, soft tone for pianissimo playing, but with sufficient resistance back of it to permit the hard blow of fortissimo playing. When the iron frame permitted the use of heavier strings, the leather hammer proved insufficient, and we find Alpheus Babcock, of Boston, taking out a patent in 1833 on a hammer covered with felt. Two years later, P. F. Fischer of London (a friend of Henri Pape) obtained an English patent for piano hammer felt. It is surmised that this patent is really for an invention of Henri Pape of Paris, who at that time experimented with hair felt for hammer covering, cutting up soft beaver hats for that purpose.

Getting very good results therewith, but not being able to slice this hairy hat felt thin enough for the treble hammers, Pape induced a hatter to make a hair felt in sheets tapering from a quarter of an inch to one-sixteenth of an inch thick. Pape in 1839 exhibited pianos having hammers covered with such felt, and it seems that the credit for the invention of tapered hammer felt belongs to Pape.

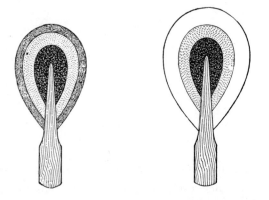

Hammers Covered with Leather and Felt

We now find the following combination in the hand-made hammers of those days: Directly over the wooden head, a covering of hard sole leather, then elkskin, and over that a covering of hair or wool felt up to about the last two treble octaves, which were covered with buckskin. The elkskin was soon replaced by a firm felt called underfelt, which was not only more economical, but also firmer than elkskin, possessing the required elasticity.

Gradually the sole leather was replaced by another underfelt, so that we now have the entire hammer made of three thicknesses of felt, each layer of its required firmness. The use of deerskin as a covering for the last two or three octaves was continued, especially in square pianos which had only two strings, more for protection, however, than for tone results. Felt making had not advanced sufficiently to produce a material so closely interknitted as to withstand the cutting of the wires on the thinly covered treble hammers.

The ever-increasing thickness of the strings, to produce greater volume of tone, necessitated a more forceful hammer than could be produced by the hand-made method, and many attempts were made to construct machines for gluing the felt to the wooden head. About 1835 Wilke, piano maker at Breslau, invented a machine in which a full set of hammers could be covered with felt at one time. It seems that hammers made on this machine were not considered as good as the hand-made, because nearly all European makers continued the hand method until about 1867, when the American pianos, shown at the Paris exposition, made a lasting impression. In America two in-

Machine-Covered Felt
Hammer, 1871

ventors patented hammer-covering machines in 1850. Rudolf Kreter of New
York patented a most ingenious but very
complicated machine. Its main fault was
that, because of manifold attached springs
and levers, it was impossible to use felt
over half an inch thick, and the cry was
for a larger, heavier hammer. This machine, which had many elements of the
present hammer-covering machines, came
into possession of Alfred Dolge in 1871,
who later on sold it as a curiosity to Brooks
of London.

Frederick Mathushek's patent of 1850 was for a hammer-covering machine of much simpler construction than Kreter's. It was patterned after the Wilke machine, the frame built of wood, with 10 iron screws, five each for down and side pressure. About 1863 Benjamin Collins, a piano and hammer maker of Boston, came out with an improvement on the Kreter machine. In Kreter's as well as Mathushek's machine, the covered hammer had to stay in the machine until the glue had thoroughly hardened. Collins, taking Kreter's iron frame machine as a pattern, changed it so that the caul or form into which the hammer is pressed could be locked, after the felt was glued on, and the caul with the hammers removed from the machine in order to repeat the operation with another set. But even Collins' machine, like others, was too light in construction to make the heavy hammers demanded for

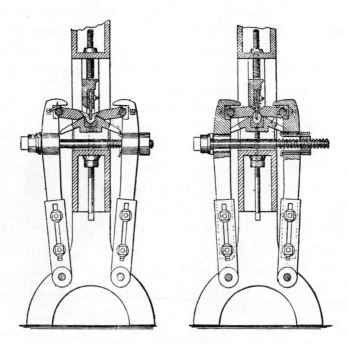

Dolge Hammer-Covering Machine, 1887

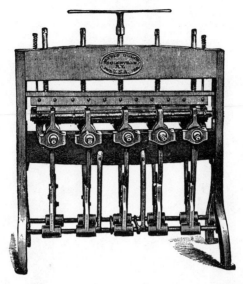

Dolge Hammer-Covering Machine, 1887

the large concert grand pianos. Most makers increased the strength of the Mathushek machine, which was generally adopted because of its simplicity, but it was very difficult to produce the desired pointed hammer with the thicker felt required.

In 1887 Alfred Dolge patented an improved hammer-covering machine, built upon the principle of drawing the felt upward, by the aid of an inclined plane on which the side cauls travel. This principle and the ease with which great pressure can be brought to bear with less physical exertion, as compared to the old style machine, has made this Dolge machine very popular. Undergoing more or less changes this machine is now in use in most of the prominent shops and factories. With the use of the heavier covering machine, the so-called " single coat " hammer made its appearance. The illustrations show a single coat grand hammer made on the Dolge machine from felt one and one-half inches thick, and an upright hammer made of felt one and one-fourth inches thick.

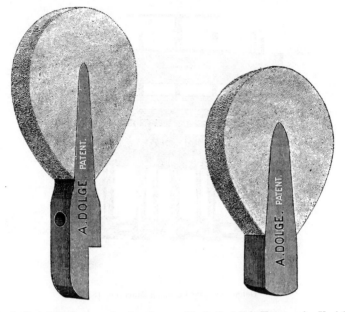

Single Coat Felt Hammer for Grand   Single Coat Felt Hammer for Upright
              Pianos   Pianos

Opinions differ very much as to the value of single coat hammers, considering their increased cost, in comparison with the double coat. The latter is universally used at present, single coat being the exception. As far back as 1873 the author made, in his factories at Dolgeville, N. Y., for Steinway & Sons, hammer felt one and three-fourth inches thick in bass and weighing 22 pounds to a sheet, which measured 36 inches wide and 43 inches long. This extraordinary thick felt was used for concert grand piano hammers, and although splendid results were achieved, the heavy hammer affected the touch too much. It is now generally agreed that felt weighing 17 to 18 pounds to a sheet is sufficiently heavy for grand hammers, and 13 to 14 pounds is the usual weight of felt used for upright hammers.

While the modern hammer-covering machine does turn out a much more uniform hammer all through the scale than could possibly be produced by the best artisan by the handmade method, further progress and improvements are necessary in order to produce a perfect hammer which will require less needle work on the part of the voicer or tone regulator. With the present machines, the operator has no control of the pressure exercised; he does not know but has to guess whether the felt is pressed down sufficiently or not. The rigidness of the covering machine does not permit of any variation in pressure to be used, so necessary on account of the uneven texture of the felt. The author has given this subject most serious thought for the past forty years, and has made many costly experiments, which finally culminated in the construction of a machine as shown in the illustration.

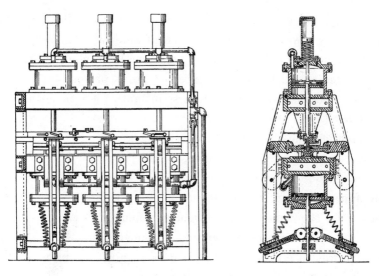

Dolge-Gardner Compressed Air Hammer-Covering Machine, 1910

Compressed air is used, and the required pressure can be gauged to a nicety and regulated as the texture of the felt or firmness required by the piano maker may dictate. Having three independent cylinders, more or less pressure can be applied, as may be desirable, at either section of the set of hammers. Martin

Gardner, for years master mechanic in the Alfred Dolge Felt Company factories, Dolgeville, Cal., built this machine under the author's instruction and supervision, and designed and originated many important detail improvements. Similar to the Collins machine, the cauls are removable after the felt is glued on to the molding, and it is estimated that two expert gluers can cover about two hundred and forty set of hammers in ten hours on one machine. While speed and saving of floor space are desirable in modern manufacturing, the main object sought for in this machine is the production of a hammer having an even gradation in texture. It is entirely within the control of the operator to give the hammer any desired degree of firmness with this machine.

Exhaustive experiments which the author has made during the past thirty years in the construction of automatic hammer-covering machines, to be operated by steam or hydraulic power, have led to the conclusion that compressed air is preferable in every respect, because the cylinders are instantly and independently controlled by a turn of a valve.

Mention must be made of a patent obtained in 1893 by John Ammon, a New York piano maker, for a process of gluing a strip of tapered hammer felt together and then inserting the same into a wooden hammer head, having two prongs on top. Ammon's motive was to economize felt. It does require much less felt by Ammon's method than gluing the felt around the molding, but the hammer designed by Ammon is utterly impracticable for many reasons, principally because it is impossible to get the treble hammers of sufficient firmness to produce a satisfactory tone.

Ammon Hammer

Alfred Dolge saw in Ammon's invention the embryo of a hammer which might, to a considerable extent, solve the vexing problem of preventing the flattening out of the hammer through usage. It is impossible to produce a well pointed hammer with the present method of hammer covering, even if the felt is forced into a sharply pointed mold of the covering machine. The hammer will invariably flatten out when it comes under the needle of the voicer or tone regulator and, of course, much more so through striking the strings, because it has no bracing or support of any kind and can give way freely. Consequently, after short usage, all felt hammers show a flat surface on top, so inimical to good tone production. To combat this flattening out of the hammers Steinway & Sons saturate the felt about half-way up with a chemical solution, which finally hardens that part of the felt sufficiently to check the flattening out to some extent. This led the author to the idea of making a hammer molding in which the upper half is split open by a saw-kerf, thus obtaining two prongs which are shaped by the ordinary wood-steaming process into a

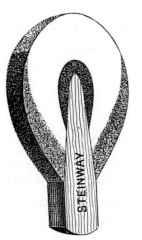

Steinway Saturated Hammer   Molding for Ammon-Dolge Hammer   Ammon-Dolge Hammer

clasp. The clasp-like prongs reach beyond the center of the glued-up felt. As shown in the illustration, the felt is forced into the clasp and then secured by a metal agraffe, passing through both prongs of the clasp, tightening the prongs so firmly on the felt that a flattening out of the felt is impossible, except through its wearing off. It is readily perceivable that the foundation of the hammer so constructed must be of a firmness and solidity not attainable by the old method of covering. Not only that the center part of the felt is glued together very tightly, but the felt itself is pressed between the firm shoulders of the clasp, thus becoming one solid body with the wooden head. The author had a grand piano containing such hammers at his home, and although his five boys used this piano almost daily for their pratice for several years, the hammers showed very little usage and wear. It is, of course, important that only the very best, most densely interknitted felt, should be used for hammers of this type. Instead of reducing the cost, as Ammon intended, the improved hammer of this type costs fully twenty-five per cent. more to produce than the ordinary. The author is of the opinion that this improvement in hammer making will finally prevail, especially since much greater durability is required for the hammers in the self-playing piano than the present form of construction admits of.

The Soundboard

The science of acoustics as developed by Chladny, Tyndall, Helmholtz, and in its direct relation to the piano, especially by Siegfried Hansing, has given us much enlightenment as to the proper and correct laying out of a scale, also the laws controlling the production of sound by percussion and otherwise, but none of these scientists can advise as to the scientifically correct construction of the soundboard. The much coddled theory of " tone waves '' found its most obstinate opponent in the soundboard of the pianoforte, disproving forcibly almost every argument brought forward in favor of this theory. Not finding any assistance from scientists, the piano maker had to rely entirely upon empiric experiments, to construct a soundboard best adapted to his scale. All the experiments, and their names are legion, ended in coming back to the plain soundboard as constructed by the clavichord and harpsichord makers of the early days, namely, a board of as large a size as the case of the piano would permit, made of the best quality of well-seasoned fir, strengthened by bars or ribs glued on crossways. The various writers on piano construction differ materially regarding the importance of the soundboard in relation to tone development in the piano. The careful and learned Dr. Oscar Paul, laboring under the ban of the '' wave theory,'' insists that the soundboard is the very soul of the piano and that tone quality as well as volume depend altogether upon its construction. Indeed, he holds that the tone is produced by the soundboard and not by the string.

Siegfried Hansing in his book '' The Pianoforte and Its Acoustic Properties,'' shows the fallacy of this contention beyond contradiction. He bases his argument on Pellisow's proven doctrine that the ear does not perceive sound through so-called tone waves, but because of the shock or jolt by which the sound is created. Consequently, Hansing looks upon the soundboard as a drum, upon which the vibrations of the strings, caused by the striking of the hammer, are delivered as shocks or jolts.

Hansing disclaims the existence of the ear harp, assumed by Helmholtz and others, as an impossibility and maintains that the ear is an apparatus to measure the intervals between shocks, distinguishing the higher tones by their shorter, and the lower tones by their longer, intervals. He does not believe that a properly constructed soundboard ever has any transverse vibrations which affect the tone, as demonstrated by the successful experiments of

Mathushek and Moser, whose double soundboards were glued together so that the grain of the one crossed the grain of the other at right angles. This method of construction makes any transverse vibration impossible, and instruments containing such boards are not inferior in volume and quality of tone to any other.

Hansing thus proves that the soundboard does not give forth sounds, but that it only augments and transmits the sound originating with the string, through a tremor, which is the effect of the motion producing the sound; namely, the percussion of the string by the hammer. This important discovery will assist materially in the further search for soundboard improvements, but even Hansing admits that for the present the piano constructor has to rely on empiric experiments for final results.

To mention a few of the most telling experiments made to improve the efficiency of the soundboard, we find Jacob Goll of Vienna using iron and copper with reasonable success in 1823; but, no doubt, the primitive conditions of the metal industries of those days made the use of metal too expensive, as compared to wood. Henri Pape of Paris, that king of piano empirics, experimented not only with all kinds of wood and metal, but tried even parchment. All these materials transmitted the sound of the strings, except the parchment, which proved totally unfit for use in the treble sections.

During the writer's engagement with the Mathushek factory in 1867-69, exhaustive experiments were made to find the most responsive thickness for a soundboard. With boards from fully one inch in thickness, without ribs, graduated down to boards only three-sixteenths of an inch thick in treble, and with proportionately heavy ribs, numberless tests were made. Curious to relate, all of the pianos had a satisfactory tone, differing, of course, in quality. The thick boards responded with a thick, somewhat stiff, woody quality, the pianos with the thinner boards had a more sympathetic, soulful, but weaker tone. The most satisfactory tone quality was found in the pianos which had the " regulation " soundboard, three-eighths of an inch thick in treble, tapering off to one-fourth of an inch in bass, ribs placed at nearly equal distances apart, except in the last treble octave, where they lay somewhat closer together. These trials and tests proved conclusively that the soundboard does not produce sound by aid of sound waves, but simply transmits and augments the sound produced by the vibration of the string. They further proved that the soundboard is not nearly as much of a factor in tone production as the string, the proper length, thickness and position of which, together with the most advantageous striking point for the hammer, are the all-important factors to be considered in piano construction.

Attempts to increase the volume of tone by using double soundboards, connected by wooden posts or otherwise, the imitation of the violin or cello form, carefully worked out corrugated soundboards, etc., have all been in vain and are discarded for good. Several ingenious devices to sustain the resistance of the soundboard against the downward pressure of the strings are recorded. Among them Mathushek's " equilibre " system, patented in 1879, is perhaps the most scientific, but the result achieved is not in proportion to the increased cost. Mathushek surmised, what Hansing established as a scientific fact, that the soundboard is not affected by so-called sound waves, and when he discarded his equilibre system because of its high cost, he returned to the thick soundboard without ribs. In 1891 he patented his duplex soundboard, which is a combination of two boards, cross-banded and glued together. The boards are made thickest at the center where the bridge rests, in order to withstand the pressure of the strings.

On October 2, 1900, Richard W. Gertz obtained a patent for a Tension Resonator for Pianos, the purport of which is to regulate the pressure in the arch of the soundboard against the strings and to assist the vibratory efficiency of the entire soundboard,

Bottom of Grand Piano showing Richard W. Gertz's Tension Resonator

thereby increasing the intensity of tone produced by the striking of the hammer against the string.

Another function of this resonator is to restore the original arched form of the soundboard when, through age or atmospheric influences, the same has given away to the pressure of the strings.

The tension rods with the conical shaped head, inserted into the rim, draw together the entire rim upon which the soundboard is fastened, and force the latter back to its original arched form, reinstating and enlivening the vibratory action of the entire board.

Radiating from the center of the piano to all parts of the rim the tension rods can be screwed up, either simultaneously to bring pressure upon the entire board, or individually if any part of the soundboard should show a pronounced flatness. They are furthermore of great value in maintaining the correct form and shape of the rim. This invention has been applied to all the grand pianos made by Mason & Hamlin since the granting of the patent.

Experience so far has shown that the best material for soundboards is the wood of the fir tree, growing in the mountain regions of Southern Europe and North America.

Whether or not the development of the steel industry will furnish the piano maker eventually with rolled sheets for soundboards, made of proper vibratory metal, and in tapered form, is speculative. It is not improbable, however, that the piano of the future may have a metal soundboard. We do know that the sound in the piano originates with the steel string, and that it is only transmitted by the soundboard, materially assisted by proper construction of the wooden frame of the piano. We also know that the iron frame has no deleterious influence upon the tone quality, and since all piano construct-

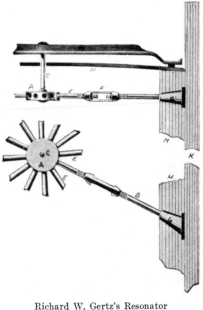

Richard W. Gertz's Resonator

View of Soundboard Rim and Tension Rods

ors are still seeking for a clear, bell-like, singing quality of tone, may not the solution be found in a soundboard of steel, so constructed as to successfully withstand the pressure of the strings, and to assist the steel strings in tone production?

Evidently the soundboard is the only part of the modern piano which calls upon the inventor for further investigation, on scientific lines, until the laws are found upon which to build a piano, not necessarily with a louder, but with a more soulful tone, such as the old clavichord possessed in limited quantity.

PART ONE

CHAPTER IV

PART ONE

CHAPTER IV

THE DEVELOPMENT OF THE MANUFACTURE OF PIANO MATERIALS AND SUPPLIES

PERHAPS no other class of manufacturing depends more largely upon auxiliary industries, each of itself of considerable magnitude, than the piano industry. It is furthermore true that the piano industry could not have made its marvelous progress, had not the auxiliary industries kept pace with the inventive piano maker, oftentimes anticipating his wants and providing superior material which permitted the improvement of the piano. Wire for strings and felt for hammers are two of the materials which have been continually improved by the manufacturers in advance of the piano maker's demands. It is therefore proper that the development of the supply industries should be recorded in these pages.

All inhabited parts of the globe contribute, more or less, the raw material for a piano. Asia and Africa supply the ivory and ebony for the keyboard. Sweden, England and America, iron ore for strings, pins and plates. North and South America, Australia and Africa, wool for felts, while Europe, North and South America, the Philippine and West India islands supply the various kinds of wood.

Wood Used in Piano Construction

It is not so many years ago since the piano maker of Germany was obliged to go to the forest and buy at auction such logs as he might select for his purpose. If a sawmill was near by, he had his logs delivered there, giving the sawyer special instruction as to how to saw each log. Oftentimes the logs had to be transported to his factory yard, where they had to be sawed into planks and boards by two men moving a big handsaw up and down, one man standing on top of the log, the other in a pit under the log. The writer saw, at a prominent factory in London, this process still in vogue in 1879.

With the introduction of power-driven woodworking machinery, the millmen and lumber dealers began to specialize, and supplied the piano maker with selected boards or planks, sawed to the thickness and length required. Receiving the lumber from the mill, it was carefully stacked up for air seasoning. As soon as the sap had hardened, the planks were brought into the shop and there again carefully stacked up about 7 feet from the floor, to get the benefit of the even temperature of the closed room. This awkward and slow process of seasoning lumber after being air-dried was done away with by the introduction of the steam-heated dry-kiln. Endless experiments have been made to force the sap out of the wood, by boiling, or using tremendous pressure upon the lumber as soon as it came from the saw, in order to do away with the costly air drying process, but none has turned out a success for lumber to be used in pianos. Wood dried so forcedly loses all its strength, life and pliability, and since every part of the piano is supposed to assist in tone production, it follows that wood deadened by forced drying is unfit for use. Hence, a well stocked lumber yard is to this date a positive necessity.

Some of the large piano manufacturers of America carry as much as three to five million square feet of lumber constantly in their yards. A New York corporation invested $400,000 not long ago, in a stock of hardwood veneers 14 to 28 feet long, to be used for bent rims on grand pianos, merely for fear that such long veneers of the required straight grain, length and width could not often be found in the market. The investment is considered a good one from a financial point, since hardwood is rapidly advancing in value, far in excess of the interest account.

For the manufacturing of veneers, inventors have been prolific in devising improved sawing appliances as well as rapidly-working automatic machines for cutting with knives. An entire log can be placed in front of the knives, which are up to 16 feet long, and veneers cut off, as thin as one thirty-second of an inch, continuously until the log is used up.

Soundboards

The manufacture of lumber for soundboards has been followed up as a specialty for over 100 years. The first specialists in this line were owners of forests in the mountains of Bohemia and Tyrol. Instead of sawing the logs into boards, they were split, like the old-time American fence rail, into boards of about one inch thickness. The clavichord or piano maker of 100 years ago would not have thought of using sawed lumber for his soundboards. He believed in the theory that sound waves traveled along the grain of the wood, and since the saw would not follow the grain, unless the tree had grown up perfectly straight (which no tree ever does), the piano maker imagined that the imperceptible crossing of the grain by the saw would interfere with the sound waves. To-day, with a production of approximately 650,000 pianos per year, all the lumber for soundboards is sawed, either with gang or circular saws, and the pianos are better than ever.

The Bohemian and Swiss manufacturers of soundboard lumber prepared their product most carefully. After cutting out all knots, shakes and other imperfections, the rough boards were smoothed off by handplaning, cut into lengths of from 4 to 8 feet and then carefully packed in boxes 2 feet wide, containing 60 layers each. Length and width of board dictated the price of the lumber, boards 8 feet long, 4 boards to the layer, bringing nearly twice as much per square foot as boards 4 feet long and having 5 or 6 to the layer. In America, soundboard lumber was sold as it came from the sawmill, and the piano maker could hardly ever utilize more than forty per cent. of what he bought.

The author revolutionized this branch of the supply business by commencing in 1874 to manufacture finished soundboards for the trade at his mills in Dolgeville, N. Y. This innovation was welcomed by the piano makers, who could now carry a full stock of boards on hand, exposing the finished board to a thorough seasoning in their factories, for as long a time as desired, with less investment than was necessary to carry a sufficient stock of soundboard lumber in their yards. I and my associates invented a number of special devices and machines for gluing up and planing the entire boards, none of which was patented. Among these machines the great cylinder planer with bed and knives five feet wide must be mentioned. Every builder of woodworking machinery then in business refused to accept the order for such a machine, claiming that a width of three feet was the limit of safety for a planing machine cylinder. I constructed a machine planing five feet in width which was such a success that similar machines are now in use in many factories of Europe and America. Two men can plane 300 soundboards to perfection on such a machine, within 10 hours, while it is an easy matter to finish off 400 boards per day on the modern cylinder sandpapering machine. The best workman could not finish over 10 boards per day with a handplane.

Fully ninety per cent. of the soundboards used are now supplied to the piano trade by concerns making a specialty of the business. The forests of Bohemia and Tyrol having been exhausted, the European makers have to get their supply of lumber from Galicia and Roumania. In America the forests of the Adirondacks and White Mountains have from the beginning been the source of supply. Even these great forests are passing rapidly and new sources of supply must be sought. The author, after thorough personal investigation, found splendid material on the west coast of North America, more particularly in the mountain forests of Oregon and Washington, and consequently started a soundboard factory at Los Angeles, Cal., in 1903, supplying not only the American trade, but exporting largely to Germany also.

The best soundboard lumber comes from the mountain districts of the temperate zone, at an altitude of 3,000 to 5,000 feet above sea, where timber growth is thriftiest. Trees not over 100 years of age are the most desirable, the wood being strong and elastic. Trees under 70 years of age are not matured and have too much undeveloped sapwood.

Several of the American soundboard manufacturers are also making a specialty of ribs, bridges, wrest planks and complete backs for upright pianos.

Piano Cases

Case making for the trade has been a specialty in America for over 50 years, and nearly all manufacturers of commercial pianos buy their cases ready made. It is readily understood that a manufacturer making a specialty of cases, producing as many as 10,000 to 30,000 per year, can afford to make a much larger investment for labor-saving machinery and devices than a piano maker who turns out 500 to 2,000 pianos per year. The tendency of the age is for economic specialization in all branches of industry, and the " compiler " of the various ready-made parts of a piano does, beyond doubt, produce a better commercial instrument, than if he should attempt to make each part of the piano in his own shop.

The tremendous growth of the piano industry has, on the other hand, developed individual concerns, which turn out from 5,000 to 20,000 pianos per year. Such firms, of course, avail themselves of the advantages of labor-saving machinery in all departments. Some of these large concerns own forest lands, have large saw-mills, and, of course, make their own cases, keys and actions, even casting their own iron plates.

The London manufacturers were the first to introduce power-driven machinery in their factories. As far back as 1850, some of their leading firms were producing from 2,000 to 3,000 pianos per annum, a quantity which made the use of steam-power machinery an economic proposition. Machinery is only economic when it can be continually employed. The piano maker with a limited production cannot avail himself of that advantage. Consequently, as a matter of commercial and industrial evolution, the specialists, such as case makers, key and action makers, have become indispensable to the industry. They made possible the production of a reliable, satisfactory instrument, at a price within the reach of the masses.

Development of the Piano Felt Industry

Felt is a fabric formed of wool or hair, or wool and hair, by taking advantage of the natural tendency of the fiber to interlace and mat together by aid of the moisture and heat during the continuous process of rolling, beating and pressure. The invention or discovery of the felting process dates back to the age of our cave-dwelling ancestors, whose sole wardrobe was a sheepskin coat, which through use became densely matted. Julius Cæsar organized a light brigade, which had felt breastplates as a protection against the enemies' weapons. In the ruins of Pompeii a complete plant for scouring and pressing felts has been found.

The first attempt at using machinery for the production of felts was made in England. The patent granted to P. F. Fischer of London, 1835, describes a piano hammer felt, which is firm on one side and soft on the other, and made in sheets, tapering in thickness. As stated elsewhere, this description is identical with Henri Pape's invention, and can undoubtedly be traced to him.

Whitehead Brothers of Manchester, England, are said to be the first who made the manufacturing of piano hammer felt a specialty. They were followed by Billon and Fortin of Paris and Weickert (1847) of Leipsic, Germany. Naish of Wilton, England, started in 1859. These firms controlled the market until the author started his factories in 1871.

There are two essential requisites for a good piano hammer felt.

First, it must be well felted to insure wearing quality, because the continual pounding of the hammer against the steel strings in the piano is liable to cut the fiber of the felt if the fiber is not closely connected. With this thorough felting, however, a pronounced elasticity is indispensable, in order to enable the hammer to rebound quickly from the string. From these two requisites arises the art of making felt for piano hammers.

A short description of the process of felt making will interest many readers. Wool of the merino sheep, raised either in North America or Cape Colony in Africa, is best adapted for hammer felt. In the scouring process, the weight of the wool, as it comes from the sheep's back, shrinks about seventy-five per cent.; that is to say, 100 pounds of raw wool will yield only 25 pounds of workable wool after scouring. After the wool is thoroughly dried and opened up by passing through so-called picker machines, it is thoroughly carded and then formed into sheets. Since almost every piano maker has his own peculiar notions as to the thickness and tapering of the felt, there were no standards in the beginning and the felt had to be formed by hand, putting one layer of wool over the other as the tapering would dictate. A sheet of felt weighing about 12 pounds when finished, measuring one inch in thickness in bass, and tapering down to one-eighth of an inch in treble, being about 38 inches square, would measure 10 inches in thickness in bass, one inch in treble and be about 54 inches square before the felting began. This unwieldy mass of wool is hardened down and fulled, until the sheet has shrunk to the above-mentioned size and thickness. No chemicals are used by any good felt maker in the fulling process, only soap and hot water being applied.*

In 1874 the author invented a process by which the wool is fed through the cards in accordance with a correct mathematical calculation, so as to form on an apron or belt the correct thickness and taper required. This apron carries the carded wool sufficient for six full sheets of felt, making about 100 sets of hammers.

The apron passes through a set of hardening rollers, which continuously unite each thin web as it comes from the carding machine, thus assuring a most positive interknitting of each layer of wool with the other, and furthermore a uniformity of taper not attainable by the hand-laying process.

The author received for his hammer felts the highest awards at the World's Fairs of Vienna, 1873; Philadelphia, 1876; Paris, 1878; and Chicago, 1893. The felt made by the above described process was preferred by all the leading makers of America and extensively used by many of the foremost piano makers of Europe.

---

* Many piano makers have the erroneous idea that the fine white dust, which they observe when sandpapering the hammers, is composed of chalk. The admixture of chalk would almost kill the fulling process. The white dust referred to is pure wool, finely ground by the action of the sandpaper file of the piano maker.

The felt factories founded by Alfred Dolge have been amalgamated with a number of other felt factories, producing principally commercial felts, and the product has lost its identity.

Piano Hammer Making

Hammer making as a specialty and rising to the dignity of an industry began in America with the invention of Mathushek's hammer-covering machine, in 1850. In England the handmade hammers were for many years produced as a house industry. American machines (Dolge model) were introduced in the London shops about 1880. Germany started this special industry about 1845, when Merckel of Hamburg supplied the action maker Isermann, and many piano makers, with handmade hammers. He introduced machines of his own construction in 1860. Hammer-covering machines of the American pattern were generally adopted in Germany about 1870.

In America hammer covering, especially for the commercial pianos, is largely controlled by the felt and action makers. Several firms make a specialty of hammer covering, but all the larger piano manufacturers make their own hammers.

The Piano Wire Industry

Records tell us that iron wire for musical instruments was drawn at Augsburg as early as 1351, but Fuchs of Nuremberg was perhaps the first who made the manufacturing of piano wire a specialty, supplying the clavichord and harpsichord makers of the 18th century.

About 1820 a Berlin firm succeeded in producing a wire which was soon preferred to Fuchs's make, to be again driven out of the market by Webster & Horsfall of Birmingham who brought out their piano wire, made of cast steel, in 1834.

This cast steel wire was so superior to the iron wire that the English firm soon had a monopoly.

But in 1840 Martin Miller of Vienna came out with a wire superior to Webster's and a strong competition began, especially when Rollason & Son, Smith & Houghton and others also took up this industry in England.

Miller's wire continued, however, to be in favor with most of the German piano makers, until Moritz Poehlmann of Nuremberg started to make his world renowned product about 1855. In the first competitive test, Poehlmann's wire proved to be of greater density than Miller's, but not of equal tensile strength. Miller's wire would, however, stretch much more than Poehlmann's, consequently would not stand in tune as well as Poehlmann's much denser, better hardened wire. At the Paris Exposition of 1867 the Jury on Piano Wire tested the various makes exhibited, on a machine loaned by Pleyel, Wolff & Company. Poehlmann's wire proved so far superior to any other make that he received the highest prize. As a natural consequence all the leading piano manufacturers of Europe and America adopted the Poehlmann make for their pianos. Moritz Poehlmann deserves particular credit for his never-ceasing efforts to improve his wire, not only as to tensile strength, but also even gradation of sizes and excellent polish, so necessary a protection against rust. Poehlmann's remarkable success not only incited his competitors to greater effort, but caused the starting of a number of new wire factories in Germany.

In America Washburn & Moen of Worcester have made very good piano wire since 1860. The American wire always had an exceedingly high polish, hardly ever attained by the European makers, but it often lacked the requisite density and necessary uniformity of tensile strength.

OFFICIAL TESTS OF TENSILE STRENGTH OF MUSIC WIRE

1. *Official Test by the Jury of the World's Exhibition, Paris, 1867.*

Pleyel, Wolff & Company's testing machine used.

Moritz Poehlmann's wire broke at a strain of............Lbs.	Nos. 13	14	15	16	17	18
	226	264	292	296	312	348

English wires broke at a strain of..	... 214	...	...	...	274

2. *Official Test by the Jury of the World's Exhibition, Vienna, 1873.*

Moritz Poehlmann's wire broke at a strain of............Lbs.	Nos. 13	14	15	16	17	18
	232	260	290	300	322	336

Martin Miller & Sons' wire broke at a strain of..................	168	192	206	232	255	280

3. *Official Test by the Jury of the World's Exhibition, Philadelphia, 1876.*

Steinway & Sons' testing machine used.

Moritz Poehlmann's wire broke at a strain of............Lbs.	Nos. 13	14	15	16	17	18
	265	287	320	331	342	386

W. D. Houghton's wire broke at a strain of	231	242	253	287	331	374
Smith & Son's wire broke at a strain of	221	242	242	287	320	331
Washburn & Moen's wire broke at strain of	176	...	198	...	242	...

The records of the World's Fair at Chicago, 1893, show the following report of the test of Poehlmann's wire made by Judges Max Schiedmayer of Stuttgart and George Steck of New York:

No. 13 Measuring .030 of an inch broke at a strain of 325 lbs.
" 14   "   .031 " " "   "   " "   "   " 335 "
" 15   "   .034 " " "   "   " "   "   " 350 "
" 16   "   .035 " " "   "   " "   "   " 400 "
" 17   "   .037 " " "   "   " "   "   " 415 "

How successful Poehlmann has been in improving his product is best illustrated by the following table of tests, which shows the tensile strength at breaking point:

Expositions—	Wire No. 13	14	15	16	17
Paris, 1867	226	264	292	312	348
Vienna, 1873	232	261	291	300	336
Philadelphia, 1876	265	287	320	331	342
Chicago, 1893	325	335	350	400	415

Since 1893 no authoritative tests are on record, but considering the severe tension to which the present-day piano maker exposes the wire, and as all the different brands of wire are used more or less, it will be admitted that Poehlmann's efforts lifted the entire piano wire industry to its present high level, to the benefit of the piano trade.

Development of the Piano Action Industry

The very first auxiliary industry of the piano trade was undoubtedly piano action making. Among the oldest firms in existence at this date, we find first Brooks of London, who started his business in 1810. L. Isermann of Hamburg, (now merged with Langer & Company, of Berlin), began business in 1842. In the same year came Charles Gehrling of Paris, who was followed by

Schwander, in 1844. Morgenstern & Kotrade of Leipsic started in 1846, Lexow of Berlin in 1854, and Fritz & Meyer, as well as Keller of Stuttgart, commenced business in 1857.

In America F. W. Frickinger, a German who had learned the art at Paris, started an action factory at Albany, N. Y., in 1837, moving later on to Nassau, N. Y. His son-in-law, Grubb, succeeded him and the business is now carried on under the firm name of Grubb & Kosegarten Brothers.

George W. Seaverns established his action factory at Cambridgeport, Mass., in 1851.

In no department of piano manufacturing has the use of automatic machinery been so largely applied, to improve the product and lessen the cost, as in the making of piano actions. In all well equipped action factories automatic machines are employed to fraise, mold, bore, also bush with cloth, or trim with leather, the various parts of the piano action. All of these machines work with positive precision. Some machines, as, for instance, the hammer butt milling machines, are marvels of human ingenuity. This machine takes the wooden block, molded to the proper form, and by entirely automatic motions turns out a perfectly

George W. Seaverns

finished butt. This economic way of producing actions has been made possible because of the fact that nearly all of the American piano makers use the same model, the only material difference being in the lengths of the pilots or tangents which connect the action with the key.

Iron Plates, Pins, Etc.

The casting, bronzing and pinning of the iron frames have kept pace in every way with the advancement of the piano. America, in particular, has for years produced the very best of castings, solid in grain, smooth in finish. The example set by Steinway & Sons, in their foundries at Steinway, Long Island, had a beneficial influence on all plate makers, whose customers demanded plates " as good as Steinway's."

The progress in the science of metallurgy has aided the plate makers in obtaining the best blending of various ores, and breaking or cracking of plates is a trouble of the past.

Even in this industry, automatic machinery begins to lessen the cost of production. The other metal parts in the piano, brass and nickel tubes for action rails, brass butts and flange rails, are manufactured by specialists. The making of wrest or tuning pins is an industry which for over 60 years has been monopolized by a limited number of manufacturers in Westphalia. They have so far managed to retain this monopoly by making excellent pins at a price so low as not to invite competition.

Very good tuning pins are now made in a factory near New York. Time will tell whether this enterprise can hold out against the low wages of Westphalia, because years ago the Westphalian manufacturers adopted the use of automatic machinery, which turns plain wire into a finished tuning pin, similar to the process of making screws.

Of other materials, such as glue, varnish, etc., nothing need be said. They are products used long before pianos were made.

PART ONE

CHAPTER V

DEVELOPMENT OF THE PLAYER PIANO, Morse, Vaucanson, Seytre, Bain, Pape, Fourneaux, McTammany, Gally, Bishop & Downe, Kuster, Pain, Parker, White, Brown, Votey, Goolman, Hobart, Clark, Kelly, Klugh, Welin, Hupfeld, Welte, Young, Crooks, Dickinson, Danquard.

PART ONE

CHAPTER V

Development of the Player Piano

ALL useful inventions are the product of evolution—the result of searching thought and creative ability. An idea may be born in one man's mind; the realization and utilization of the idea require, however, the co-operation of several minds, one improving upon the labors of the other.

The player piano is still in its development, and many bright minds are devoted to the improvement of the instrument as we know it at present. Destined eventually to displace the piano as the musical instrument of the home, adequate financial reward beckons to the inventive genius who can accomplish the extraordinary. Aside from the financial aspect, the player problem has some of that alluring attractiveness which tempts the ambitious inventor to make his bid for fame, or at least to try to satisfy his own desire for the accomplishment of the ideal.

The history of the player piano is in the making. While the fundamental idea is perhaps two hundred years old, the real development and practical application dates back only to the early seventies of the past century, and the most important improvements, those which made the player piano a commercial possibility, have been developed during the past twenty-five years. Indeed, we can look for ultimate perfection only from now on.

It would be presumptuous to pass judgment or dispense honors for what has been achieved so far. Many an ingenious device of practical value to-day may prove to be only a stepping-stone for greater achievements to-morrow, and thus soon become obsolete. The author has to confine himself, therefore, to a documentary description of what appear to be the most important inventions of the development of the player piano, in their chronological order, without attempting to discuss their merits or demerits, excepting those upon which final judgment has been passed by that infallible tribunal, the purchasing public.

Inquiring into the origin of the player piano mechanism, we find that the idea of applying automatic attachments to keyed instruments engaged many of the harpsichord and pianoforte builders of the 17th and 18th centuries, as illustrated by their efforts to augment the scope of their instruments with orchestral effects, set in motion by pedals, swells, etc. Apparently the first successful attempt to play an instrument with a keyboard by a mechanical device was made in 1731 by Justinian Morse of England. He obtained a patent, in which he describes his invention as follows:

" A new organ with either diapason or the principal in front with one or more sets of keys, the bellows to go with either the feet or the hands, by which any person, though unskilled in musick, may be taught in an hour's time to play with great exactness and with their proper graces, either single or double, with preludes and interludes, all psalm tunes, fuges, volunteries, and anthems that are usually sung in churches or chappells, or any other musick tho' never so difficult, or what length or compass soever, and that by this invention a fuller, thorough bass may be pla'd than can possibly be performed by the hands or fingers alone on the common keys; and this is performed entirely without vowls or barrels, and in a third part of the room, the musick being prickt on both sides of leaves or half-inch wainscot, eight or ten psalm tunes being contained on a board about the size of a large sheet of paper and may be worked by clockwork, jack or winch, and is made after a new method to play louder or softer by a division on the sound board; and that this organ may be made for a much lower price than all others heretofore, and therefore will be very proper to be made use of in churches or chappells in small parishes that are unable or unwilling to be at the expense of the constant attendance of an organist, or in gentlemen's houses or in private familys.''

It is to be regretted that no instrument answering the above description seems to be in existence, but, considering the severity of the patent laws of those days, it can hardly be doubted but that Morse constructed at least a working model according to his specification.

About 1740-50 Vaucanson, the celebrated automaton maker of Paris, reversed the construction of the cylinder used in automatic musical instruments of his time. Instead of projecting pegs, Vaucanson constructed a pierced cylinder for weaving flowered silks. This cylinder, according to the holes it presented when revolved, regulated the movement of needles, causing the warp to deviate in such a manner as to produce a given design indicated by the holes in the cylinder. It is said that Vaucanson used this pierced cylinder also in musical instruments.

Jacquard, of silk-loom fame, seized upon Vaucanson's idea, and in 1802 added an endless piece of cardboard to the cylinder, perforated with holes in accordance with the pattern intended to be woven. The perforated cardboard pattern of the Jacquard loom is in principle identical with the perforated music rolls of the present day.

Seytre of France patented, in 1842, a musical instrument to which he applied Jacquard's perforated cardboard. Bain of Scotland patented a similar device in 1847, and that great piano maker, Henri Pape of Paris, tried his hand on the same thing in 1851. No instruments of these inventors are in existence, and it seems that neither invention had any practical or commercial value. They are mentioned here only as the next step in advance from the stiff perforated board to the flexible cardboard.

In 1863 Fourneaux of Paris patented his *pianista,* a device

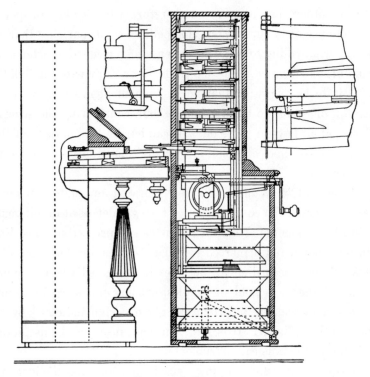

Fourneaux's Pianista

which through pneumatics pressed " fingers " upon the piano keys
as indicated by the perforated cardboards. This mechanism was
exhibited at the Philadelphia Exposition in 1876, and quite a number of these machines have been sold. The machine, set in motion
by a crank movement, could be attached to any piano, the fingers
being placed over the piano keyboard, as in the later cabinet player.
For unknown reasons this invention was not further developed,
and became obsolete because of its limited possibilities and high
cost.

About 1868 John McTammany constructed a mechanism for
automatic playing of organs, substituting for the crank and perforated cardboard of Fourneaux a foot-pedal action and narrow
sheets of perforated flexible paper with winding and rewinding

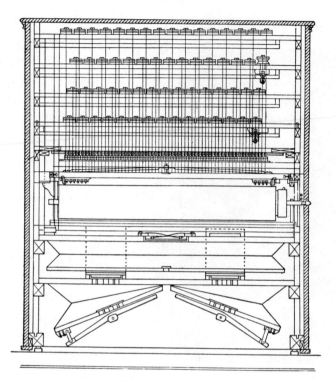

Fourneaux's Pianista

rolls. For this invention McTammany filed on September 7, 1876, a caveat with the following description: " The invention relates to an improved attachment to organs, so that any piece of music may be played in an automatic manner, in any key, on the same, and the invention consists of a mechanism worked by a fan from the bellows and by a strip of paper perforated to express musical notes, and it consists also of a transposing mechanism to play music in any desired key." The above language shows that the patent attorneys of those days were in the kindergarten class of player piano patent lingo as we read it to-day.

In McTammany's invention the action was inside the organ case, instead of being attached from the outside, as in Fourneaux's pianista. While broadly speaking the action was pneumatic, yet

John McTammany

it did not have individual pneumatics for each tone.

The next important step in the development of the player mechanism was Merritt Gally's device, patented in 1881. It created a sensation at the time, but has never been commercially exploited.

Bishop & Downe of England were granted a patent for a keyboard attachment for musical instruments in 1883. Perhaps for the reason that the mechanism had to be set in motion by turning a crank, precluding any exercise of individuality, this invention did not succeed commercially.

In 1886 G. B. Kelly invented a wind motor with slide valves opening and closing ports to pneumatic motors. This form of motor was at once adopted, and, upon the expiration of the patent, came into general use in all the factories in the world.

On May 14, 1886, Charles A. Kuster filed his application for a patent on a mechanical instrument, which was granted on April 19, 1887. Kuster's construction differed entirely from Bishop & Downe's, as well as from Gally's. It seems, however, that Kuster did not know how to make his invention popular and to secure for it proper recognition.

R. W. Pain is perhaps the first who constructed a pneumatic self-playing piano. In conjunction with Henry Kuster he built

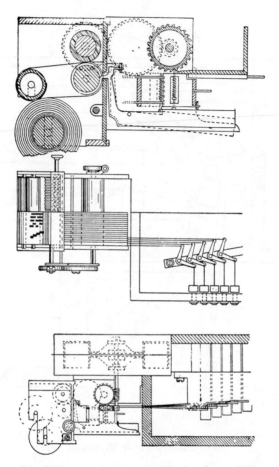

John McTammany's Automatic Playing Organ, 1868

such an instrument for Needham & Sons in 1880, having a compass of 39 notes. In 1882 he constructed for the Mechanical Orguinette Co. (which later on became the Aeolian Co.) an inside player with 46 notes, and in 1888 he produced his 65-note electric player.

On October 16, 1891, Wm. D. Parker of Meriden, Conn., in the employ of the Wilcox & White Company, made application for a patent on an automatic piano. The patent was granted March 8, 1892, for a combination piano adapted for either manual

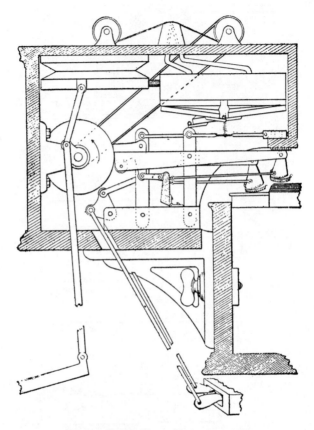

Merritt Gally's Player Mechanism, 1881

or automatic operation, having a system of pneumatic operating mechanism controlled by a perforated music sheet.

Suitable wind-inducing apparatus or motor, and such mechanism, permanently introduced into the structure of the instrument, operating upon the rear ends of the manual keys, not interfering or preventing use of the piano for ordinary manual operation. This interior player mechanism was manufactured by the Wilcox & White Company of Meriden, and sold under the name of Angelus Piano Player to piano dealers in Boston, Phila-

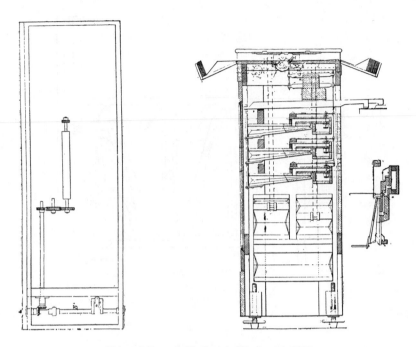

Bishop & Downe's Keyboard Attachment, 1883

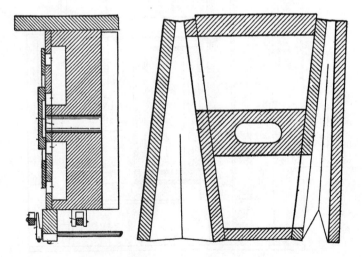

George B. Kelly's Wind Motor with Slide Valves, 1886

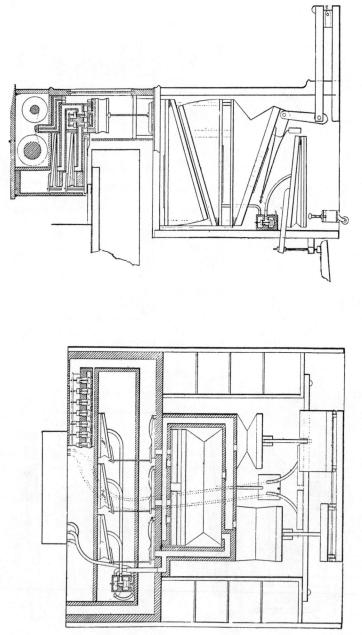

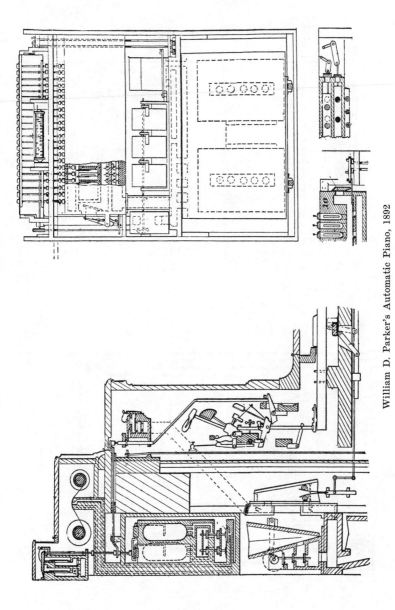

William D. Parker's Automatic Piano, 1892

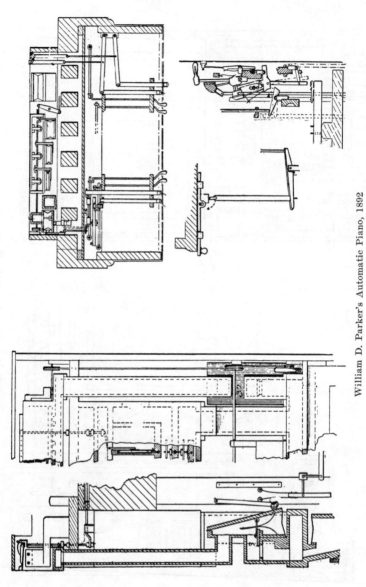

William D. Parker's Automatic Piano, 1892

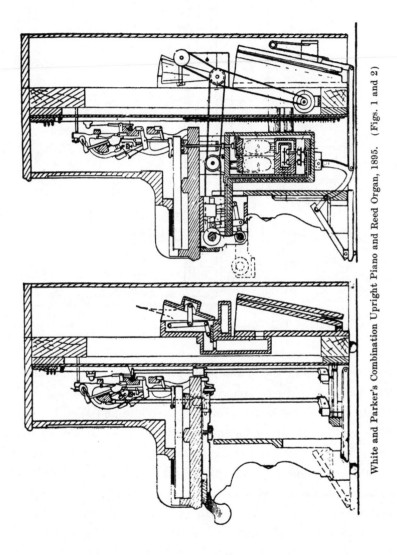

White and Parker's Combination Upright Piano and Reed Organ, 1895.   (Figs. 1 and 2)

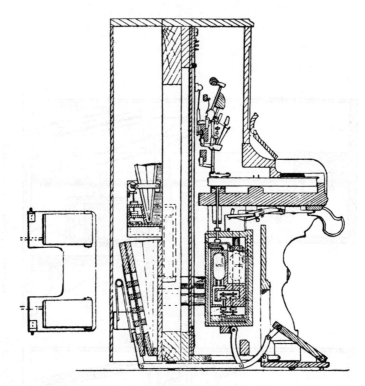

White and Parker's Combination Upright Piano and Reed Organ, 1895.   (Fig. 3)

delphia, etc., and the patent was assigned to and controlled by the Wilcox & White Company.

On November 29, 1895, Edward H. White and Wm. D. Parker filed application for a patent, which was granted December 15, 1896, for a combination of the automatic upright piano and reed organ. This ingenious invention did not prove a commercial success, mainly for the reason that the steel strings of the piano would not remain in tune with the reeds (which would remain in tune for years), and naturally on that account would not always blend with the tone produced in combination with each other.

On July 27, 1897, Wm. D. Parker obtained patents for similar attachments for grand and square pianos.

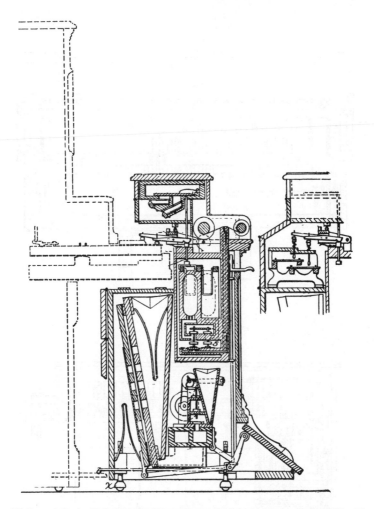

White and Parker's Automatic Piano Player in Cabinet Form, 1897.   (Fig. 1)

Not meeting with the success anticipated in introducing this interior mechanism, White and Parker on April 5, 1897, filed an application for a patent for an automatic piano player in cabinet form, and which contained reeds and could be operated either as an automatic reed organ or as a keyboard instrument player. The patent was granted October 26, 1897. This cabinet could be moved

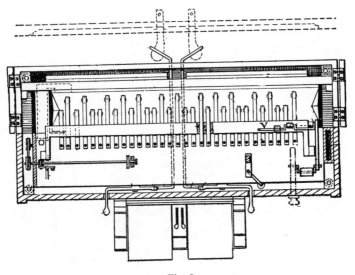

Fig. 2

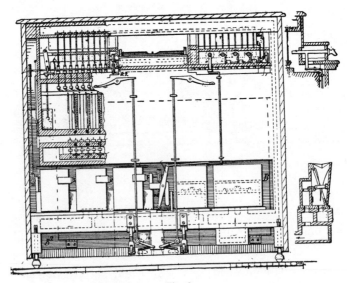

Fig. 3

White and Parker's Cabinet Piano Player

up and on to any kind of a piano, whereby the fingers of the mechanism would stand upon the tops of the keys of the piano, similar to the fingers of the human hand. The general construction being practical and durable, the instrument found immediate favor with the public.

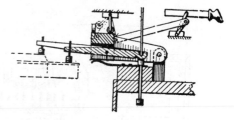

Fig. 4

After completing a number of pianos with P. J. Bailey's electric self-playing device, which did not prove a success, Theodore P. Brown of Worcester was granted patents for an interior player mechanism under dates of April 7, June 15, December 7 and 14, 1897. The pianos containing this mechanism were marketed under the name of "Aeriol Pianos," and proved a commercial success. In 1898 Brown sold his patents to the Aeolian Company, and followed the example of the Wilcox & White Company in constructing a cabinet player,

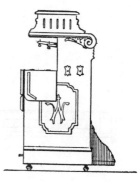

Fig. 5

Fig. 6

White and Parker's Cabinet Piano Player

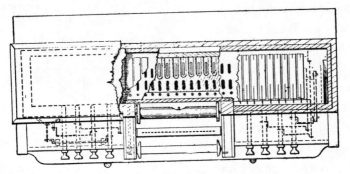

Fig. 7

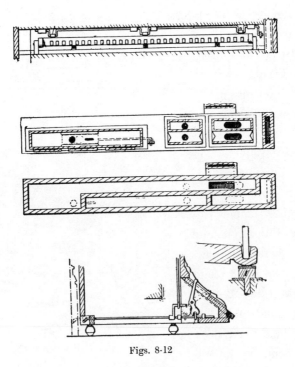

Figs. 8-12

White and Parker's Cabinet Piano Player

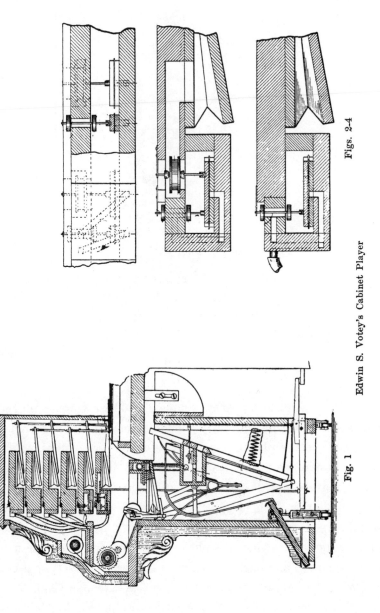

Figs. 2-4

Fig. 1

Edwin S. Votey's Cabinet Player

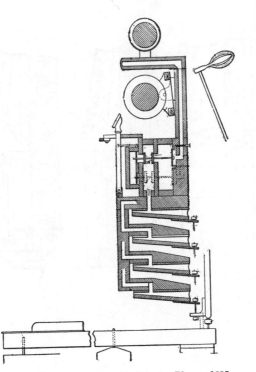

Theodore P. Brown's Interior Player, 1897

known to the trade as the "Simplex." These cabinet players, now almost obsolete, curiously enough seemed to be preferred by the public to the player piano. The fear of the piano manufacturers to add the player action to the complicated upright piano action, may, to a large extent, have been responsible for the temporary popularity of the unsightly and unhandy cabinet player. This popularity was largely increased when Edwin S. Votey's pneumatic piano attachment was put upon the market under the name of "Pianola," and pushed by a most aggressive advertising campaign on the part of the manufacturers, the Aeolian Company of New York. Votey filed his application on January 25, 1897, and a patent was issued to him on May 22, 1900.

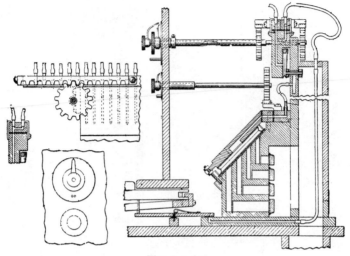

Figs. 1 and 2

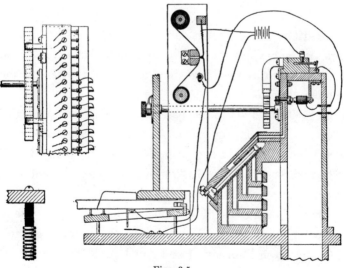

Figs. 3-5

Melville Clark's Transposing Device, 1899

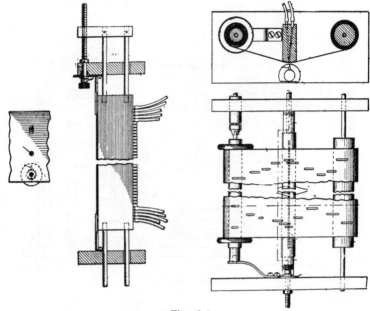

Figs. 1-4

Melville Clark's Transposing Device, 1902

Comparing the drawings of the White-Parker and Votey patents, it is obvious at first glance that the three inventors worked, although at the same time, on entirely different lines to accomplish their object.

From 1898 to 1906 many patents, too numerous to mention, were granted for improvements in player mechanism. Among them are Melville Clark's transposing device, patented on May 30, 1899, and September 30, 1902, which has been adopted by many manufacturers of player pianos.

In 1898 F. Engelhardt & Sons commenced to make their " Harmonist " player, having acquired the patents granted to F. R. Goolman, on February 1 and April 26, 1898. Their " Peerless Piano Player," a coin-operated electric pneumatic instrument, was also placed on the market in the same year. This firm controls

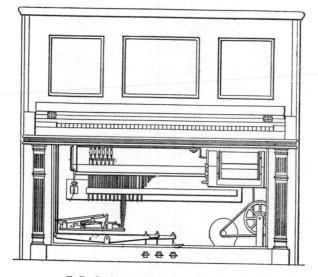

F. R. Goolman's Harmonist Player, 1898

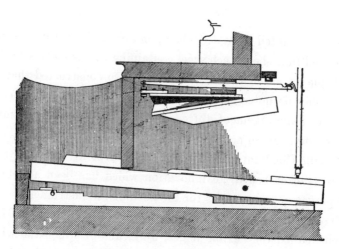

Paul B. Klugh's Auxiliary Key, 1906

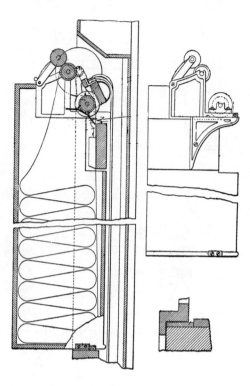

A. J. Hobart's Endless Tune Sheet, 1908

the patent granted to A. J. Hobart, on July 7, 1908, for an endless perforated tune sheet, each sheet containing five or more selections.

All player actions prior to 1898 were so constructed that they played only 65 notes of the 88 of the piano scale. This necessitated the rearrangement (often mutilation) of modern compositions written for 88 notes.

Melville Clark introduced in 1901 his " Apollo " player with an 88-note tracker board, an innovation which has been adopted by most player manufacturers for the good of the instrument.

Thomas Danquard obtained a patent, on August 2, 1904, for a device called the flexible finger, by means of which the wippen of the piano action is attacked direct, eliminating thereby the

harshness of contact and imparting
elasticity without interfering with the
function of the piano action.

To overcome the objectionable
stiffness of the interior player action,
Melville Clark patented on August 1,
1905, and in March, 1907, a construction by which the stroke button is
placed in front of the fulcrum of the
piano key. Paul B. Klugh obtained on
October 9, 1906, a patent for an auxiliary key, with the same object in
view.

Peter Welin was granted a number
of patents on applications beginning
May 1, 1902, for interior player
mechanism, in which every pneumatic
can be independently removed or ad-

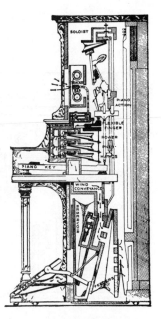

Thomas Danquard's Flexible
Finger Mechanism, 1904

justed. This mechanism is used by the Auto Grand Piano Company, which acquired the Welin patents; also by Broadwood & Sons
of London, under protection of English patents granted to Welin.

In Germany, about the year 1887, Paul Ehrlich patented his
" Ariston " mechanism, which played 36 notes. This was soon
improved by Ludwig Hupfeld by a device controlling 61 notes.
The mechanism could be inserted into an upright piano and set
in motion by a crank movement or electric motor. In 1889 Hupfeld created a new type of player with 76 notes. None of these
mechanisms had pneumatics. The " Phonola," placed on the
market in 1902, containing pneumatics, had originally a compass
of 72 notes, but it has now been changed to 88 notes.

For the better control of piano or forte playing independently
in bass or treble, the power-producing bellows of the Phonola is
divided into two sections, as shown in illustration.

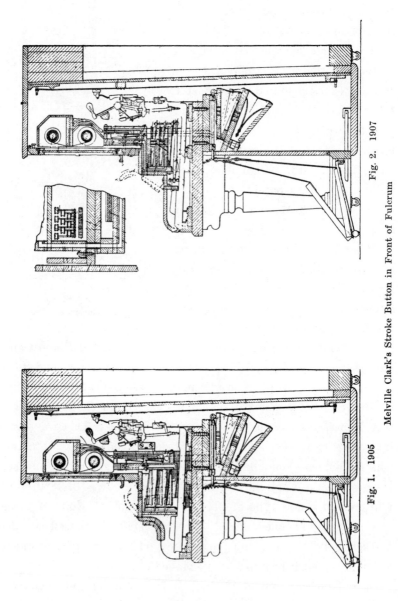

Fig. 2. 1907

Fig. 1. 1905

Melville Clark's Stroke Button in Front of Fulcrum

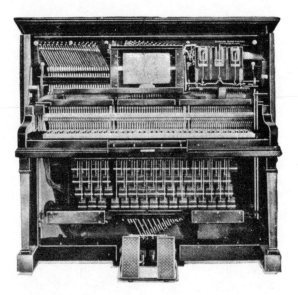

Peter Welin's Individual Valve System, 1902

Through an ingenious connection of a special pneumatic with the hammer rail, the Phonola mechanism gives the performer an opportunity for most delicate shading in pianissimo playing, by simply exercising more or less pressure upon the pedals.

The latest product of the Hupfeld factories is called the " Dea," a self-playing device which reproduces the playing of virtuosos through an arrangement of the music rolls.

The Dea and the " Welte Mignon " may justly be called the *ne plus ultra* of player development for purely mechanical expression, because they reproduce the individual interpretations of the most renowned pianists with all the accentuation and expression in its finest, most subtle *nuances*. These artistic players will ever be a most valuable assistant to the piano teacher, aiding him in instructing his pupils as to how great artists interpret the compositions of the masters. They are furthermore of inestimable value in record-

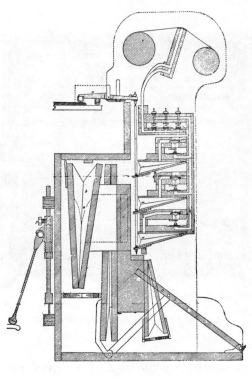

Fig. 1

Ludwig Hupfeld's Phonola Player, 1902

ing for posterity the wonderful playing of a Joseffy, Rosenthal, De Pachman, Busoni and other virtuosos.

However, the music-loving amateur requires the pleasure of his own interpretation, the only real pleasure anyone can get out of a piano. We have at present the " Metrostyle," invented by F. L. Young in 1901, enabling the amateur to follow the intention of the composer as to the proper metronomic rendering of his composition; the " Themodist," invented by J. W. Crooks in 1900; the " Phrasing Lever," patented in 1903 by Haywood; the " Temponome," invented by Danquard and Keeley in 1911; the " Artistyle " markings for the music rolls, indicating both tempo and

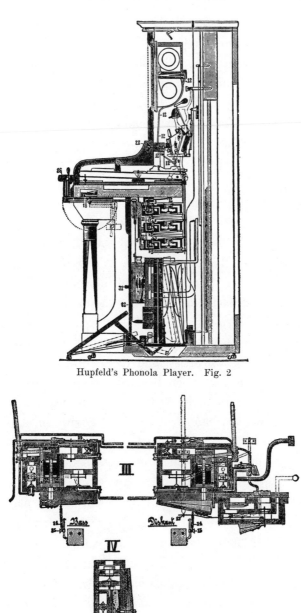

Hupfeld's Phonola Player.   Fig. 2

Figs. 3 and 4

Hupfeld's Phonola Player, Showing Divided Bellows for Bass and Treble Section

volume of tone, invented by P. K. Van Yorx; besides the many ingenious improvements of Kelly, Dickinson and other inventors, whose fertile brains are continually engaged in making player-piano history by improving and simplifying the mechanism of to-day.

As time passes on, the beauty and scope of the player piano will be appreciated in the same ratio as people learn to perform upon it properly. Teachers must be trained to give instructions on the player piano just as manual piano playing is taught at present. It not only requires practice, but earnest and intelligent study to learn the use of the expression and accentuating devices, and more especially to master the pedaling, because, after all, the secret of proper shading and phrasing in rendering a composition depends mainly upon the artistic use of the pedals. The " touch," this all-controlling factor in producing the various shades of tone on the piano, is controlled by the pedals almost entirely.

The player piano is the musical instrument for the home of the future, barring all others, and the growth of the player industry depends entirely upon the activity and enterprise of the player manufacturers. The instrument is as yet in its infancy. Eventually a player piano will be evolved with an action which will be capable of producing the long-sought-for effects of tone sustaining, losing its mechanical character entirely, and thus becoming the superior of the present-day piano, as that instrument has superseded the clavichord. Why should not the player piano finally be so constructed as to produce the powerful piano tone blended with the soulful tone of the clavichord?

The possibilities of improving the player action together with the piano action can hardly be estimated. Sufficient has been done to show that the player piano of the future will be a musical instrument *par excellence.*

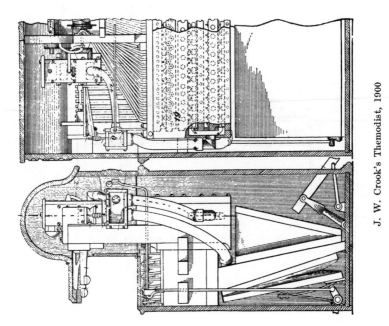

J. W. Crook's Themodist, 1900

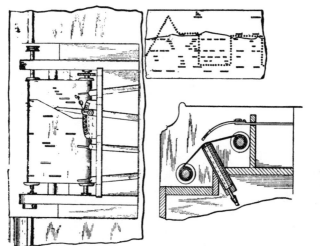

F. L. Young's Metrostyle, 1901

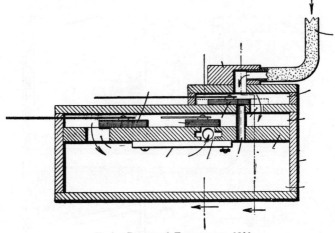

Keeley-Danquard Temponome, 1911

PART TWO

Commercial Development of the Piano Industry

CHAPTER I

ITALY, Christofori, Fischer, Sievers, Röseler, Mola.

GERMANY, Silbermann, Stein, Nannette Stein, Streicher, Schied-mayer, Ibach, Ritmüller, Rosenkrantz, Irmler, Breitkopf & Härtel, Blüthner.

FRANCE, Erard, Pleyel, Herz, Gaveau, Bord.

ENGLAND, Tschudi, Broadwood, Kirkman, Zumpe, Collard, Brinsmead, Hopkinson.

AMERICA, Chickering, MacKay, Nunns & Clark, Gilbert, Steinway.

PART TWO

CHAPTER I

History of the Commercial Development of the Piano Industry

I
T is difficult to make a piano, but much more difficult to sell it. The craft of piano making did not evolve into an industry until the commercial genius joined hands with the craftsman. It requires the lofty genius of an artist and the methodical genius of the mechanician to design and build a piano, but mercantile genius of the highest order is necessary to market this art product in such a manner as to assure for it its proper position in the marts of the world.

To achieve lasting success in the piano industry of to-day, a combination of artistic and commercial ability of the highest order has become a positive necessity. The piano, not a necessity, but a vehicle for expression of one of the high arts, appeals only to people of culture and refinement. Consequently the piano industry can thrive only in countries where wealth is accumulating. It will prosper in proportion as a country's wealth increases, and decline when a country's resources are declining.

In its early struggles for existence, the piano had to depend upon the protection of kings and princes. Schröter could not build his piano because he did not command sufficient influence to obtain financial aid from his king.

It is not to be wondered that Italy and the Netherlands produced those beautiful, artistic spinets, clavichords and harpsichords, enshrined in most artistic cases, embellished with rich carvings, or like the clavichords of Hans Ruckers, with paintings of the great Flemish masters of those days. Both the Netherlands and Italy were then at the zenith of their commercial supremacy, their ships bringing riches from all parts of the globe. This great accumulation of wealth brought about the age of Renaissance in Italy. The enormously rich nobility and the wealthy burghers generously supported Michael Angelo, Raphael, DaVinci and their contemporaries, encouraging the creation of their master works by most liberal contributions and the bestowal of honors.

Together with architecture, sculpture, painting and literature, the culture of music was revived, and we find at the end of the 17th century Bartolomo Christofori comfortably placed as musical-instrument maker to the Duke of Tuscany. The ever-open purse of the Duke permitted Christofori to pursue his studies and experiments in developing the pianoforte, while engaged in making spinets, harpsichords, lutes, etc., for the courtiers of the Duke. It was a proud moment for Christofori and the Duke when the latter could show to his court the great invention of Christofori. However, as the proud Italian noblemen of that period eschewed the idea of commercializing the creations of their artists, not many pianofortes were built by Christofori. Nor were the conditions favorable for an immediate exploitation of the invention. Italy's trade was chiefly with the Orient, where pianofortes could not be sold. The larger cities of Europe nearly all had clavichord makers of their own, and the overland transportation of so large an instrument was very costly and slow.

There is no doubt, however, that the King of Saxony came into the possession of a Christofori pianoforte at an early date, which Silbermann copied, thus making any further sales of Christofori or other Italian pianofortes impossible north of the Alps. We, therefore, hear very little of piano making in Italy at that time, except for home consumption.

About the middle of the 19th century the piano industry of Italy took a new start. Fischer of Vienna had started a factory at Naples, followed by the renowned Sievers of St. Petersburg, and later on by Röseler of Berlin, who established himself at Turin. Röseler was so successful that he soon found many followers, so that Turin boasts to-day of having 15 well-equipped piano factories, of which the establishment of Mola is the largest, producing about 4,000 pianos, harmoniums and church organs per annum. No doubt Italy produces more barrel and pneumatic street pianos than any other country, but these noisy instruments are only intended to amuse children on the public highways and cannot be classed with pianos.

GERMANY

Accepting Gottfried Silbermann of Freiberg as the father of the piano industry of Germany, we have to admit that, besides being a good organ builder and piano maker, he also was a very shrewd business man. Not only had he the good sense to copy the Christofori piano *in toto,* after Johann Sebastian Bach had condemned Silbermann's own creation in unmeasured terms, but he finally induced old Bach to indorse his Christofori copy and cleverly managed to sell to Frederick the Great seven of those instruments at the extravagant price of 700 thalers (about $500) for each instrument. Considering the purchasing power of money at that time, it is reasonable to assume that Silbermann received at least five times the amount of the actual cost of the instruments.

Saxony remained for a long time the center of piano making in Germany, and from the shops of Silbermann came nearly all the pioneers who spread the industry over the continent of Europe and Great Britain. The so-called 12 apostles (12 German piano makers), who landed in London about 1760, were nearly all Silbermann pupils, and became the pioneers of the English piano industry. Among them were Zumpe, Backers (Becker), Geib and others, whose names later on appeared in the London city directory as pianoforte makers.

Johann Andreas Stein, undoubtedly the most talented of Silbermann's pupils, went to Augsburg and made his first piano in 1768. His daughter Nannette, with her husband, Johann Andreas Streicher, later on moved to Vienna, founding the '' Vienna school '' of piano makers. Balthàsar Schiedmayer made his first piano at Erlangen in 1735. Johann David Schiedmayer continued the business at Nuremberg, and his son Lorenz moved to Stuttgart in 1809, where he became the founder of the '' Stuttgart school.'' Next we hear of Johannes Adolf Ibach, who started near Barmen in 1794. Andreas Georg Ritmüller commenced business at Göttingen in 1795, and Ernst Rosenkrantz at Dresden in 1797.

From that period on piano making increased rapidly in Germany, makers locating chiefly in the residence cities of the many principalities of those days, because the courts of the potentates were about the only customers a piano maker could then look for. Commercial methods were entirely unknown. A piano maker would build his piano and then quietly await a customer. To advertise a piano for sale would have been considered an unpardonable sin against the ethics of the craft. It required the revolutionary nerve of the pathfinders after the middle of the 19th century to brush away that prejudice. Just as soon as the industry began to develop in the commercial atmosphere of Leipsic, Berlin and Stuttgart, the piano makers of Germany commenced to make efforts to sell their products outside of their own bailiwicks. Vienna looked askance at this new movement, and consequently has hardly held its own in the onward march of the industry.

Julius Blüthner of Leipsic made good use of the opportunity which that great school, the Conservatory of Music, offered. Young people from all parts of the globe came to that school to be instructed by Moscheles, Plaidy, Wenzel, Reinecke and others, to go out into the world as teachers or virtuosos. They studied on Blüthner pianos during their sojourn at Leipsic, and sang the praise of the Blüthner piano wherever they went. Nor did Blüthner ever spare printer's ink in order to tell the world what fine pianos he was building, to the great horror of the old-school piano makers. He sent his pianos to the world's expositions and carried off prize medals for showing something new or better than the conventional.

The old renowned firms of Irmler, Breitkopf & Härtel of Leipsic and the Dresden and Stuttgart makers looked on for quite a while, satisfied with the steady home trade and their profitable export trade (mainly to North America), but, when their export business was absorbed by the American makers and their active German competitors invaded their home territories, they quickly adopted the same aggressive policy, keeping pace with the most advanced ideas and business tactics.

This persistent propaganda by all the leading firms made the piano very popular, and the demand increased in proportion. The use of labor-saving machinery was introduced by all leading firms. Establishments for the manufacture of supplies sprang up at all piano-manufacturing centers, and soon the piano " compiler " appeared, at first in Berlin, later on to be found everywhere.

Export merchants saw the possibilities of using the German piano for successful competition against the English make in foreign countries, and a lively export trade was soon established. Piano dealers became active in every city, town and hamlet. At the present time almost every schoolteacher in the villages of Germany is the agent for one or more piano makers.

The practice of " peddling " pianos—that is, to load a piano on·to a wagon, going out to the country with it, looking for a possible customer—was first resorted to by Berlin makers of low-priced pianos about 1866. It is now generally practiced in America.

After 1873 Germany started upon a wonderful career of industrial revival. That far-seeing statesman, Bismarck, not only inaugurated the beneficial policy of protection for the home market, by putting duties on foreign-made goods, but he also organized a splendid consular service, making each consul a servant of German commerce and industry. Furthermore, he subsidized the merchant marine and cheapened transportation on land, all in order to enable the German manufacturer to gain a foreign trade. How effectually the German piano trade has made use of these advantages is illustrated by the fact that over 20,000 pianos were shipped from Germany to England alone during 1909. Considering that up to 1860 England was leading the world in the production of pianos, this fact speaks volumes for the enterprise of the German piano manufacturers and the quality of their product.

German pianos to-day dominate all foreign markets, excepting, of course, North America, not on account of low prices, but mainly because of the advanced commercial methods followed by the German manufacturer and merchant, who is ever willing to accommodate himself to the demands of his customers, meeting the buyer's peculiar taste for style and tone of the piano and also his methods of transacting business.

Germany has to-day about 300 piano factories, some of them producing from 3,000 to 7,000 pianos per year. The total output of all factories is estimated at about 170,000 pianos annually. Spain has about 20 piano factories. The firm of Ortiz & Cusso of Barcelona turn out 1,000 pianos annually. The total production of Spain is estimated at 2,500 pianos per year, of which a considerable number are exported to South America. Scandinavia, Belgium, Holland and Switzerland are no factors in the world's piano markets. Good pianos are made at Copenhagen, Stockholm and Christiania, as well as at Brussels and The Hague, at Zurich and Bern, mostly for home consumption, however. Belgium has 16 piano factories; Switzerland, 12; Holland, 6; Scandinavia, 40; mostly small shops with a production of from 50 to 100 pianos per year. The total annual production of these countries probably does not exceed from 6,000 to 8,000 pianos.

FRANCE

Although Paris (which means France) was, up to 1851, far in the lead of Germany, it appears to be retrogressing, because of its overproud conservatism. It seems difficult for the leading Paris makers to realize that Germany and America are producing pianos far better adapted to the modern school of piano playing and composition than the sweet-toned instruments which dominated the concert halls in Chopin's days. The home of the Erard, Pleyel, Herz and Gaveau piano can show only 35 establishments where pianos are manufactured, all together scarcely reaching an output of 25,000 per annum. Antoine Bord in his best days turned out as many as 4,000 pianos (mostly small uprights) per year, but even this formerly enterprising concern seems now to be content to rest on its laurels. The firm of Pleyel, Lyon & Company turns out about 3,500 pianos per year, one-seventh of the total production of France.

When Johannes Zumpe went from Silbermann's shop to London in 1760, it seems that he was at once infected with the commercial bacteria, rampant in that greatest commercial and financial center of the world. No one holds the title to the name "father of the commercial piano" so indisputably as that industrious German. He found the aristocratic Tschudi, Broadwood, Kirkman and others making high-priced harpsichords, and later on equally costly grand pianos, and quickly decided to build a piano at a price within reach of the well-to-do middle class. To reduce cost, he simplified the Christofori action, adopted the square form of the clavichord and thus was first in putting upon the market a square piano at a moderate price. This piano, although without merit, either as to workmanship or tone, filled a long-felt want, and Zumpe amassed a fortune within a comparatively short time, upon which he retired at an early age. Kirkman, landing in London in 1740 as Jacob Kirchmann, a German harpsichord maker, was even more successful than Zumpe. He left an estate valued at about $1,000,000 when he died in 1778.

The financial successes of Kirkman, Zumpe, Broadwood and others attracted capital to the industry, and London became the birthplace of the modern piano factory, where steam-driven machines were employed. London piano manufacturers utilized circular saws, planing machines, etc., as early as 1815. In the days before the steam railroads, London was an ideal place for piano manufacturers. Not only did they control a fine home market, among the great landowners, rich merchants and manufacturers, but they also had absolute control of the export business to foreign countries by reason of England's supremacy of the seas. It is reported that in 1851 London had 180 firms, which produced 25,000 pianos a year, at a value of $4,000,000.

In about 1860 London had reached its zenith as the leading piano manufacturing center. Edgar Brinsmead, in his book published in 1870, claims an output of about 35,000 pianos per annum for England. Since that time Germany has not only captured most of England's export trade, but is sending to England direct not less than 20,000 pianos every year, while the total production of Great Britain hardly exceeds 75,000 pianos a year. The main cause of this state of affairs is undoubtedly the conservatism with which the English manufacturers, like the French, have clung to their old models and methods. Up to 1860 the piano makers of Germany looked to London and Paris for new ideas and improvements in construction and making. With modifications of their own, they adopted the English and French models and used English and French felt, wires and actions in their pianos. After the Paris exposition of 1867, Germany adopted the American system of piano construction, made its own wires, felts and actions, and, as a result, soon dominated over England and France in the world's markets.

London is now credited with 126 piano factories, still led by the revered names of Broadwood, Collard, Brinsmead, Hopkinson and others, who for so many years gave luster to the English piano's reputation.

Broadwood & Sons have lately adopted a progressive policy as of old, using in their new factory all known modern improvements, and with characteristic foresight are again in the lead as the only London firm who manufacture every part of their player pianos in their own factories. It is possible that the English piano industry under Broadwood's lead may retrieve its lost prestige by an energetic development of the player piano, which is destined to be the controlling factor in the piano industry of the future.

Yet the prevailing economic policy of the British Government is a great handicap for the English manufacturer, making it impossible for him to even control his own home market, as is done by the manufacturers of all other countries.

AMERICA

North America, the new world, presented entirely different conditions to the piano industry than the old world. Although without nobility or aristocracy, its natural resources produced wealth at such a rapid pace that even in its early days the piano industry of America was very lucrative. In 1860 we find mammoth piano factories in Boston, New York, Baltimore and Philadelphia rivaling in every respect the old renowned establishments of London.

That excellent piano maker and inventor, Jonas Chickering, had the good sense to associate himself, in 1830, with John MacKay, an enterprising commercial genius, who spread the fame of the Chickering piano over the entire United States as it was then known. At the World's Fair, London, in 1851, Chickering exhibited the first American pianos shown in Europe, and carried off the highest honors. Meyer of Philadelphia, Nunns & Clark of New York and Gilbert & Company of Boston were also represented at that exposition, all of them making creditable exhibits. After the death of his partner, MacKay, Chickering, being far in the lead of all other American piano manufacturers, did not continue the aggressive business policy inaugurated by MacKay, and lacking an inspiring leader, the industry progressed very slowly from 1840 to 1855, when Steinway & Sons appeared. Their methods of persistent publicity were as revolutionary as those later on adopted by Blüthner in Germany. They never relaxed in letting the public know that they manufactured a fine piano. William Steinway, with far-seeing judgment, was not satisfied only to use printer's ink with telling effect, but he also began to educate the public to appreciate good music. Steinway Hall was erected, the Theodore Thomas orchestra generously supported and the greatest piano virtuosos from Rubinstein to Joseffy engaged for concerts, not only in New York but in all large cities of the United States and Canada.

Chickering & Sons followed Steinway's example and erected Chickering Hall in New York, also one in Boston. Knabe, Weber and Steck also engaged great soloists for concert work in all leading cities, creating a popularity for the piano in proportion to the growth of wealth in the United States.

Official statistics show that during 1869 the United States produced about 25,000 pianos at a value of $7,000,000,—$3,000,-000 more than London received for the same number of pianos in 1851. The output for 1910 is estimated at 350,000 pianos, valued at about $100,000,000.

PART TWO

CHAPTER II

The Commercial Piano, Joseph P. Hale.
The Stencil, Department Stores, Consolidations.

PART TWO

CHAPTER II

The Commercial Piano

UP to this time nearly all the pianos were manufactured by men who were expert piano makers. Excepting William Steinway and Albert Weber, all the piano makers of those days were more superior as craftsmen than as business man, valuing glory as piano constructors higher than financial success. About 1870 Joseph P. Hale, one of America's typical self-made men, came to New York from Worcester, Mass., where he had accumulated a fortune of $35,000 in the crockery trade. Looking about for an opportunity to invest his money in an active business, he bought an interest in the Grovesteen piano factory. After a short period he severed this connection and started a piano factory on his own account.

With the eminently practical trading instinct of the Yankee, Hale looked upon the piano as a strictly commercial proposition. Without the remotest knowledge of music, tone or theory of piano construction, utterly without patience for scientific experiments, he dissected the piano, figuring the cost of case, plate, action, labor, varnish and other material, with one point in view—how he could reduce the cost of the piano. He inaugurated a system of manufacturing and merchandising heretofore unknown to the American piano trade. Hale is, beyond question, the father of the " commercial " piano of America, and has done splendid pioneer work in his sphere, to the benefit of the entire trade. Unhampered by

Joseph P. Hale

tradition or prejudice of any kind, he manufactured pianos as he would have manufactured bedsteads. A genius as an organizer, he carried the division of labor to the last point, so that he could reduce his labor cost to less than half of what his competitors paid. Buying his cases, keys, actions, etc., from specialists at bottom prices, for cash on delivery, he was not obliged to carry a big stock of lumber or other material. Even when his output had reached the at that time imposing number of 100 pianos per week, he would not carry more than one week's supply of stock on hand.

It will be readily understood that Hale could sell his pianos far below the cost price of a high-grade piano and still make a good profit. These revolutionary methods caused bitter antagonism on the part of his competitors of the old school. Hale went on with his business complacently, and argued that the makers of high-class pianos were all wrong in antagonizing him, because, by his low price, he was bringing the piano within the reach of the working classes. Once introduced there, out of each 10 buyers of his cheap pianos, at least one would develop within 10 years into a good piano player, who would then not be satisfied until he possessed a high-class instrument.

Hale's prophecy has come true. The number of firms making commercial pianos increased steadily, but so did the output of the makers of high-class pianos, and to their list names like Baldwin, Mason & Hamlin, Everett, Conover and many other makers of fine concert grands have since been added. Hale and his followers made it possible for the dealer, especially in the rapidly-growing western States, to market large numbers of pianos among the farmers, artisans, etc.—tenfold more than would have been possible if they had been restricted to the sale of high-class makes only.

Hale was the first American piano manufacturer who discarded the agency system. His goods were for sale to anybody, anywhere, as long as the buyer was able to pay for the same. To avoid clashing among his own dealers, he started the stencil system. He would stencil his pianos with any name desired by the buyer, which the law permitted. Thus the dealer, especially the big jobber of the west, commenced to sell some pianos with his own name on the fallboard, or even cast into or screwed on to the iron plate. In time the western jobber began to see that he might save that great item of freight from New York or Boston to Chicago by manufacturing his own goods at home, and about the year 1880 the first factories were started in Chicago. Cincinnati soon followed, and to-day the western factories produce nearly half of the pianos made in the United States.

The tremendous increase of output, from 25,000 pianos in 1869 to 350,000 in 1910, was only made possible through the educational, artistic and advertising propaganda by the makers of high-grade pianos on the one hand, and the aggressive selling methods of the makers of commercial pianos on the other. Many of the large western houses own and successfully run factories in which pianos of the highest grade are made, as well as factories turning out commercial pianos by the thousands.

Stencil

The much-abused and scandalized stencil has been legitimatized, inasmuch as many manufacturing concerns trade-mark one or more names other than their firm name, and use such trade-mark names for specific pianos made in factories built especially for this purpose. Again, dealers often obtain a trade-mark for a certain name, which they use on pianos built especially for them, all of which is now considered quite proper and accepted by universal usage.

Department Stores

While the manufacturing of a large number of pianos has become a comparatively easy matter, being merely a matter of factory space, machinery, system and proper organization, the distribution of the manufactured goods is becoming a more and more vexing problem. The general demand has of late years impelled some of the leading department stores in the large cities to add pianos to their list of commodities. In these stores the one-price system has been introduced with more or less success. The so-called mail-order houses are also distributing pianos, and it appears as if the small dealer will eventually have to quit the field, unless he is strongly supported by the manufacturer. The keen competition has induced some of the larger manufacturing concerns to become their own distributors, having salesrooms in most of the leading cities.

Consolidation

Several large manufacturers of high-grade pianos have found it to their interest to combine with large concerns having a superior selling organization, like Weber and Steck, who joined the Aeolian Company, or with large manufacturers of commercial pianos, as in the case of the American Piano Company, a combination of Chickering & Sons, Knabe & Company and Foster, Armstrong & Company, whose combined output per year is over 15,000 pianos of all grades. There are a number of concerns in the middle west whose annual individual output exceeds 10,000 pianos, while a production of from 3,000 to 5,000 pianos per year is at present rather the minimum for up-to-date firms. It is, perhaps, safe to say that each of the three largest western manufacturing firms turns out nearly 20,000 pianos per year, or together more than twice as much as the production of the entire United States in 1869.

How profitable large production coupled with independent distribution can be made is best illustrated by the fact that a Chicago house managed to sell 60,000 pianos of one style or pattern. What economy in manufacturing may be practiced in making such an immense number of pianos of one kind!

PART TWO

CHAPTER III

THE ART PIANO, *Geronimo, Trasunti, Hans Ruckers, Shudi, Broad-wood,* Sir Alma Tadema, *Steinway,* Marquandt, Norman, Sir Edward Poynter, Theodore Roosevelt, Denning, *Bösendorfer,* Empress Elizabeth, *Ibach's* Jubilee Grand, *Baldwin,* Barnhorn, Guest, *Blüthner, Erard, Pleyel, Lyon & Co., Chickering's* Louis XIV Grand, *Everett's* Sheraton Grand, Samuel Hayward, *Knabe's* " Nouveau Art " Grand, *Weber's* Louis XIV Grand.

THE PEDAL PIANO, *Schöne,* Schumann, Mendelssohn, *Pleyel, Erard, Pfeiffer, Henry F. Miller.*

PART TWO

CHAPTER III

Art Pianos

ART is described as the "harmonious beautiful." An artist must therefore not only have a highly developed sense of truth, the grand, noble and beautiful, but also the ability to give form to his ideals in an absolutely pleasing manner.

Piano making has not as yet been developed to a positive science with fundamental laws, but it has ever been an art, calling for a familiarity on the part of the piano constructor with all of the liberal arts, more particularly music, architecture, sculpture and painting. An inborn talent for music is the first requisite of an artistic piano maker. His sense of harmony must be acute, so that he may distinguish the finest shadings in tone color. He must be capable of mentally hearing the *klangfarbe* which he desires to impart to his piano, or create in it. He draws his scale irrespective of form or size, because so far he only seeks to produce tone. After succeeding in getting the tone quality and quantity he desires, he begins to construct the frame and casing of his piano, for which a knowledge of architecture and talent for designing are imperative. He next calls on the sculptor for plastic decoration, and on the painter for higher embellishment by appropriate pictures to finally achieve the harmonious beautiful.

Art is a passionate expression of ideal conception and develops only after a nation has accumulated sufficient wealth to enable some of its higher intellects to devote themselves to art and science without regard to financial reward. The true artist dreams, thinks and works for art's sake only. He is altogether too sensitive for barter and trade, and needs the freedom of financial independence, the enjoyment of luxuries and the inspiration of the beautiful as a necessary stimulant and requisite.

The first art pianos were constructed by the early Italian makers. After Geronimo had invented his wing-formed harpsichord, he embellished the outer case of the same with artistic carvings, as shown on the instrument of his make at the South Kensington Museum in London. Alessandro Trasunti and other Italian makers improved greatly on Geronimo's efforts and built special cases detachable from the body of the instrument. These cases were decorated with exquisite carvings, embellished with inlaid ivory designs and often with pictures painted by masters.

That celebrated maker, Hans Ruckers of Antwerp, called on his friends among the great Flemish painters to enhance the beauty and value of his harpsichords by painting pictures upon them. Indeed, his connection with the artists was so intimate that he, as well as his son and his nephew, were elected members of the "Painters Guild, of St. Luke." Many specimens of the old Italian and Flemish school are to be found in the collection of old instruments of Paul De Wit of Leipsic, Wilhelm Heyer of Cologne, Morris Steinert of New Haven, the Kensington Museum of London and the Germanic Museum at Nuremberg. The paintings upon many of these instruments oftentimes represent a value much greater than that of the piano alone.

Cost is never considered in the building of an art piano. The designer and executing artists are given full liberty to work out their ideas in accordance with the desired style. Burkat Shudi built for Frederick the Great a highly decorated harpsichord, for which he received one thousand dollars, an enormous amount, considering the money value of those days; his successors, John Broadwood & Sons, not long ago built for Sir Alma Tadema an art grand costing many thousand dollars. In richness of design and brilliancy of execution this instrument is unique. The art grand of Erard is an exquisite specimen of that artistry so peculiar to French genius and handicraft when unlimited freedom is given to fantasy, regardless of cost. Mr. Marquandt of New York is said to have paid forty thousand dollars for an art grand piano built by Steinway & Sons, after special design of Sir Alma Tadema. Johnston Norman of London executed the embellishments under Sir Alma's personal direction and Sir Edward Poynter painted his picture, " The Wandering Minstrels," upon the lid. It took fully five years to finish this marvel of combined arts.

At the White House in Washington, D. C., is the one-hundred-thousandth piano built in the factories of Steinway & Sons. It was presented by that firm to President Roosevelt, for the American people. The designs, models and decorations for this piano are the combined work of the most noted sculptors and architects of America. The painting is by Thomas W. Denning. The total cost of the piano was about $20,000.

Ludwig Bösendorfer furnished the Empress Elizabeth of Austria with an art grand, in the decoration of which the sculptor's art predominates to an overwhelming degree, showing a most masterly treatment of wood in its highest capacity for the display of artistic genius. In contrast to the above we have Rudolf Ibach Sohn's Jubilee grand, being the fifty-thousandth production of his factories. Its graceful lines and chaste decorations are eminently pleasing and restful.

The house of Ibach has been in the front rank in the propaganda for artistry in piano case designing, and their " Memorial," published in 1894, the one-hundredth anniversary of the founding of their firm, ought to be in the hands of every studious piano maker. It contains a most excellent collection of designs, many of which would have a place in this work, if space permitted.

That there are no limitations to the artist's desires or inclinations in designing and embellishing piano cases is shown in the Baldwin art grand. The realistic tendency of the modern school is depicted in a masterly manner in the sculpturing of Mr. C. T. Barnhorn, also in the general design of the case by Mr. I. H. Guest, both of Cincinnati, Ohio. The Blüthner art grand is impressive because of the severity of the design, an example of the dominating boldness of the " new school."

The Weber Piano Company has made the building of art pianos a specialty for many years. The accompanying picture represents one of their Louis XIV style grand pianos, designed by W. P. Stymus, Jr.

The art grand piano of Pleyel, Lyon & Company is a beautiful specimen of Renaissance design, while the upright shows a most effective application of the Gothic style.

The Chickering grand in Louis XIV style is a typical production of Chickering & Sons' art department. The Sheraton grand of the Everett Company, designed by John Anderson, with paintings by Samuel Hayward, is a specimen of the Everett Company's art work. The " Nouveau Art " grand of Knabe & Company is from their catalogue of art pianos, in which all dominant styles are represented.

Nearly all the leading firms of piano makers during the past twenty years have added special departments to their establishments for the creation of art pianos, employing their own designers and executing artists. The architects of modern mansions insist that the design of the piano as well as of the furniture must be in harmony with the architecture of the room in which it is

Alessandro Trasunti's Art Harpsichord, 1531

Hans Ruckers' Double Spinet, with Paintings, Antwerp, 1560

John Broadwood & Sons' Art Grand, Built for Sir Alma Tadema

Ludwig Bösendorfer Art Grand.   Built for Empress Elizabeth of Austria

Rudolf Ibach Sohn Jubilee Art Grand

Julius Blüthner Art Grand

Erard Art Grand

Designed by Coupri

Pleyel, Lyon & Company Renaissance Art Grand

Pleyel, Lyon & Company Gothic Upright

Steinway & Sons Art Grand Piano made for Frederick Marquandt
of New York City.   Cost $40,000

Steinway & Sons One-hundred-thousandth Piano, at the White House, Washington, D. C.
Paintings by Thomas W. Denning.   Cost $20,000

Baldwin Art Grand

Weber Louis XIV Art Grand

Chickering & Sons Louis XIV Art Grand

Everett Piano Company Sheraton Art Grand

William Knabe & Company "Nouveau Art" Grand

to be placed. This extended use of correct styles in art pianos has favorably influenced the general design of the commercial piano of the present day, the form and exterior of which are of a much more agreeable and pleasing character than the cold conventional designs of former years. Thus we find the ennobling influence of art penetrating the industry, and quietly fulfilling its mission of elevating character and taste.

The Pedal Piano

Since the church organ had been developed to perfection long before the piano was invented, and the first piano makers were recruited almost entirely from the organ maker's guild, it is reasonable to suppose that " pedal pianos " were constructed in the early days of the piano industry, although we have no record of any up to the year 1843, when the author's uncle, Louis Schöne, constructed pedal pianos for Robert Schumann and Felix Mendelssohn at Leipsic. Schöne constructed, for Mendelssohn, a pedal mechanism to be used with a grand piano, but Robert Schumann preferred his pedal action connected with the regular upright piano. The keyboard for pedaling was placed under the keyboard for manual playing, had 29 notes and was connected with an action placed at the back of the piano where a special soundboard, covered with 29 strings, was built into the case. As is well known, Schumann wrote some of his best music for this novel instrument.

Erard and Pleyel also built pedal pianos in Paris, and it can hardly be doubted that Henri Pape also tried his hand at it, because there has ever been a demand for such instruments, by organists, for practice purposes. In America the Henry F. Miller & Sons Piano Company has for years made a specialty of building pedal pianos for organists.

Carl J. Pfeiffer of Stuttgart has devoted himself of late years to the improvement of this instrument, with very satisfactory re-

Carl J. Pfeiffer's Action for Pedal Upright Pianos

Carl J. Pfeiffer's Attachment for Pedal Grand Piano

Carl J. Pfeiffer's Upright Piano for Pedal Practice

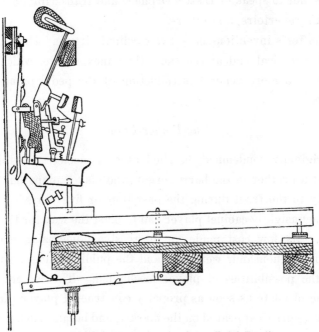

Carl J. Pfeiffer's Mechanism for Organ Pedal Practice

sults. Using the iron frame and overstrung system, his pedal tones are sonorous and powerful and the pedal action almost the same in touch as the organ pedal. His independent pedal can be easily attached to a grand piano, as shown in the illustration, while for upright pianos the pedal is placed under the framework of the piano. A very ingenious and valuable invention is Pfeiffer's mechanism for organ pedal practice, which can be built into any upright piano and used without affecting the touch for hand playing. As the illustration shows, the pedal mechanism is so constructed as to relieve the piano action instantly when the foot is removed from the pedal. These two practical inventions of Pfeiffer's have been thoroughly tried out by prominent organists and are highly recommended, not only for practice purposes, but also for the music lover who enjoys the study of Bach's immortal preludes and fugues or Schumann's beautiful sketches for pedal pianos, not to speak of Liszt's Orpheus and transcriptions of Gottschalk's repertoire, and others.

Pfeiffer's inventions have two cardinal virtues. They are eminently practical and at the same time inexpensive, which ought to aid in a more general introduction of the pedal piano in the future.

The Player Piano

Originally condemned, laughed at as a useless plaything, or at best a brother to the barrel organ, the player piano has forged rapidly to the front during the past four or five years.

The unsightly cabinet player had to blast the way for the player piano. Its low cost made an aggressive advertising campaign possible. Thousands were sold and the public became acquainted with the possibilities of player mechanism. The cabinet player became obsolete as soon as properly constructed player pianos at moderate prices appeared on the market, and became such favorites that the most obstinate opponents of the player piano among the piano manufacturers, were forced to recognize its commercial importance.

With the introduction of the 88-note compass, the artistic possibilities are almost without limitations, and the time is not far distant when music will be specially written for the player piano, of such technical complexion as to preclude its performance by hand.

The player piano is opening up an entirely new and much larger field than the piano proper ever had. Considering the increase from 50 factories producing 25,000 pianos in 1869, to 200 factories turning out 350,000 pianos in 1910, it seems difficult to form any estimate of the magnitude which the industry may assume in the future, when the player piano has reached its ultimate development.

PART TWO

CHAPTER IV

EXPORT, Steinway, Aeolian.
METHODS OF MARKETING, The Agency System.

PART TWO

CHAPTER IV

Export

A MOVEMENT of a most peculiar character must be mentioned in this connection, namely, the transplanting of American manufacturing methods, by American manufacturers, to Europe. When Sebastian Erard closed his shops in Paris and went to London to start a factory in the British metropolis, he was driven there by the terrors of the French revolution. He returned to Paris as soon as peace was restored, maintaining his London establishment, however, in charge of his nephew, Pierre. This is the only instance on record where a piano manufacturer removed his business from his own country to another. Now the American manufacturers are going over to Germany and England, establishing branch factories for their products, to better supply their European and export trade.

Steinway & Sons started their Hamburg factories about 1880. The Aeolian Company a few years ago established a factory at Gotha, Germany, for making the Steck pianos and is now erecting a large factory near London for the Weber piano.

Owing to high price of labor and to undeveloped shipping and banking facilities, the American piano manufacturer cannot look for any extended export business. As a matter of fact, there is nowhere on the globe such a good market as the United States at the present time. Because of the prevailing high standard of living, an American city with a population of 100,000 can and does buy more pianos than any South American republic with 2,000,000 inhabitants, of which only a small fraction are able to wear shoes. Australia, with its 5,000,000 people, does not take over 3,000 pianos per year. Japan is beginning to make its own pianos, while China, with a population of over 400,000,000, buys hardly any pianos. The same can be said of almost all other Asiatic nations.

It is, therefore, the home market to which the American manufacturer will have to look for any expansion of his business, although a limited business offers almost everywhere for American player pianos of competitive value or superior quality.

Methods of Marketing

To increase sales, the product must be brought nearer and nearer to the masses, by lowering the cost of production and marketing. The system of marketing through agents, who control a restricted territory, practiced by the leading makers of America for so many years, has served its purpose and is not in harmony with progressive merchandising. Joseph P. Hale discovered that truth 40 years ago. By breaking away from it he made more money in his time than any other piano manufacturer.

Makers of high grade as well as commercial pianos who still adhere to the agency system will eventually be compelled to sell their pianos as any other product is sold, namely, to whomsoever is able to pay for it. The much desired one-price system is utterly impossible as long as regularly appointed agents control the sale, and although leading houses publish their retail prices to the public, competition forces deviation in many instances.

In 1881 the author found at Milan, Italy, a piano dealer who carried in stock grand and upright pianos of all the leading makers of the world. It was a most interesting study to play and compare the Erard with the Steinway, the Chickering with the Pleyel, the Broadwood or Collard with Bösendorfer or Blüthner, and Schröter with Schiedmayer, so interesting that I gave up a whole afternoon to that pleasure, until night overtook me. Questioning the dealer as to whether it was not at times embarrassing for him to extol the merits of the different makes, he replied that he, as a dealer, never attempted to influence his customers in their selection of a piano. The prices were all marked in plain figures. He knew that all of the pianos were of the highest grade, and since tastes as to tone, case, etc., differ, he preferred to have his customers select whatever appealed to them as best. Whenever a piano was sold he would order another one of the same make to keep his assortment complete. This man carried about 400 pianos permanently in stock and did the largest retail business in Italy. I left his warerooms thoroughly convinced that this was the proper way to handle the piano selling business. He was a merchant, high-toned, enterprising, carrying on his business in a most honest, respectable manner.

In the large cities of the continent of Europe, and more especially in London, one can find pianos of celebrated makers in several warerooms, although the maker may have his own city showroom. The time will come when piano manufacturers will fix the wholesale and retail price for their product, and then sell to any or all dealers in any city or territory without any other restrictions than the maintenance of retail prices, as established by themselves. Unless this system is adopted the manufacturers will, because of the practices of the dealer (born of the agency system), be more and more driven into combinations, by the strength of which they will be able to control the dealer or do their own distributing. This again will, as a matter of logical evolution, lead to the formation of greater combinations, ending in the so-called trust, as illustrated in the steel, woolen and other dominant industries.

PART TWO

CHAPTER V

THE TRUST MOVEMENTS OF 1892, 1897 AND 1899

PART TWO

CHAPTER V

The Trust Movements of 1892, 1897 and 1899

IN the spring of 1892 I was invited to take an active part in the formation of a piano trust. My studies in economics had convinced me long ago that the trust was not only the logical development of our factory system, according to the law of evolution, but in some instances the only salvation for an industry, which, because of too many rivaling establishments, suffered on the one hand from an unreasonable expense account, and on the other from over-competition, both of which reduced profits to a minimum.

The piano industry was not in dire straits, still the expense of carrying on the business was out of all proportion to the intrinsic value of the product, and the selling methods were anything but ethical. The greatest evil, however, was that the industry as a whole was suffering from lack of sufficient working capital.

I agreed to investigate the proposition and then give my opinion as to the feasibility of carrying it to a successful conclusion. My first step was to collect statistics as a basis for calculation. The status of the piano industry in the United States presented itself as follows:

On January 1, 1892, 132 firms and corporations were engaged in the manufacturing of pianos and organs in the United States,

turning out about 91,500 pianos and 92,750 organs per year, of a
total selling value of............................... $22,235,000
Cost of labor and material amounted to............   13,362,500
                                                     _____
Leaving a margin for profit and expenses of......... $ 8,872,500

If all or at least a majority of the manufacturing concerns
could be merged into one great corporation, it would be possible
to carry on a business of manufacturing pianos and organs, making only four kinds of instruments: namely,

First, artists' pianos and organs, which should be of the highest grade and command the highest prices paid now for such instruments.   Second, a first-class instrument.   Third, a medium-grade
instrument.   Fourth, a low-grade instrument.

It was proposed to capitalize this corporation at fifty million
($50,000,000) dollars.   Fair and just value was to be allowed to
each concern for its property.   The affairs of the corporation were
to be managed by a Board of Directors, elected by the share-
holders and chosen from the ranks of the most experienced men
engaged in the manufacture and sale of pianos and organs.

The General Purchasing and Contract Company was organized
under the laws of West Virginia, with a capital of $1,000,000.
This contract company was to conduct the purchase of the various
piano and organ concerns, and, as soon as a sufficient number of
options were secured, the American Piano and Organ Company
was to be started.

On May 12, 1892, the contract company entered into an agreement with a syndicate, composed of a number of leading New York
bankers who obligated themselves to provide capital to the amount
of $5,000,000, to facilitate the purchasing of such manufacturing
concerns as either needed money to cancel their liabilities or preferred to sell for cash instead of taking the securities of the American Piano and Organ Company for their plants and chattels.

One of the main reasons why the leading bankers were invited to assist in the enterprise was to insure their active support of the securities of the American Piano and Organ Company as soon as they were listed on the Stock Exchange. Being interested by prospective loans up to five million ($5,000,000) dollars, for which they would hold the securities of the American Piano and Organ Company, these bankers would, for their own interests, give the strength of their influence and manifold connections to the enterprise and to the marketing of these securities.

The financial basis of the undertaking being arranged in a proper and satisfactory manner, the emissary of the contract company took the field, submitting to the piano and organ manufacturers the proposition.

It will be observed that the scheme was a bankers' proposition. Its aim was to procure the necessary outside capital to put the industry on a proper footing and upon a safe financial basis for legitimate expansion. Neither the scope nor aim of the proposition were, however, properly understood and comprehended by the majority of the manufacturers, and the negotiations leveled down in most cases to a bargaining; the seller asking an unreasonable price and the buyer trying to obtain options at workable values. The amusing fact developed that almost every seller objected to " water " and found fault with what he considered an over-capitalization; at the same time he would ask such an enormous price for his own property that, if a corresponding amount was allowed to all sellers, it would have been necessary to increase the capital stock of the American Piano and Organ Company threefold, thereby making it, of course, of proportionately less value.

In spite of the bitter opposition of the trade press, the supply trades and other interests that erroneously feared to suffer if the trust should become a fact, a sufficient number of strong firms and corporations saw the great advantage to be obtained, to assure the success of the undertaking, when the great panic, starting in April, 1893, put a sudden stop to all further negotiations and the scheme was abandoned.

1897

During the trying years of free-trade experiment, from 1893 to 1897, the piano industry stood up well as compared with other industries. Comparatively few failures were recorded, and at the end of that long period of business depression the industry could even boast of an increase in production. This remarkable showing had not been overlooked by the banking fraternity, but it was also known that the piano manufacturers were very heavy borrowers through all those years. However, the fact that the industry did enjoy this credit proved its inherent strength and soundness, and the trust idea was again taken up in earnest.

Many of the manufacturers who in 1892 had stood aloof, or had directly opposed the trust idea, now looked rather favorably upon the proposition and it appeared as if the project might be carried through. Nearly all those who had supported the movement of 1892 again took an active part in the new effort. On September 24, 1897, the " Columbia Investment Company " was organized and incorporated under the laws of New Jersey with a capital of one million ($1,000,000) dollars. This company entered upon an agreement with a syndicate of bankers who obligated themselves to advance up to five million ($5,000,000) dollars for the purpose of acquiring the various piano factories. All the contracts and agreements were similar to those of the 1892 attempt.

Several of the largest manufacturers declared their willingness to join the consolidation, but the difficulty arose how to deal justly and fairly with all the desirable concerns. While apparently the manufacturer sold his business to a new company, he was still largely interested as a shareholder in this concern. To assure lasting success, all deals had to be made on a sound business basis and real value had to be shown for the shares issued to the vendors.

Notwithstanding the fact that a number of the largest manufacturers had either executed agreements or had reached the point of willingness to sell to the Columbia Investment Company, the enterprise had to be abandoned because of the state of the money market, which made the sale of new securities impossible for a long time to come.

1899

In the early part of 1899 the trust scheme was again revived, but upon an entirely different basis and plan than that applied in 1892 and 1897. To eliminate the large expense connected with the obligations to an underwriters' syndicate, it was proposed to invite only such concerns into the combination as could take care of their own liabilities. The allotment of shares of stock was to be based on a proper ratio to the net profits shown for the previous five years, with due consideration of the value of all tangible assets.

Although this new plan appealed strongly to a number of the leading manufacturers, petty jealousy, the fear that one or the other might be treated more liberally and the reluctance of being among the first to sign, even after an agreement had been reached, made the negotiations so wearisome and tedious that the proposition was dropped for good after one month's work in the field.

The piano trade was not ready to make the proper start on its predestinated career of greater development. Only a few of the manufacturers had the broad vision for such a perspective as this combination scheme offered. Besides, an unexpected wave of prosperity such as the piano industry had never before experienced began to make itself felt and almost everybody was perfectly satisfied with existing conditions.

In the light of the marvelous development of the piano trade since 1892, the above related efforts are of historical value.

Like all other large industries, the piano industry, by force of conditions, will eventually be driven to the economic necessity of combination in order to stay in the procession for industrial development and to perform its duty to the people, providing musical instruments of quality at lowest cost and, furthermore, to take proper care of its wage workers by providing adequate pensions for them when their economic efficiency comes to an end. The great railroad combinations, the Standard Oil Company, the United States Steel Corporation, the International Harvester Company, the packers and many other large combinations are pursuing this policy as a part of the duties which they owe to the people at large. Despite all the opposition by sensational writers and unthinking people against the so-called trusts, the fact is patent that all of these combinations do serve the public better than it was ever served before. The most noticeable illustration is found in the great department stores, which have adopted the one-price system in their piano departments. Their example will eventually force every piano dealer to do likewise.

PART THREE

Men Who Have Made Piano History

CHAPTER I

ITALY, Guido of Arezzo, Spinnetti, Geronimo, Christofori, Fischer, Sievers, Röseler, Mola.

GERMANY, Silbermann, Stein, Nannette Stein, Streicher, Bösendorfer, Seuffert, Ehrbar, Schweighofer, Heitzmann, The Ibachs, Ritmüller, Rosenkrantz, Irmler, The Schiedmayers, Kaim & Günther, Dörner, Lipp, Wagner, Pfeiffer, Rohlfing, Knake, Adam, Heyl, Vogel, Lindner, Meyer, Mand, Gebauhr, Thürmer, Steinweg, Grotrian, Zeitter & Winkelmann, Buschmann, Rachals, Scheel, Blüthner, Rönisch, Feurich, Isermann, Weickert, Poehlmann.

ENGLAND, Shudi, Broadwood, Collard, Challen, Hopkinson, Brinsmead, Chappell, Eavestaff, Squire, Grover, Barnett, Poehlmann, Strohmenger, Witton, Allison, Monnington & Weston.

PART THREE

CHAPTER I

Men Who Have Made Piano History

Introduction

ONE of the remarkable peculiarities of the piano industry is the great value of an established name. His name is the piano maker's trade-mark, and that concern is fortunate that controls a name which is impressive, euphonious, easy to spell, easy to pronounce, easy to remember—in short, of such a character that it cannot be easily confounded and always will make a lasting impression.

Shakespeare's often quoted phrase, "What's in a name? That which we call a rose, by any other name would smell as sweet," does not hold true in the piano business. The maker's name on a piano carries everlasting responsibility with it. But this is not the only significance of the maker's name on a piano. Every piano maker who loves his art for the art's sake, is, as a matter of course, a man of pronounced individuality, and he impresses his individuality upon his creation. Thus it comes that we hear virtuosos and connoisseurs speak of the Erard, the Broadwood, the Blüthner, Steinway or Chickering "tone," signifying that each maker's pianos have an individuality of their own in tone and *klangfarbe*. This individuality is so carefully guarded that we find older firms always reluctant to adopt new methods of construction or other innovations. They fear that any change may rob their instruments of their most cherished individuality, their characteristic tone and *klangfarbe*.

Not only the tone quality and volume reflect the maker's individuality, the workmanship of the entire piano is guaranteed by the maker's name, and his name will live or die as his instruments are built to last or not. The reputation of the instrument which a piano maker produces follows him beyond his grave, often for generations.

In due appreciation of the overshadowing importance of a proper name and its commercial value, many of the leading members of the craft did not hesitate to give up their family name, no matter how honorable it was made by their ancestors. Whenever necessary or advisable, they changed the same, so as to give it the desired distinction. We find Burckhardt Tschudi changing his name to Burkat Shudi, Ehrhardt to Erard, Schumacher to Schomacker, Steinweg to Steinway, etc., and quite properly so! Would not an unpronounceable name on the fall board kill the best piano as a commercial proposition? Not to think of its impossibility on a concert program!

Names once identified with a good piano are never changed, even if in course of time no scion of the founder is connected with the firm or corporation making the piano. Neither genius nor talent can be transferred from father to son, or grandson, by mere teaching or example. Artists are born, and very seldom do following generations show any trace of their progenitors' inborn ability. If that were not so, we would have more Rafaels, Rubens, Shakespeares, Goethes, Wagners or Darwins. On the contrary the real genius usually exhausts his talents during his lifetime, and new blood has to be injected to maintain the standing of firms founded by men who ranked far above their contemporaries. Notable exceptions simply prove this rule. To maintain the exalted position of a leading firm, proper respect must always be paid to the honor of its illustrious founder or founders, by unceasing efforts to better the product and, with due reverence to its artistic reputation, to improve volume and quality of tone in harmony with its fundamental individuality. This requires genius, and wherever artistic, mechanical and commercial genius are combined, success is inevitable. Each by itself may make a mark, an impression, but only the combination of the three under guidance of a strong mind can achieve lasting success in the piano business. The history of the piano industry from its beginning to the present day proves that.

Italy

In the town of Arezzo a boy was born toward the end of the 10th century who was christened Guido. Intended to wear the cloth, Guido was sent to a monastery to study the Holy Book and lead a life of abstinence and devotion, but Guido had a soul, and that soul was full of music. Books did not interest him unless they spoke of music. He invented a new system of music, so revolutionary in its character that the staid old monks drove Guido out of the monastery.

The name of Guido of Arezzo is indelibly marked in history, for establishing the principle and system of notation of music. By his new system a scholar could acquire within five months as much knowledge of music as would otherwise require ten years of study. After his fame spread through the civilized world Guido was called back into the fold and instructed even the Pope in his new method. He died as prior of Avellano, May 17, 1050.

Correctly, or not, Guido is also credited with the invention of the movable bridge on the monochord, and of the keyboard. He was so great a genius, so strong a character, that historians of later days did not hesitate in crediting to him all the progressive events and inventions in the realm of music happening in Guido's time, some going so far as to ascribe to him even the invention of the clavichord.

No records are available, telling us anything regarding the Venetian Giovanni Spinnetti, who invented the spinet about 1503; nor of Geronimo of Bologna, who gave us the harpsichord in 1521, but the instruments of these two makers which are still in existence are speaking examples of their genius and talents.

Padua claims the honor of being the birthplace of Bartolomo Christofori, but in 1710, when 27 years of age, we find Christofori enjoying an easy life at the court of the Duke of Tuscany at Florence, engaged in building clavichords, spinets and other musical instruments for the prince and his courtiers. Whether Christofori allowed his genius to drive him to over-exertion, or whether the sybaritic life at the court of the wealthy and luxurious prince shortened his life is not known; he died in 1731 when only 48 years old, leaving to the world his great invention, the piano e forte.

Italy has not produced another great piano maker since Christofori. Mola of Turin has built up a very large business and is to-day the mainstay of the industry in his country, but he has not gone on record as an independent constructor. Röseler, who also founded a large establishment at Turin about 1850, and was appointed by the King of Italy a cavalliero, came from Berlin. The genial Sievers, who wrote a valuable treatise on piano construction and established a factory at Naples about 1865, came from St. Petersburg, and Carl Fischer, preceding Sievers at Naples, came from Vienna.*

---

* Fischer's sons came to New York about 1840, founding the firm of J. & C. Fischer.

Germany

Gottfried Silbermann, born near Frauenstein, Saxony, January 14, 1683, served his apprenticeship as cabinetmaker and then studied organ building, following the example of his talented elder brother Andreas. We find Gottfried, about 1712, at Freiberg, Saxony, erecting fine church organs. His Bohemian escapades compelled him to leave the staid old Saxon city rather hastily, to seek shelter and work at his brother Andreas' atelier at Strasburg. His weakness for the gentler sex involved him, however, here also in serious affairs, culminating in the futile effort to escape with a nun from the convent, and he had to tramp back to far-away Freiberg after a stay of several years at Strasburg. A fine mechanic, as illustrated by the many great church organs of his creation, his commercial talents were no doubt even stronger. Although a man of the world, a great entertainer and liberal spender, he accumulated a respectable fortune. In his art he was quick to adopt the inventions of others and thoroughly understood the value of clever advertising. Both Gottfried and his nephews at Strasburg, who succeeded their father in business, were the first in the piano industry who effectually resorted to *réclame* to let the world know what they were doing, and managed to get their name into print much oftener than any of their contemporaries, which has led many a historian to the error of calling Gottfried the inventor of the piano, or the hammer action.

Gottfried Silbermann died in 1756, having erected 30 large church organs and made quite a number of pianos. His nephew, Johann Daniel Silbermann, continued the business, devoting himself to the making of grand pianos exclusively. He died on May 6, 1766, at Leipsic, having no successor. The Strasburg branch of the Silbermann family continued, however, to make pianos until the death of Johann Friedrich Silbermann on March 8, 1817.

Johann Andreas Stein had a creative mind. An organ builder by profession, he learned piano making in Gottfried Silbermann's shop. About 1754 he established himself at Augsburg, making pianos, and while there he built the great organ in the Church of St. Francis. In 1758, seeking a larger field, he went to Paris, taking some of his pianos along, but the gay metropolis was apparently not ready for pianos. Disappointed and almost penniless Stein returned to Augsburg, where he again began to build pianos. He invented the '' hopper action '' and many other improvements.

Mozart, in a letter to his mother, pronounced Stein's pianos superior to any others that he had played upon. Stein's pianos were copied everywhere, especially by the Vienna makers, so that Stein may rightfully be called the father of the Vienna school. He built about 700 pianos and several church organs. He was born at Hildesheim in 1728, and died at Augsburg, February 29, 1792, in his 64th year.

His talented daughter, Nannette, had learned the art of piano making under her father's tutelage, besides being an accomplished pianist. She played in concerts and had also played for Mozart and Beethoven. Soon after her father's death she moved to Vienna, where she continued the business with her brothers, Andreas and Friedrich. In 1794 she married Johann Andreas Streicher, and although her husband soon took an active part, the piano business was carried on under the name of Nannette Streicher, geb. Stein, until 1822, when her son Johann Baptist Streicher was admitted to partnership and the firm name was changed to Nannette Streicher & Sohn.

Johann Andreas Streicher, born at Stuttgart, on December 13, 1761, attended the renowned Karl Schule at Mannheim, together with Friedrich Schiller, whose friendship he retained ever after. Leaving the school Streicher devoted himself entirely to the study of music, especially the piano, and gained renown as a virtuoso, composer and teacher. It was but natural that Beethoven, while living at Vienna, should become a warm friend of such congenial people, who always kept open house, and assembled the celebrities of the day, such as Hummel, Cramer, Moscheles, Henselt and Kullak, around their table. This friendship never lessened to the last days of the great composer. Indeed Nannette exercised a motherly care over that " great child," Beethoven, superintending his much neglected household and looking after his daily wants. In 1816 Nannette built for Beethoven's special use and by his request, a grand piano with a compass of 6½ octaves, which was considered quite an accomplishment in those days. Nearly all of Beethoven's compositions were created on pianos built by Nannette Streicher. She closed her eventful career by passing away at Vienna, in January, 1833, her husband following her in May of the same year. Their son, Johann Baptist Streicher, born at Vienna in 1796, continued the business with great success, and added valuable improvements, so that the Streicher pianos achieved world-wide reputation. He changed the firm name to J. B. Streicher & Sohn in 1857, when his son Emil was admitted to partnership. The latter retired from business soon after his father's death in 1871, without a successor.

Among the many illustrious names which gave Vienna its prestige as the home of the grand piano, that of Ignatz Bösendorfer stands foremost. Born at Vienna in 1795, a pupil of Brodmann, he established his business at Vienna in 1828. After 30 years of active life, during which time he added many valuable improvements to the development of the piano, he retired and his talented son Ludwig took the reins.

Having had the benefit of a most thorough education and extended travels, young Bösendorfer soon became a factor in the piano world, and made his pianos known far beyond the boundaries of his home. He improved on the piano made by his father, ac-

Ludwig Bösendorfer

cepting modern ideas as far as his inborn admiration for the " Vienna tone " would permit, and produced pianos which to this date hold their own successfully in competition with other celebrated makes.

Appreciating the valuable assistance of the virtuosos, Bösendorfer erected a concert hall in 1872. Hans von Bülow gave a recital at the opening. Bösendorfer's grand pianos are to this day the favorite instruments of many of the leading virtuososos, and his factory ranks foremost in the production of artistic pianos. In recognition of his services to the industry, the Emperor of Austria appointed Bösendorfer purveyor to the court, conveyed the title of Imperial Commercial Counselor, and bestowed the decoration of the " Golden Cross of Merit with the Crown," upon him.

Friedrich Ehrbar, born on April 26, 1827, in Hanover, was another of those remarkable men who carved their fortunes out of the rock of privation and adversity. When two years of age a cholera epidemic took from him, within one week, his father, mother and sister. His childhood was spent in a home for orphans. Showing a decided talent for music as well as mechanical ability, when still a schoolboy, by making guitars for himself and comrades, the organ builder, Frederici of Hanover, consented to take him as an apprentice. He had to serve fully seven years. Although after that his master was anxious to retain his services at good wages, Ehrbar was intent on going to Vienna, the high school of piano making. In 1848 he started on his journey. He went from Hanover along the Rhine to Frankfort, Nuremberg and via Regensburg to Vienna. At Hanover he met Henry Steinweg, who had also started out on his "Wanderschaft," and the two young piano makers formed a lasting intimate

Friedrich Ehrbar

friendship. Reaching Vienna, Ehrbar was so captivated with the beautiful "Kaiserstadt," that he immediately resolved to make his home there. He was fortunate in finding employment with that celebrated master, Seuffert. Although the original understanding was that he should serve for three years as a student at a nominal wage, he proved himself such an adept that his master relieved him from this obligation after the first nine months. His further progress was so rapid that Seuffert intrusted him in 1854 with the production of six pianos for the Munich exposition of 1855. Ehrbar had the satisfaction not only of receiving a prize medal, but furthermore of seeing all six pianos sold at the exhibition.

Seuffert died in 1855 and Ehrbar managed the business until 1857, when he acquired ownership. At the World's Fairs of Lon-

Johannes Adolf Ibach

don in 1862 and Paris in 1867, Ehrbar's pianos were awarded first prizes. The Emperor of Austria honored him with decorations and the title of purveyor to the court, and at the Vienna Exposition of 1873 he served as juror for the musical instrument exhibits.

Progressive by nature, Ehrbar was among the first of the Vienna makers who adopted the full iron frame for all of his pianos. In 1877 he erected the Saal Ehrbar, a notable addition to the concert halls of Vienna. He retired from active business on January 1, 1898, and died at his country home near Vienna on February 25, 1905, in his seventy-eighth year. The business is continued under the able direction of his son, Friedrich Ehrbar.

I. M. Schweighofer's Söhne is Vienna's oldest firm.

J. Fritz & Sohn, established in 1801, Karl Dorr in 1817, Otto Heitzmann and Josef Schneider's Neffe in 1839, are all builders of good pianos, sustaining the time-honored reputation of the Vienna piano industry.

Following the good old German custom to go " wandern," that is, to travel for a number of years on foot from country to country, stopping for a while at a city wherever an acknowledged " master of the craft " had his domicile, to learn and to earn, young Johannes Adolf Ibach left the monastery of Beyenburg, just as soon as his education was completed. He studied organ and piano making with several of the best masters of Germany, and returned to his home a master of the art. He was intrusted with the remodeling of the great organ at Beyenburg and did such excellent work that his standing as a master was at once established. Like most organ builders of those days, he longed, however, to build pianos, that instrument which had taken such a

Carl Rudolf Ibach

a strong hold and promised a much greater field for invention and business expansion than the church organ. We find him, therefore, soon giving his entire attention to pianos. He knew how to build them, and in spite of the great depression in business, caused by the Napoleonic wars, Ibach's business grew steadily, unfortunately, however, undermining the health of the indefatigable worker, so that at the age of 59, he had to give his business into the hands of his eldest son, Carl Rudolf Ibach, who was then only 21 years of age. The young man filled his place well, and from 1825 dates the rise of the house of Ibach. To find a greater market for his product and to enrich his knowledge of the world and business, young Ibach took to travel whenever he could. He visited France and Spain, and never lost an opportunity to attend the then just inaugurated expositions and fairs, oftentimes putting

Rudolf Ibach

his pianos in competition with others and always rewarded with the customary honors.

Like his father, he sacrificed his health for his ambition, and died at Barmen, April 25, 1863, leaving the care of his business upon the shoulders of his son, Rudolf Ibach, who changed the firm name to Rudolf Ibach Sohn. Although only 20 years of age when his father died, young Rudolf inaugurated a most aggressive campaign, just as soon as he had found his bearings. He was an exceptionally strong character, a genius in many ways, artistic in his inclinations and desires. He soon developed a commercial keenness and foresight, which, coupled with the daring born of faith in his own strength and ability, brought astounding results, and in a few years under Rudolf's leadership the factory had to be enlarged to meet the growing demand for Ibach pianos. In his extended travels he came in contact with the leading musicians and composers of his day. Himself a very magnetic and interesting man, he drew others to him. Richard Wagner honored him by dedicating a life-size photograph with the inscription " Seinem freundlichen Tongehilfen Rudolf Ibach dankbarlichs Richard Wagner, 1882.'' What a strong indorsement of the piano maker, Rudolf Ibach!

Liszt, Sauer, and many other virtuosos have played the Ibach grands. Rudolf Ibach was not satisfied to serve art only as "Ton Gehilfe." With his resistless energy he started a campaign to give his pianos an artistic exterior and called on the masters of decorative art for assistance. In 1883, and again in 1891, he invited competitive designs for artistic piano cases, awarding adequate cash prizes to the winners, so that the leading architects of Germany found it

J. G. Irmler

worth their while to participate. It was not only the benefit of obtaining exquisite designs for the Ibach pianos which resulted from this enterprising movement; it reached farther and impelled other piano makers to follow Ibach's example.

Foresightedness was one of Ibach's characteristics. While he was occupied in expanding his business in all directions, he sent his younger brother, Walter Ibach, into the world to study the methods of other piano makers. Walter went to Brussels, then spent considerable time at Gaveau's atelier in Paris and prepared himself at London for his American visit, where he was for several years active in George Steck's factory. He also studied felt and hammer making in the author's factories at Dolgeville, N. Y. After an absence of nearly 10 years, Walter Ibach returned to Barmen in 1883, a master of his art, to assist his brother Rudolf,

Oswald Irmler

whose duties and cares had grown almost beyond one man's endurance. Like his father and grandfather, Rudolf Ibach had gone beyond his strength, and passed away at the early age of 49 years, on July 31, 1892. The great business which he built up is carried on by his sons, under the guidance of their uncle, Walter Ibach.

In 1795 Andreas Georg Ritmüller began making pianos at the old university town of Göttingen. It is not known where he learned his trade, but his pianos were well built and the business founded by him has continued with marked success to the present day.

Ernst Philip Rosenkrantz, born July 10, 1773, served his apprenticeship with Heinrich Ludolf Mack of Dresden, and started on his own account in 1797. His son Friedrich Wilhelm succeeded him after his death in 1828. He gained a worldwide reputation for his instruments, doing especially a large export business to North America. The firm has maintained its reputation for high grade instruments and enjoys an enviable position among the Dresden makers of to-day.

Born at Obergrumbach near Dresden, Johann Christian Gottlieb Irmler studied piano making with the masters at Vienna and came to Leipsic in 1818, where he founded the house of J. G. Irmler. He built very good grand, square and upright pianos,

and some of his earliest productions can be found at the
Germanic Museum in Nu·
remberg. Enterprising to
an unusual degree, Irmler
saw his small shop grow into
a large industrial establishment, and his pianos sold in
all parts of the globe. He
died December 10, 1857. His
sons, Otto and Oswald Irmler, had gone through the
school of piano making in
the leading shops of Vienna,
Paris and London, and as-
sumed the management after
their father's death. The
young men introduced steam-
driven machinery in their works in 1861, probably as the first in the
piano industry of Germany. Otto Irmler died October 30, 1861,
at the age of 41, and the management fell to the younger brother,
Oswald, then only 26 years of age.

Johann David Schiedmayer

For 44 years Oswald Irmler directed the destiny of the time-
honored firm with marked ability and success, taking his sons,
Emil and Otto, in partnership in 1903. He died October 30, 1905,
leaving an establishment to his sons, which ranks among the best
in Germany.

The firm of J. G. Irmler has been honored by the appointment
as purveyors to the courts of the Emperor of Austria, the Kings
of Wurtemburg, Sweden, Roumania, and other potentates, and received distinguished awards for its products wherever exhibited.

Johann Lorenz Schiedmayer

Leading virtuosos such as Bülow, Friedheim, Henselt, Felix Mendelssohn, Sofie Menter, Carl Reinecke and others, have used the Irmler grand pianos in their concerts.

It is not known of whom Balthasar Schiedmayer, born in 1711, learned his art, but he built his first grand piano at Erlangen in 1735. He died in 1781 and was succeeded by his son, Johann David Schiedmayer, who was honored by the appointment of piano maker to the Elector of Brandenburg. He removed to Nuremberg, continuing there with great success until his death in 1806. His son, Johann Lorenz Schiedmayer, sought a larger field for his activities and we find him in 1809 located at Stuttgart, laying the foundation for one of the most renowned firms of Germany. In 1845 he admitted his sons, Adolf and Hermann, to partnership, changing the firm name to Schiedmayer & Söhne. Always progressive, this firm produced upright pianos as early as 1842. At the World's Fair in London in 1851, their product carried off the gold medal, and in 1881 Adolf Schiedmayer received the title of " Counselor of Commerce " from the King of Wurtemburg. Adolf Schiedmayer died in 1890, and his brother Hermann in 1891. Adolf, Jr., born in 1847, is the present head of the house, maintaining the honored traditions with great success.

He wears the title of " Privy Counselor of Commerce " and is also president of the Piano Manufacturers' Association of Germany. The firm is, by appointment, purveyor to the courts of Wurtemburg and Roumania.

The younger sons of Johann Lorenz Schiedmayer, Julius and Paul Schiedmayer, devoted themselves exclusively to the building of harmoniums. They spent several years at London and more especially at Paris with Debain and Alexander, and

Adolf Schiedmayer

established themselves in Stuttgart in 1853 under the firm name of J. & P. Schiedmayer. They produced most excellent instruments, improving upon the products of the French masters, but since the upright piano began to crowd the harmoniums from the markets, J. & P. Schiedmayer were forced to begin the manufacture of pianos in 1860, and finally changed their name to the " Schiedmayer Pianofabrik." They soon achieved great prominence, being among the first makers of Germany to adopt the overstrung system and full iron frame. In course of time the firm was appointed purveyor to the courts of the Emperors of Germany, Russia and Austria, the Queen of England and the Kings of Wurtemburg, Bavaria, Italy, Spain, Roumania, etc. Distinguished by the award of 45 diplomas of honor and prize medals, at the fairs where their

Hermann Schiedmayer

pianos were exhibited, the firm was awarded the grand prize at the World's Fairs of Paris in 1900 and St. Louis in 1904.

Julius Schiedmayer was appointed Counselor of Commerce by the King of Wurtemburg, and chosen as juror of the piano exhibits at the World's Fairs of London, 1862; Stettin, 1864; Paris, 1867; Vienna, 1873; and Philadelphia, 1876. He also received decorations from the Emperor of Austria and the Kings of Wurtemburg and Italy, in recognition of his valuable services. He died at Stuttgart, January, 1878, his brother Paul following him in 1891.

Under the energetic guidance of Paul's son, Max Schiedmayer, the renowned firm is constantly adding to its prestige and honor. Like his illustrious uncle and father, Max Schiedmayer has served as juror at exhibitions, notably at the great World's Fair of Chicago in 1893, and at Brussels in 1910.

In 1819 Kaim & Günther began to make pianos at Kirchheim near Stuttgart, building up a large business. The firm was eventually dissolved, the grandson of Kaim doing business under the firm name of "Kaim & Sohn." Günther's sons adopted the firm name of "Günther & Söhne." The latter have the appointment as the purveyors to the court of Wurtemburg.

Among the noteworthy firms of Stuttgart must be mentioned F. Dörner & Sohn, established in 1830, Richard Lipp & Sohn, in 1831 and Hermann Wagner in 1844. The firm of A. J. Pfeiffer was founded in 1862. The present head of the house, Carl J. Pfeiffer, has devoted much attention to the construction of pedal pianos for pedal practice of organ players. He has also been very industrious in collecting models of piano actions for the Royal Museum at Stutt-

Julius Schiedmayer

gart, and has assembled there the most complete collection of piano actions in existence. In recognition of his services Pfeiffer has been appointed purveyor to the court of Wurtemburg, and also Royal Counselor of Commerce.

Germany can boast of a long list of old established houses in all parts of its domain. The house of Gebrüder Rohlfing of Osnabrück dates back to 1790. H. Pfister started at Würzburg in 1800; Gebrüder Knake of Münster in 1808. In the year 1828 Gerhard Adam of Wesel, G. L. Nagel of Heilbronn, Ritter of Halle, G. Heyl of Borna, and I. G. Vogel & Sohn of Plauen, commenced business. I. P. Lindner of Stralsund made his first piano in 1825, and Meyer & Company of Munich in 1826. In 1832 Carl Mand began his career at Coblenz, and in 1834 C. J. Gebauhr had the courage to establish himself at Königsberg, on the far

Paul Schiedmayer

eastern border of Germany. In the same year Ferdinand Thürmer opened his shop in Meissen, to be followed a year later by Heinrich Engelhardt Steinweg at Seesen. His son Theodor Steinweg removed his business to Brunswick, after the elder Steinweg left with his family for America in 1850.

Joining in 1865 the meantime established firm of Steinway & Sons in New York, Theodor Steinweg sold his business to three of his workingmen, Grotrian, Helfferich and Schulz, who adopted the firm name of Theodor Steinweg Nachfolger. This firm ranks to-day among the foremost of Germany under the able management of Wilhelm Grotrian and his sons.

Traugott Berndt started in Breslau in 1836, and the highly respected firm, Zeitter & Winkelmann of Brunswick in 1837.

In Hamburg, Gustav Adolph Buschmann commenced making pianos as early as 1805. Mathias Ferdinand Rachals followed in 1832. Rachals, born at Mitau, June 3, 1801, had studied with Brix of St. Petersburg and Sachsossky of Cassel. His pianos were of the highest order, and he was especially successful in constructing a detachable piano for tropical countries. Rachals died September 6, 1866, and was succeeded by his son, Eduard Ferdinand, who continued to spread the fame of the firm. Born at Hamburg, May

4, 1837, he learned piano making in his father's shop, and afterward studied in the leading factories of Paris, London and Zürich. Rachals possessed a most artistic temperament, played the piano to perfection and enjoyed practicing on brass instruments, playing classic quartets with friends for his own amusement. The business prospered under his able management until death ended his usefulness. He passed away April 24, 1902. His son Adolf Ferdinand

Mathias Ferdinand Rachals

went to the United States in 1892, where he worked in several of the prominent piano factories, including a long stay at Dolgeville, N. Y., for the study of hammer making. At the World's Fair of Chicago in 1893, M. F. Rachals & Company received a special diploma for their excellent instruments. Adolf Ferdinand Rachals succeeded his father in 1902.

Carl Scheel of Cassel worked for Erard from 1837 to 1846, during the later years as superintendent. He had learned so much in Paris that his business, founded in 1846, was a success from the start. An acknowledged master of his art, he attracted many young men, desirous of studying under him, among whom Georg Steck later made a name for himself in New York.

A most remarkable success, achieved in a comparatively short time, assures Julius Blüthner a prominent place in history. Born March 11, 1824, at Falkenhain, he learned his trade with Hölling

Edward Ferdinand Rachals

& Spangenberg of Zeitz, and studied under Alexander Bretschneider, the renowned builder of grand pianos, at Leipsic, until 1853, when he started in business on his own account. Handicapped by lack of a broader education, Blüthner had to dig his way to prominence. He was fortunate in the possession of a highly developed sense of hearing, and it is said that in later years no one in his extensive establishment could " voice " a piano so accurately as he.

Ambitious to contribute something more to his art than mere industrial activity, Blüthner made many experiments to improve the piano. In order to enhance the volume and singing quality of tone in the upper octaves, he revived Hans Ruckers' fourth string system, calling his device the " Aliquot System." He also invented a grand action. Calling to his aid able young men of literary ability, Blüthner used printer's ink to great advantage and his fine instruments soon found a market in all quarters of the globe, so that his production in 1882 had risen to an annual output of 1200 grand and 1800 upright pianos. Blüthner published, in conjunction with Gretschel, a treatise on piano making, of which several editions have been sold. The King of Saxony honored him with the appointment of Privy Counselor of Commerce, and he also received decorations from his King, the Duke of Saxe-Coburg and the Grand Duke of Mecklenburg-Schwerin. He died at Leipsic in 1910 in his eighty-seventh year.

None of the modern makers of Germany has done as much to procure for the German piano the prominence which it enjoys at the present time as Carl Bechstein. Born at Gotha on June 1, 1826, Bechstein was imbued with all the poetic and musical instinct so typical of the Thuringians. It was natural that he should choose piano making for a profession, and so proficient had he become that at the age of 22 he was given the responsible position of managing the business of G. Perau, one of Berlin's best known makers of that time. After four years' faithful service wanderlust got the better of Bechstein, and we next find him at London, later at Paris, studying under that genial empiric, Pape, and getting an insight into modern business methods with Kriegelstein.

Equipped with new experiences in piano making, a thorough knowledge of Parisian commercial tactics, enriched with broader views, world-wise, Bechstein returned to Berlin and built his first grand piano in 1856. A man of the world, amiable, even magnetic to a certain degree, he easily attracted artists and litterateurs to himself, gaining thereby a publicity which redounded largely to the ever-increasing prosperity of his business. Carl Bechstein

Carl Bechstein

received numerous decorations, both from his King and Emperor, as well as other rulers, and was appointed purveyor to the courts of nearly all the reigning emperors and kings of Europe. He died at Berlin in 1908 at the age of 82.

Among the many firms that, during the past 50 years, have been more or less active in expanding the piano industry of Germany, C. Weidig of Jena, founded in 1843; Carl Rönisch of Dresden, founded in 1845; and Julius Feurich of Leipsic, established in 1851, deserves special mention.

Carl Rönisch, born at Goldberg, Silesia, in 1814, experienced all the privations of poverty in his youth, but his inborn talent and determination finally got the better of adverse conditions. Without capital, but having unlimited faith in his ability, he began to make pianos at Dresden and in time had the satisfaction of shipping the product of his factory to all parts of the globe. Indeed, Rönisch was one of the pioneers in exporting German pianos. His grands and uprights became so popular in Russia, that he found himself compelled to erect a factory in St. Petersburg. Rewarded with highest awards at all expositions, wherever his pianos have been exhibited, Rönisch was also personally honored with decorations of distinction, and appointed purveyor to the Court of Saxony. He died July 21, 1893, at the age of 80. The great business is successfully carried on by his sons, who have been his associates for many years.

There are a large number of aggressive young firms in Germany, making history, inspired by the glorious records of the older houses, but it is not the province of this work to dwell upon present and future.

In the supply industries Germany has produced three self-made men who assumed the leadership in their re-

Carl Rönisch

spective branches from the day they entered the arena. The piano industry is indebted to L. Isermann, Moritz Poehlmann and August Moritz Weickert for furnishing actions, wires and felt of such quality as to make the perfect piano of the present day a possibility.

I. C. L. Isermann, born on July 1, 1813, near Hanover, served his apprenticeship as a cabinetmaker, and shortly thereafter traveled on foot through Germany, Italy, Switzerland and Belgium, working at his trade in most of the larger cities. About 1835 he landed in Paris, the mecca of all young German artisans of that time. He found employment in one of the piano action factories. Just as soon as he had mastered that art he made further studies in other factories to become familiar with the various models of actions then in use and the different methods of manufacturing. Thoroughly grounded, he returned to the Fatherland

J. C. L. Isermann

and in 1842 started the first piano action factory in Germany at Hamburg. It was an innovation and seemed a bold undertaking, because up to that time all piano makers in Germany made their actions, following their own notions regarding construction. Isermann demonstrated at once, that he could produce a better action for less money than the piano maker, and his business prospered far beyond his expectations. His success was so remarkable that it invited competition. Very soon all piano makers quit producing their own actions, and the piano action industry, founded by Isermann, spread to all the leading manufacturing centers of Germany. Because of the reliability and excellent workmanship of his goods, the honesty and integrity of his dealings, Isermann always had more business offered to him than he could take care of, although his establishment had been constantly enlarged, eventually employing about 550 persons.

In 1870 his son, C. W. Isermann, assumed management, and in 1904 young Ludolf Isermann, the grandson, joined the firm. I. C. L. Isermann died on November 5, 1898, in his eighty-fifth year, having made his strong mark as a captain of industry in a field created by himself. C. W. Isermann died on December 29, 1900, in his sixty-first year.

Harassing labor conditions impelled Ludolf Isermann to leave Hamburg and join the firm of F. Langer & Company of Berlin, perpetuating the work of his illustrious grandfather and father, under most favorable and promising auspices. Although established only since 1882 the firm of Langer & Company enjoys a most enviable reputation for the high quality of its products and controls one of the largest establishments of its kind.

August Moritz Weickert

I. D. Weickert, born August 23, 1751, the fourth son of a family of 14 children, learned the profession of an optician and established himself at Leipsic in 1783. Thrift and industry soon brought prosperity, with greater promises for the future. When the Napoleonic wars devastated Germany, paralyzing business for many years, Weickert's hard-earned savings gradually disappeared and he and his family often had to suffer indescribable hardships. These sufferings, worry and anxiety finally caused the untimely death of this energetic man in 1816. He left his family almost in poverty, but the era of peace was dawning in Europe, and although only 15 years of age, the son, August Moritz, together with his most remarkable mother, hung on to what little there was left of his father's business.

C. W. Patzschke

After the optical business was re-established, so to speak, the young man added the sale of hardware and gradually built up a reputation for his firm. When he became personally acquainted with the renowned English tool maker, Stubbs, during the latter's visit to Leipsic, he improved his opportunity to open up direct business connection with this English firm and thus laid the foundation for the great hardware business, which under his personal management, extending over 60 years, grew to magnificent proportions.

In 1847 F. W. Patzschke, a hatter by trade, had made some experiments in producing tapered felt for piano hammers. Lacking capital, he appealed to the merchant, Weickert, who agreed to make the necessary advances. For several years the results were so disappointing that Patzschke became discouraged and forced Weickert to assume control and management. Weickert secured the services of his old partner's son, C. W. Patzschke, as manager of the factory and pushed the business energetically. With keen foresight he anticipated the great future in store for this new industry and re-invested all the profit for years in new machinery and improved buildings, aiming always to produce the best felts that could be made. For many years Weickert enjoyed a monopoly for his product. Other factories were started in Ger-

many, following in Weick-
ert's footsteps as much as
possible, but his business
continued to grow, in spite
of competition, and enjoys
to-day a position as undis-
puted leader in the industry.

Carl Moritz Weickert
died on May 22, 1878, highly
respected by all who knew
him as a man of indomi-
table energy, business ability, sagacity and one whose
noblesse of character, honesty and integrity compelled
admiration. His son, Otto
Weickert, extended the felt
manufacturing business to

Otto Weickert

enormous proportions, establishing distributing depots in all the
larger markets. After fifty years of active participation in the
management, he turned the business over to the care of his son
Max and his nephew Fritz Weickert, who maintained the conservative policy of the house with due regard for progressive
advancement.

The technical management of the factories has remained in the
hands of the Patzschke family. Rudolf Patzschke, a grandson of
F. W. Patzschke, has succeeded his father as superintendent of the
extensive works at Wurzen, near Leipsic.

The fact that three generations of Weickerts have continuously worked with three generations of Patzschkes, for the benefit
of their business, may be looked upon as the key to the remarkable
success of the time-honored firm of I. D. Weickert.

Moritz Poehlmann

Moritz Poehlmann, born at Ober Redwitz, January 27, 1823, began the manufacture of cast steel wire for piano strings about 1855. Although he demonstrated, from the very beginning, that his wire was superior to any other on the market, he met with great difficulties in obtaining sufficient outlet to make his business profitable. It required all of that inborn determination, which says, " I will," to believe in final victory, during the years of disappointments and severe trials.

Poehlmann studied to improve the tensile strength, polish and uniform thickness of his wire, and has succeeded in outclassing all his competitors since the Paris exposition of 1867. Like Isermann and Weickert, he became the father of an industry, which multiplied, especially in Germany, mainly for the reason that through Poehlmann's efforts German music wire achieved an international reputation. Moritz Poehlmann died March 26, 1902, in his eightieth year. The business is carried on by his son, Richard Poehlmann.

ENGLAND

Turning to England with its rich history of glorious achievements, we find the grand old house of John Broadwood & Sons, after a career of 178 years, in renewed glory at the head of the

English piano industry. The founder, Burckhardt Tschudi, born at Schwanden, Switzerland, on March 13, 1702, came to London in 1718, to follow his trade of cabinet making. He soon found employment with Tabel, a Flemish harpsichord maker. In 1732, Tschudi established himself as harpsichord maker in that historic house, 33 Great Poulteney Street, which the later firm of Broadwood & Sons occupied for their showrooms and city offices until 1903. It was

John Broadwood

in this house where the " Wonder-child," Wolfgang Amadeus Mozart, practiced on the harpsichord which Tschudi had built for Frederick the Great, King of Prussia.

Tschudi seems to have been the first to change his name for expedience' sake, for he traded under the name of Burkat Shudi. Besides being an excellent mechanic, Shudi was also a very shrewd business man, who knew the value of advertising. He courted the friendship of all leading musicians who came to London, and formed an intimate friendship with the great Handel, who introduced Shudi's harpsichords to the English nobility, and no doubt assisted materially in securing Shudi's appointment as maker to the court of the Prince of Wales. The composer Haydn was also one of Shudi's intimate friends and was so much at home in Shudi's house that he wrote many of his compositions there.

With creditable shrewdness Shudi presented to Frederick the Great, as the defender of the Protestant faith, one of his harpsichords, after Frederick had won the battle of Prague, for which he received in return a ring bearing a portrait of Frederick. In 1776 he was commanded to build two harpsichords for the " New Palais " at Potsdam, and later on Frederick ordered a harpsichord of Shudi at a cost of $1,000. Besides profiting by the prestige, Shudi certainly made a good cash profit on these instruments.

John Broadwood, born at Cockburns, Scotland, in 1732, came to London about 1752. A joiner by trade, he eventually found his way to Shudi's shop and ingratiated himself so strongly in his master's favor that he not only was accepted in partnership, and the firm name changed to Shudi & Broadwood, but he also married Shudi's daughter in 1769, whereupon Shudi retired from business entirely. Shudi died on August 19, 1773. Broadwood now took Shudi's son in partnership, but assumed sole control again in 1783.

John Broadwood was a man of exceptional ability in many ways. He kept in close touch with all the leaders in his art, associating intimately with Americus Backers, Stodart and other inventors of his day, always keeping open house for his friends among the musicians and other artists, so that 33 Great Poulteney Street became a meeting place for all the brilliant people of London of that time. His receptive mind enabled him to profit by this intercourse with intellectual people, and he never hesitated to ask the aid and judgment of his artistic or scientific friends, when working on his great innovations in piano construction. When Broadwood reconstructed the square piano, he was not satisfied to experiment merely as an empiric. He called upon his friends, the great scientists, Dr. Gray and Cavalla, of the British Museum, to benefit by their knowledge of acoustics. He would ever search for scientific laws to learn cause and effect, hence his inventions were all of permanent value. In 1795, he admitted his son James Shudi Broadwood to partnership, changing the firm name to John Broadwood & Son, and in 1808 his son Thomas joined the firm, the name being again changed to John Broadwood & Sons.

After the death of John Broadwood, in 1812, James became the head of the house. Brought up in the intellectual and artistic atmosphere of that house in Great Poulteney Street, where his grandfather had built harpsichords for kings and nobility, where Mozart, Handel and Haydn had practiced, and where his father had built his pianos under the advice and according to the demands of Muzio Clementi and other masters of the piano, James S. Broadwood was eminently qualified to add to the glory of the house, as a piano maker and a business man. Thoroughly in sympathy with the liberal views of life current in the world of artists, James inaugurated those celebrated Saturday dinners at 33 Great Poulteney Street, where he assembled around his sumptuous table all of the great musicians, or whoever, in London, could lay claim to superior achievement in art and literature. No wonder that the praise of the Broadwood piano was sung in all modern languages. Even Beethoven, with all his loyalty to Nannette Streicher, joined the chorus of Broadwood admirers.

Henry Fowler Broadwood succeeded James in 1834 as head of the house, his valuable inventions adding largely to the luster of the great firm. It was during this time that Chopin gave his last recital in England at the concert hall of the Broadwood house in Great Poulteney Street. Henry Fowler Broadwood passed away in 1893 at the age of 82, having guided the affairs of the house for over 50 years.

Walter Stewart Broadwood and Thomas Broadwood became partners in 1843, George Thomas Rose and Frederick Rose in 1857. George Daniel Rose joined in 1883, and James Henry Shudi

Broadwood, the inventor of the barless steel frame, in 1894. W. C. Dobbs, a grandson of Henry Fowler Broadwood, was admitted to partnership in the same year. Thus six generations, counting from Shudi in direct descent, have guided the destiny of this great house. James H. S. Broadwood died February 8, 1911.

Conforming to the changed conditions in manufacturing and business methods, the Broadwoods have lately erected new works, equipped with up-to-date machinery and appliances of the most approved character. In 1903 the historic showrooms on Great Poulteney Street had to be taken down, and one of London's most celebrated landmarks passed into oblivion.

With traditional progressiveness the house of Broadwood has taken the lead in England by producing entire player pianos as a specialty in their factories and have established modern showrooms near fashionable Bond Street. It should be mentioned here that the Broadwoods have uninterruptedly been purveyors to the Court of St. James since the reign of George I.

The firm of Collard & Collard traces its origin to Longmann & Broderip, who established a publishing house in 1767, and also built some pianos. Muzio Clementi, who had become wealthy, and whose compositions were published by Longmann & Broderip, invested part of his money in their piano factory, finally associating himself with F. W. & W. P. Collard, under the firm name of Clementi & Company. Clementi's great reputation as a virtuoso and composer was a distinct advantage to the young firm, but its lasting reputation was established through the mechanical and inventive genius of F. W. Collard, who obtained several patents for improvements as early as 1811. Upon the retirement of Clementi, the firm was changed to Collard & Collard. Under the aggressive management of Charles Lukey Collard, who became sole owner in 1859, the firm forged rapidly to the front, and achieved worldwide fame.

In 1804 Thomas Butcher started a piano shop and took William Challen as a partner in 1816. Upon Butcher's retirement in 1830, Challen became sole owner. He succeeded in turning out excellent upright pianos and amassed a fortune. Retiring in 1862, he left the business to his son, C. Challen, who admitted his son, C. H. Challen, to partnership in 1873, from which time the firm has been known as Challen & Son.

John Brinsmead

The firm of J. & J. Hopkinson was founded in 1835 by John Hopkinson at Leeds. In 1846 he took his brother, James, as partner and moved the business to London. John Hopkinson was a thorough piano builder and invented many improvements, which gave his firm great prominence. He retired from business in 1869 and died on April 4, 1886.

John Brinsmead started in business in 1837. In 1862 he patented a repetition action, for the further improvement of which seven patents were granted, the latest in 1885. His sons, Edgar and Thomas James, took active part in the management of the ever-growing business, which soon was counted among the leaders of its kind in England. The firm was appointed piano makers to the Prince of Wales, and, in 1911, to King George V. Forty prize medals and diplomas were awarded to them at various expositions for meritorious exhibits.

Thomas James Brinsmead

In 1870 John Brinsmead was elected honorary member of L'Académie Nationale of France, and in 1878 was decorated with the cross of the Legion of Honor. Many of the leading artists have used the Brinsmead pianos in their concerts and have indorsed their fine qualities.

Thomas James Brinsmead died November 9, 1906. Edgar William Brinsmead died November 18, 1907. John Brinsmead died March 17, 1908, at the age of 92. The business is continued at the present day by H. Billinghurst, a grandson of John Brinsmead.

During the palmy days of England's supremacy in the piano industry of Europe, many firms sprang up who have held their own successfully to the present day. Chappell & Co., who began business in 1811; Eavestaff & Son, established in 1823; B. Squire & Son, in 1829; Grover & Grover, in 1830; Samuel Barnett & Son, and Poehlmann & Son (Halifax), in 1832; Strohmenger & Son, in 1835; Witton, Witton & Company, in 1838; Arthur Allison & Company, in 1840; and Monnington & Weston, who started in 1858, are counted among the progressive and successful houses of today, that readily adopted modern methods of manufacturing, and whose product upholds the fame of the piano industry in England.

PART THREE

CHAPTER II

FRANCE, Erard, Pleyel, Kalkbrenner, Wolff, Lyon, Herz, Pape, Kriegelstein, Gaveau, Bord, Schwander, Herrburger.

SPAIN, Estela, Guarra, Chassaign, Montana.

BELGIUM, Berden, Van Hyfte, Vits, Boone fils, Gevaert, Günther, Oor.

NETHERLANDS, Allgäuer, Cuijpers, Rijken and de Lange.

SCANDINAVIA, Hornung & Möller, Ekstrem, Malmsjö, Hals.

RUSSIA, Diederichs, Schröder, Becker.

JAPAN, Yamaba, Nishikawa & Son.

PART THREE

CHAPTER II

FRANCE

BORN in the old historic city of Strasburg on April 5, 1752, Sebastian Erard manifested, as a child, exceptional mechanical talent. When only eight years of age we find him taking a school course in architecture and practical geometry. His mind, even then fertile in inventions, would suggest new problems and he would find his own way of solving them. He had the desire to learn the use of tools, and at an early age entered his father's shop to learn cabinet making.

When Sebastian was 16 years of age his father died, and from then on it fell to Sebastian's lot to care for his mother with her three small children. Not wavering long, he started on foot for the journey to Paris. Arriving there in 1768, he found employment with a harpsichord maker, and earned such good wages that he could well take care of those he had left behind at Strasburg.

The study of the harpsichord became a passion with him, and he soon was the peer of his employer, who, evidently an empiric, could never answer Erard's searching questions as to the scientific reasons or causes in harpsichord construction. Indeed, it was but a short time after his connection with the harpsichord maker that Erard could teach his master. He began to construct instruments according to his own ideas, and they found so much favor that Erard's fame spread rapidly, so much so that the Duchess of

Villeroy, a great patroness of art, sought him out and engaged him to build an instrument for her use, placing a well-equipped workshop in her own palace at his disposal, with perfect liberty to follow his own inclinations and desires, just as Christofori had done at the palace of the Duke of Tuscany.

It was here that Erard constructed his first piano in 1777. It is said that it was superior to any other piano of that time. Although he enjoyed the respect and most liberal protection of the duchess, Erard when 25 years of age had greater aspirations. He left the palace and started his own shop in the Rue de Bourbon. Because of his connection with the aristocracy, fostered by his influential protector, the Duchess of Villeroy, Erard's success was immediate. With his brother, Jean Baptiste, he founded in 1785 the firm which for many years thereafter reigned supreme in all the concert halls of the civilized world. No other firm, before or after Erard, occupied so exalted a position in the musical world as the house of Erard, from 1796 to 1855.

That Erard had become a man of culture and refinement is illustrated by the fact that he managed to keep in close touch with the French aristocracy, and that he had sufficient influential friends at the king's court, so that at a time when the luthiers of Paris, who suffered in business because of Erard's competition, demanded the closing of his shop because he was not a chartered member of the guild, the king issued a special charter for Erard as privileged piano and harp maker, independent of the guild. What splendid advertising! Erard had downed the guild that had set out to ruin him, and he stood now above it by special edict of the king!

The French Revolution drove Erard to London, where he immediately started a piano and harp factory. As in Paris, so in London, Erard managed to obtain the entrée to the inner circles of the English aristocracy, and, because of his interesting and magnetic personality, made warm friends among the peers of

England. At the proper time he understood how to make good use of his influential friends. When he made the most unusual request for a renewal of the English patent on his repetition action, he depended upon his personal friends in the House of Lords to carry his point. By their support success was his!

His forced stay in England was not only advantageous to him in a financial way—and Erard surely was a good financier—he profited largely by getting more

Sebastian Erard

closely acquainted with English systems of piano construction and manufacturing methods, which knowledge he put to excellent use in his Paris factory upon his return there in 1796. In fact, Erard's prominence as a manufacturer dates from that time, and for many years the pianos built by him in Paris followed the English models very closely.

However, Erard was too great a genius to follow a beaten path long, and he soon developed many useful inventions, which assured him immortality in the piano world and made his pianos the favorites of all the great artists (excepting Chopin) for almost two generations, an unparalleled record!

It is needless to say that Erard was a princely entertainer. For many years the Salon Erard was the center of the intellectual life of Paris, and the Salle Erard the place where Liszt and all

à Monsieur Alfred Dolge
Amical Souvenir du successeur de
Sebastian Erard.   a Blondel
Paris 20 avril 1911.

the great virtuosos of the day played before most distinguished audiences.

Erard divided his time between Paris and London. His brother Jean Baptiste had charge of the Paris establishment and his nephew Pierre managed the London works. Jean Baptiste Erard died in 1826, and Sebastian Erard on August 5, 1831. He made his nephew, Pierre Erard, sole heir of his business and of his great estate. Pierre made Paris his domicile in 1834, going to London off and on to look after the business affairs there. He died at Paris in 1855. The Paris factory, under the management and ownership of Mons. A. Blondel, is still producing excellent instruments, which are preferred by leading virtuosos, maintaining the exalted position created by the great genius and wonderful personality of Sebastian Erard.

At the village of Ruppersthal, near Vienna, lived a schoolmaster by name of Pleyel. He was twice married and became the father of 38 children, living to be 99 years of age. His twenty-fourth child, born in 1757, was baptized "Ignace." The boy seemed to be talented, and his father therefore soon began to teach him the Latin language, and also obtained a good music teacher for him. Ignace was a prodigy, and made such astounding progress in his music studies that the wealthy, music-loving Count Erdoedy agreed to pay the great composer, Haydn, the large sum of $500 per year, for five years, for teaching and boarding young Ignace, who was then 15 years of age. After finishing his studies with Haydn, Ignace went to Italy, where he spent some time at the court of Naples, and by request of the king composed an opera, also a number of orchestral works.

Ignace Pleyel

From 1783 to 1793 Pleyel occupied the chair as chapel-master of the cathedral of Strasburg. During that period he composed most of his works, which had an unusually large sale all over Europe. In 1793 he resigned as chapel-master and accepted a lucrative engagement at London, where he appeared in concerts in direct competition with his old master Haydn. It seems that London did not appeal to him, and he soon returned to Strasburg.

During the French Revolution, Pleyel was suspected of royal tendencies and was repeatedly condemned to death. Stoutly maintaining his loyalty to the republic, he was, as a test, compelled to compose music to a revolutionary drama. Constantly watched by two gendarmes, Pleyel finished the work in seven days. It was received with so much approval by the populace that his loyalty to the republic was never again questioned. The harassing expe-

Camille Pleyel

rience was, however, too much for sensitive Pleyel and he soon after removed to Paris. In 1805 he went into the music publishing business and also started a piano factory in 1807. In 1824 he transferred his business to his oldest son Camille and retired to a country seat near Paris, where he died on November 14, 1831.

Camille Pleyel, born at Strasburg in 1792, studied music with his father, and later on studied piano with Dussek. He demonstrated that he also had considerable talent as a composer, and one of his biographers says that, if he had not been a music seller and piano maker, he would probably have become a great composer. He associated himself with Kalkbrenner, the renowned musician and piano virtuoso. Together they spent several years at London, studying piano making with Broadwood, Collard and Clementi. They adopted for their pianos the upright action of Wornum, and the Broadwood for their grand pianos, and organized their factory according to the modern methods originated in London, all of which were great factors in the remarkable success of the firm.

Both principals being accomplished pianists of high order, it was but natural that they were in close touch with the brilliant men of the profession. Camille Pleyel formed a very intimate friendship with Frederic Chopin, who became an enthusiastic advocate of the Pleyel piano, which he played in all his concerts, with a few exceptions. Salle Pleyel, erected about 1829, was the place where Kalkbrenner, Hummel, Hiller, Moscheles, Mme. Pleyel and many others scored their triumphs, and where Frederic Chopin made his bow to Paris in 1832. Anton Rubinstein, at the age of 10, played there in 1841, followed by Saint-Saëns, who made his début at the age of 10, in 1846.

Auguste Wolff

Camille Pleyel died at Paris, May 4, 1855, succeeded by his partner, Auguste Wolff, the firm having been changed to Pleyel, Wolff & Company. Under Wolff's intelligent management the business expanded so that the production rose in 1889 to 2,500 pianos per year. Wolff died in February, 1887, since which time the concern has been guided by Gustave Lyon. The firm has been incorporated under the name of Pleyel, Lyon & Company. As far as I know, this company is the only establishment in the piano industry that has installed a practical pension system for aged employees.

Like Clementi, Cramer, Kalkbrenner and Pleyel, the great piano virtuoso, Henri Herz, entered upon piano making after his reputation as a musician was established. Born on January 6, 1806, at Vienna, he played in concert at Coblenz when only eight

Henri Herz

years of age. When 10 years old he was admitted as pupil at the Paris Conservatory, where he obtained the first prize in 1818. He then made extended concert tours through France, Germany and England, meeting with great success. His compositions were also very popular, and when he met the piano maker, Klepfar, about the year 1825, he established a piano factory at Paris. The enterprise was not a success in the beginning, and, in order to replenish his exchequer, Herz undertook a great concert journey through the United States, California, Mexico and the West Indies during 1849 and 1850. Upon his return to Paris he devoted himself largely to the improvement of his pianos, and established his fame among piano makers by the practical simplifying of the Erard grand action. His model has been almost universally adopted and is known as the Erard-Herz action. When he erected his new factory he provided a large concert hall, which, under the name of "Salle Herz," became famous because of the concerts given there by many of the masters of the piano world.

Herz's grand pianos were distinguished by their rich and refined tone, evenness of register and excellence of touch. Wherever exhibited these instruments were awarded high prizes, and always ranked among the best. Herz was appointed professor of

music at the Paris Conservatory in 1842, and held that
position until 1874. Decorated by the King of Bel-
gium, he was also appointed
purveyor to the Empress of
France. He died in Paris on
January 5, 1888.

One of the most interest-
ing leaders of the French
piano industry of that period
was Johann Heinrich Pape,
born at Sarstedt, Germany,
on July 1, 1789. He arrived
at Paris in 1809; but shortly
after went to London, studying there for over a year,
returning to Paris in 1811.

Charles Kriegelstein

He took charge of the Pleyel factory and began to build pianos
after English models. In 1815 he started in business on his own
account, and commenced a carnival of experiments, the record
of which is almost amazing. It seems as if Pape's mind just
bubbled over with ideas, some so bizarre and queer as to border
on the ridiculous. He took out over 120 patents for piano improvements and published a booklet describing his inventions.

Had Pape, only to a small degree, possessed the orderly mind
of a John Broadwood, or a Sebastian Erard, he would, beyond
doubt, have become a great benefactor to the industry. As it was
his experiments and vagaries are only interesting, but without
value, excepting his experimenting with hat-felt for hammer-
covering, which led the way to a permanent improvement.

Jean Schwander

It is safe to say that Pape's restless mind did not permit him to turn out a number of perfect pianos in succession. He made many very good pianos in his big factory, but, before one of his often brilliant ideas was thoroughly worked out to practical usefulness, he would come out with another idea of improvement, which necessitated yet another change in the piano then under construction. His reputation as an inventor spread all over Europe, and while in his prime, from 1835 to 1855, Pape had in his factory young men from all parts of the Continent studying under him. Many of them became well known later on, among his most talented pupils being Frederick Mathushek and Carl Bechstein.

Toward the end of his career Pape was beset with a mania for building pianos in all kinds of impossible forms—cycloid, hexagon, etc.—to which the buying public did not take, and, although he at one time owned one of the largest piano factories of Paris, employing over 300 men, he died a poor man on February 2, 1875.

Jean Georges Kriegelstein, born at Riquewihr in 1801, founded the firm of Kriegelstein & Company at Paris in 1831. He invented many improvements and was especially successful with a small upright piano, which he constructed in 1842. Although only

42½ inches in height, it had
a rich tone and was espe-
cially even in its registers.
He retired from business in
1858, and died at Paris on
November 20, 1865. His son,
Charles Kriegelstein, born
at Paris, December 16, 1839,
followed in the footsteps of
his father, with marked success, obtaining high honors
for his pianos, wherever exhibited. The business is now
under the management of
Georges Kriegelstein, son of
Charles, who maintains the
high reputation which his
predecessors acquired.

Josef Herrburger

J. G. Gaveau started to make pianos at Paris about 1847, and
in course of time built up a large business, turning out about 2,000
high-class pianos per year.

Jean Denis Antoine Bord, born at Paris in 1814, was the
first in Paris to make a commercial upright piano of good quality.
He started his business in 1840, and brought his production
to over 4,000 pianos per year in 1878. He died on March 4,
1888.

Action making, as a specialty, had its cradle in Paris, and for
many years Paris supplied nearly all the piano makers on the
continent of Europe. Jean Schwander, born at Lauterbach,
Alsace, in 1812, came to Paris in 1830, and learned action making
at Kriegelstein's factory. He started his own shop in 1844, and
Kriegelstein became his first customer. Schwander turned out

Johann Friedrich Schröder

such excellent work that his business expanded very rapidly. After taking Josef Herrburger in partnership in 1865 and accepting him as son-in-law, the concern assumed commanding proportions.

Josef Herrburger, born at Dauendorf, Alsace, in 1832, went to Paris in 1853 and began to work for Schwander in 1854. He demonstrated not only great ability as an organizer, but also as a mechanician with inventive talent. He designed many valuable machines and appliances for action making and invented several valuable improvements for piano actions. The Schwander action factory became known as the best equipped establishment of its kind, its products were shipped to all parts of the civilized world and young piano makers from all over the Continent came to the Schwander factory to study modern methods of action making. Jean Schwander died in 1882 and Josef Herrburger retired from business in 1900, succeeded by his son, Josef Herrburger, Jr., who established a branch factory in New York, maintaining the exalted standing of the old firm in both hemispheres.

SPAIN

Barcelona is the center of piano manufacturing in Spain. We find that Pindo de Pedro Estela established his shop in 1830,

Hermanos Guarra and Louis Izabel in 1860, Chassaign Frères in 1864. At Madrid, Montana commenced business in 1864.

BELGIUM AND HOLLAND

Belgium can boast of older firms. François Berden & Company commenced business at Brussels in 1815. In the city of Ghent four firms started within a few years, about the middle of the 19th century. B. Van Hyfte was established in 1835, Emile Vits in 1839, Boone Fils in 1839 and V. Gevaert in 1846. J. Günther of Kirchheim started in Brussels in 1845, and J. Oor in 1850.

Carl Nicolai Schröder

The Netherlands has three firms of excellent standing—Allgäuer & Zoon of Amsterdam, established in 1830; J. F. Cuijpers of Hague, started in 1832, and Rijken & de Lange of Rotterdam, in 1852.

SCANDINAVIA

The respected firm of Hornung & Möller of Copenhagen, founded in 1827, has always been in the lead. G. Ekstrem & Company started at Malmö in 1836. I. G. Malmsjö of Göteborg established in 1843 and Brodrene Hals, who started at Christiania in 1847, are all known beyond their own country as makers of high-class pianos, and from their shops the piano manufacturers of America have drawn many of their best workmen.

Jacob Becker

The firm of Gebr. Diederichs was established in St. Petersburg in 1810. No record of this old firm is available; it is, however, safe to assume that they came to Russia from Germany.

Johann Friedrich Schröder, born at Stralsund in 1785, started to make pianos in St. Petersburg in 1818 and built up a respectable business. After his death in 1852, his son, Karl Michael Schröder, born in St. Petersburg in 1828, having studied with Erard and Herz at Paris, made good use of what he had learned and began to build excellent grand pianos, which found great favor with the artists, bringing his firm into the front rank of European piano makers. His pianos were awarded the highest honors wherever exhibited, and Schröder was honored with decorations by the Emperors of Russia and Austria, and the King of Belgium, and was elected a member of the Legion of Honor in recognition of his services. He died at Frankfort-on-Main, May 5, 1889.

His son, Carl Nicolai Schröder, continued the progressive policy of his father, following closely all modern movements in piano construction, as well as factory organization and equipment. The firm has been appointed purveyor to the Emperors of Russia, Austria, Germany, and the Kings of Denmark and Bavaria. After

Carl   Nicolai   Schröder's
death the management of the
establishment passed into the
hands of his sons, John and
Oskar Schröder.

Jacob Becker went from
Neustadt-an-der-Hardt, Germany, to St. Petersburg and
established his business in
1841.   Becker was an independent thinker and experimented with many innova-
tions. His pianos, especially
his concert grands, were excellent   instruments,   often
used by leading virtuosos.
Becker retired from business

A. Bietepage

in 1871, to be succeeded by Michael A. Bietepage, under whose
energetic management the business took on commanding proportions. The firm received appointments as purveyor to the Emperors of Russia and Austria, the King of Denmark and the Grand
Dukes Constantin and Nicolai of Russia. M. A. Bietepage was
honored by election as hereditary honorable citizen of St. Petersburg and commander of the St. Stanislaus Order. In 1904 Bietepage retired and the firm is now controlled by Carl Schröder.

JAPAN

Although Japan was represented at the Paris Exposition of
1878 with a square piano, the piano industry is developing only
slowly there. Torakusu Yamaba established his business of making musical instruments in 1880. In 1885 he produced the first

Torakusu Yamaba

organ made in Japan and organized The Nippon Gakki Siezo Kabushiki Kwaisha (Japanese Musical Instrument Manufacturing Company) in 1889 with a capital of 30,000 yen. In 1907 the capital was increased to 600,000 yen, of which nearly 500,000 yen is paid up. Yamaba is president of the company, which owns extensive factories at Hammamatsu. This company produces now about 600 pianos, 8,000 organs and 13,000 violins per year, mainly patterned after American and German models.

Nishikawa & Son of Yokohama, established in 1885, manufacture about 200 pianos and 1,300 organs per year. The senior member of this firm was a maker of Japanese lutes and other musical instruments, and is still making violins. His son learned piano making at the Estey factory in New York.

PART THREE

CHAPTER III

AMERICA, Crehore, Osborn, Babcock, MacKay, Stewart, The Chickerings, Bacon & Raven, James A. Gray, William Bourne, McPhail, The Lindemans, Schomacker, The Knabes, Steinways, Hazeltons, Fischers, Stieff, Weber, Steck, etc., Kimball, Cables, Wulsin, Starr, Healy, Wurlitzer, etc., Estey, The Whites, Packard, Votey, Clark, etc.

PART THREE

CHAPTER III

AMERICA

THE history of prominent piano men and firms of the United States portrays not only the restlessness of the American people, differing from the conservatism of the old world, but also demonstrates in a large degree that America is the land of unlimited opportunities and possibilities. Nowhere else have firms founded on meritorious production and sane business methods gone so quickly into oblivion, and nowhere else have such stunning successes been achieved as in the United States.

The progress in technical as well as commercial development has been rapid because America could draw from the old world its best minds, or benefit by their products, assimilate and improve them. It had the whole civilized world to draw from, and was never slow in producing original ideas. The seemingly endless natural resources of a whole continent were at the command of the industry, and its only drawback in the early days was the lack of a sufficiently large clientèle of cultured people who would buy the instruments, as compared with Europe. Hence we find that, although square pianos were made in America at about the same time as in England and Germany, it took about fifty years longer to develop the industry to anything like the magnitude which it had approached in Europe.

Benjamin Crehore, who had established a reputation as an expert maker of violins, cellos and other musical instruments, exhibited a harpsichord in 1791, and soon thereafter built pianos at Milton, near Boston. In his shop he had John Osborn, Alpheus and Lewis Babcock as pupils. In 1810 the Babcock brothers began to make pianos in Boston. The great panic of 1819 ruined their business, but we hear of Alpheus Babcock again in 1821, in partnership with John MacKay, that commercial genius who later assisted so strongly in building up the fame of the Chickering firm.

John Osborn, the most talented of Crehore's pupils, started in business in 1815. It was in Osborn's shop that Jonas Chickering learned the art of piano making. Born in New Ipswich, N. H., on April 5, 1798, Chickering came to Boston about 1817, after he had served his apprenticeship as a cabinetmaker and joiner. Well educated and possessing decided mechanical talents of a high order, Chickering was attracted to the art of piano making and was fortunate in finding a master like Osborn as teacher. He studied with Osborn until 1823, when James Stewart, who had come from Baltimore to go in partnership with Osborn, but soon quarreled with him, proposed partnership to Chickering, which the latter accepted, and the firm of Stewart & Chickering opened their shop on Tremont Street in that year.

Stewart was one of those restless, unsettled inventors, who needed the methodical and painstaking young Chickering to give to his inventions the practical form. It soon developed, however, that Chickering was not only the better workman of the two, but also the far more scientific piano maker. The firm was dissolved in 1826. Stewart went to London to take a prominent position with Collard & Collard. Jonas Chickering continued the business, making excellent pianos, but his talents were more in the line of inventing and constructing than merchandising. He also suffered from lack of capital, so that his progress was rather slow until John MacKay, who had left Babcock, joined him as a partner. This closed the chain of Chickering's connection with Crehore, the founder of the Boston school, consisting of Osborn and Lewis Babcock, pupils of Crehore; and Alpheus Babcock, partner of MacKay, the latter joining Chickering.

MacKay had had considerable experience as a merchant, having traveled much to England and other foreign countries, and was unquestionably a commercial genius. With sufficient capital at his command, and faith in Chickering's excellent pianos, MacKay started an aggressive selling campaign, making the Chickering piano known in all the cities of the United States. Chickering, freed from all financial and business cares, devoted his whole time and attention to the development and improvement of his piano, and many of his best inventions were perfected during the period of his partnership with MacKay, which came to an untimely end in 1841. MacKay, having gone in a ship of his own to South America to procure fancy woods for the Chickering factory, never returned from that voyage, nor was his ship ever heard from.

Once more Jonas Chickering had to assume entire charge of the business. He continued MacKay's aggressive policy with great energy, maintaining the highest possible prices for his pianos, and spending money liberally for the necessary publicity. He exhibited his pianos at every important exposition, going to the World's Fair of London in 1851 with a number of instruments; engaged prominent virtuosos to play his grand pianos in concert; and took active part in the musical life of his home city, acting as vice-president of the great Handel and Haydn Society as early as 1834, and later on as its president for seven years.

While paying proper attention to the commercial and artistic necessities of his great establishment, Jonas Chickering was ever true to his love for scientific research and experiments, to improve his pianos. He was not an empiric, who would experiment haphazard with an idea. Whenever he had discovered a possible improvement, he would work out the problem in its entirety on his drawing board, until he had proven to his own satisfaction its practicability, and not before would he turn it over to his mechanics for execution. It was this painstaking care down to the smallest detail which assured the Chickering piano the place of honor in the first ranks.

When at the height of his prosperity Jonas Chickering met with a great calamity. On December 1, 1852, his factory was totally destroyed by fire, involving a loss of $250,000. Undaunted, Chickering at once designed plans for a new and larger factory, which was soon erected, and stands to this day on Tremont Street, Boston, as a monument to the exceptional ability, talent and courage of Jonas Chickering. Even now, nearly 60 years after its erection, this factory is considered one of the best for its purpose.

Jonas Chickering died on December 8, 1853, in his fifty-sixth year. The extraordinary nervous strain of the short period from the destruction of his old factory to the completion of the new works had, no doubt, affected his constitution. He had educated all of his three sons as practical piano makers and admitted them

to partnership in 1852, when
the firm was changed to
Chickering & Sons. The
three brothers made a rare
and most fortunate combination.

Thomas E. Chickering,
the eldest son, soon ex-
hibited pronounced commercial talents and, as a man of
the world, represented the
firm with excellent results in
social circles, making friends
among artists, literary and
scientific men. His promising career was prematurely
cut short by his death on
February 14, 1871.

Thomas E. Chickering

This sad event made C. Frank Chickering, born at Boston on
January 20, 1827, the head of the firm. Having inherited his
father's talents as a designer and inventor, he had been in charge
of the construction department since his father's death in 1853.
While studying, as a young man, he had impaired his health and,
upon the advice of his physician, in 1844 he went on a voyage to
India in a sailing vessel. He took with him a number of
pianos, which he sold in India at good prices, and thus the firm
of Chickering became the first exporters of American made
pianos.

In 1851 Frank accompanied his father to London to take care
of their exhibit at the World's Fair. The prolonged stay in what
was then the home of the most advanced piano construction was
of great and lasting advantage to young Frank. It gave him the

C. Frank Chickering

opportunity to study and compare the work of the best brains of the industry as it then existed in Europe, and furthermore he became acquainted with the advanced manufacturing methods of the celebrated London establishments. Returning from abroad, Frank utilized his experiences with effect, greatly improving the Chickering pianos.

Appreciating the importance of New York as an art center, Chickering & Sons opened extensive warerooms there under the direct management of C. Frank Chickering, and in 1875 erected Chickering Hall, on Fifth Avenue. In this hall, virtuosos like Bülow, Joseffy, de Pachmann, Henry Ketten and many others gave their never-to-be-forgotten concerts on the Chickering grand pianos, designed and constructed by C. Frank Chickering.

Chickering Hall was chosen as a permanent home by leading glee clubs, such as the Mendelssohn, the English Glee Club, the New York Vocal Society and by those eminent apostles of classic chamber music, the New York Quartette, composed of C. Mollenhauer, M. Schwarz, George Matzka and F. Bergner, and the Philharmonic Club under the able leadership of Richard Arnold. Remenyi and Wilhelmi appeared as soloists with Gotthold Carlberg's Orchestra, and Frank Van der Stucken conducted symphony concerts for several seasons in Chickering Hall, to be followed by

Anton Seidl and the Boston Symphony Orchestra with Franz Rummel, Xaver Scharwenka and Richard Hoffmann as soloists. The great building contained, besides the concert hall with a seating capacity of 2,000, the showrooms for the Chickering pianos, offices, repair shops and also the drafting rooms, where C. Frank Chickering designed and worked out his inventions.

It was but natural that in New York, as in Boston, Frank should be in close

George H. Chickering

touch with artistic and literary circles. Among his personal friends was one J. H. Paine, a composer and critic of considerable ability. He was generally known as " Miser " Paine, and would gladly accept Chickering's hospitality and aid at all times. He was considered a poor man by all who knew him. One day he brought to Frank Chickering a bundle wrapped up in a bandanna handkerchief, asking Chickering to kindly place the package in his safe. Chickering assumed that the bundle contained manuscripts of Paine's compositions and accepted the charge. About 17 years thereafter Paine died, without leaving a will or any disposition of the aforesaid bundle. Chickering sent for Paine's legal representative, the bundle was opened in his presence and found to contain over $400,000 worth of bonds and currency. Chickering delivered the valuable package to the lawyer, who was obliged to hunt up distant relatives of Paine to distribute the heritage.

C. Frank Chickering was in all respects one of nature's noblemen. In appearance he reminded one forcibly of the Grand Seigneurs of Louis XIV's time. He died in New York, March 25, 1891.

George H. Chickering, the youngest of the brothers, was born at Boston on April 18, 1830. After acquiring an excellent education, he turned to the bench and worked under his father's tutelage. For many years George made every set of hammers used in their concert grands. He was an exceedingly neat and artistic mechanic. After 1853 he took charge of the factory management and performed his arduous duties most faithfully until his death, on November 17, 1896. All three of the brothers, like their father, took an active part in the artistic life of their home city and each of them served in turn with honor as president of the Handel and Haydn Society.

The Chickering pianos were always awarded the highest honors wherever exhibited, and, at the World's Fair at Paris, 1867, C. Frank Chickering was decorated by the Emperor of the French with the Cross of the Legion of Honor.

The business of this renowned firm is successfully carried on by a corporation which has joined the American Piano Company, maintaining the high character of its products. True to the traditions of the honored name, Chickering & Sons have of late years been instrumental in reviving interest in the beauties of the old clavichord, and are building such instruments for those who enjoy the study of the compositions of Johann Sebastian Bach, Scarlatti and others who wrote for the clavichord. The factory on Tremont Street, Boston, has become a landmark of that historic city, but Chickering Hall, New York, had to give way to a modern building for business purposes.

Next to Chickering & Sons, the Bacon Piano Company of New York is most closely connected to the founders of the industry in America. Robert Stodart of London started in New York in 1820. In 1821 Dubois joined him and the firm was Dubois & Stodart until 1836, when Stodart retired and George Bacon and Chambers joined. Five years later Dubois and Chambers withdrew and Raven joined, the firm being changed to Bacon & Raven, which was again

James A. Gray

changed to Raven & Bacon, when George Bacon died in 1856 and his son, Francis Bacon, entered as partner. In 1904 the firm was incorporated under the title of the Bacon Piano Company, with Chas. M. Tremaine as president and W. H. P. Bacon, son of Francis, as vice-president.

James A. Gray, born at New York in 1815, learned his trade with Firth & Pond of New York from 1831 to 1835, when he was called to Binghamton, N. Y., to superintend Pratt's piano factory. In 1836 William Boardman of Albany induced him to take charge of his establishment, and two years later the firm became Boardman & Gray. Possessing decided talents as an inventor, Gray made many very interesting experiments, among which his isolated iron rim and frame and the corrugated soundboard are the most noteworthy. For a time he had great faith in the value of those

A. M. McPhail

inventions. He even took a number of pianos containing the same to London for exhibition in 1850, but after a comparatively short time he discarded all of them, preferring to build a fine piano along conventional lines. He educated his sons, James S. and William James, as thorough piano makers, and the time-honored firm maintains its reputation for high-class production to this date. William Boardman, who retired at an early date from the firm, died January 5, 1881, at the age of 81 years. James A. Gray took a more or less active part in the business until his death on December 11, 1889. His sons, William James Gray, born June 13, 1853, and James Stuart Gray, born September 7, 1857, are continuing the business with success.

One of the pioneers who attempted to force civilization in its higher development upon the " Far West " was William Bourne. He started a piano factory at Dayton, Ohio, in 1837, at a time when the savage Indian was still a " near neighbor." Evidently Bourne did not find the expected encouragement at Dayton, and removed in 1840 to Cincinnati. Even here his art was not appreciated, and he therefore accepted in 1842 a position in the Chickering factory, where he remained until 1846, when he organized the firm of William Bourne & Company. A piano maker of the old school, Bourne could turn out nothing but thoroughly first-class pianos. Since his death, in 1885, the business has been continued by his son, Charles H. Bourne.

William Lindeman

A. M. McPhail started his business in Boston in 1837. Born at St. Andrews, New Brunswick, he came to Boston as a boy, and was apprenticed to the renowned piano maker, Gilbert. He learned to make pianos so well that he soon established a high reputation for his own product. He was a piano maker of the old school, who took pride in his work and considered the artistic success more than the commercial, although in his long career, from 1837 to 1891, he met all of his obligations with never failing promptness. As a citizen he took a great interest in educational, artistic and musical affairs, and also served as representative in the Massachusetts Legislature. He retired in 1891, and died at Omaha, October 6, 1902. The business is carried on by the A. M. McPhail Company, a corporation.

Among the many illustrious Germans who have done so much for the uplifting of the piano industry in New York, William Lindeman deserves particular credit for being the first who had the courage to combat successfully the unworthy prejudice and attitude of the people of his day toward the German element.

Henry Lindeman

Born at Dresden, Germany, in 1795, where he also learned his art of piano making, Lindeman came to New York in 1834 and established his business in 1836. Although his pianos were of the highest order, success came slowly, but when his son Henry brought out his " Cycloid " piano, a rather happy compromise between a grand and square piano, in 1860, the firm secured a strong hold upon the piano-buying public. The Civil War interfered seriously with a more rapid development, and it was left to Henry to push the firm into the front rank.

Henry Lindeman, born in New York on August 3, 1838, was admitted to partnership in 1857, and after the death of William Lindeman on December 24, 1875, assumed the management and continued the work of his father. Henry's son, Samuel G., was admitted in 1901, and the firm name of Henry and S. G. Lindeman was adopted.

In 1838, shortly after Lindeman's appearance in the arena, Johann Heinrich Schumacher, who changed his name to John Henry Schomacker for expedience' sake, established himself in partnership with William Bossert in Philadelphia. Schomacker, born in Schleswig-Holstein on January 1, 1800, learned piano making in the master schools of Vienna. About 1830 he established himself at Lahr, Bavaria, and came to America in 1837. For one year he worked with E. N. Scherr, one of Philadelphia's best-known makers of those days. Schomacker was not only an excellent and thorough piano maker, but also a very forceful man with almost boundless ambition. His partner was conservative and perfectly satisfied with a moderate income. Schomacker finally decided to go his own way, and the partnership was dissolved in 1842. With restless energy Schomacker

John Henry Schomacker

first improved his pianos, and in 1845 he was awarded the silver medal of the Franklin Institute of Philadelphia for the " best " piano exhibited. At the American Institute Exhibition in New York in 1848, he received the first prize, a silver medal, in competition with a number of American pianos, and at the great World's Fair at the Crystal Palace in New York, in 1853, he carried off the gold medal. To meet the demands of his ever-growing business, he erected in 1855 the great factory which stands to-day at Catherine and Eleventh streets, Philadelphia. In 1856 he organized his business into a close corporation under the title of Schomacker Piano Company. With his ambition satisfied, he quit the field of activity in 1872, and died on January 16, 1875.

His son, Henry C. Scho-
macker, born in Philadelphia
in May, 1840, served his apprenticeship under his father
and spent several years in
Germany, studying under
the leading masters. The
company, under the able
management of I. B. Wood-
ford as president, and Henry
C. Schomacker as secretary,
is maintaining the glory of
the old firm, producing most
excellent pianos of the highest order.

While Lindeman in New
York and Schomacker in
Philadelphia earned laurels
for the German school of
piano making, William Knabe was busy preparing himself for his
great career in Baltimore. Born at Kreutzberg, Germany, in 1803,
he received a superior education, intending to follow a learned profession. When the time for ultimate decision came, William preferred, however, to learn the art of piano making. He served the
customary apprenticeship and acquired further experience while
working for various masters in Germany. Coming to Baltimore in
1833, he found an engagement with Henry Hartje, who had won
quite a reputation as an inventor. Conservative and careful, Knabe
waited until he had mastered the English language and had become thoroughly familiar with the business conditions of the new
country. It was, therefore, not until 1839, that he ventured in

business, associating himself with another German
piano maker, Henry Gaehle,
under the firm name of
Knabe & Gaehle. The en-
terprise was moderately
successful and the association continued until 1854,
when Gaehle withdrew.
From that time on Knabe
was able to demonstrate his
exceptional ability as a
piano maker and business
man without hindrance. His
pianos were second to none
in the market, and he handled the commercial end of
his business so cleverly

Ernest Knabe

that by 1860 his firm almost controlled the entire market
of the southern States. The Civil War temporarily destroyed
that market, and the firm of William Knabe & Company went
through a trying period for over five years. Wearied from over-
anxiety, care and worry, Knabe passed away in 1864, leaving the
care of the great business, which he had founded and built up to
magnificent proportions, to his sons, William and Ernest. Both
had enjoyed a most liberal education and had been thoroughly
trained by their father in the art of piano making. William, being
by nature of a quiet, retiring disposition, took upon himself the
management of the factories, while Ernest assumed without any
wavering the grave responsibilities as head of the house. When
Ernest Knabe took the reins the outlook was very gloomy. Not
only was their main market, the rich southern States, entirely

destroyed by the Civil War then raging, but their customers for the same reason could not meet their obligations. The work in the big factory, with its hundreds of employees, dragged along in an uncertain way and the day seemed to be near when the factories would have to be temporarily closed.

Ernest found a solution. He concluded to make a prolonged trip through the northern and western States which were not so seriously affected by the war, determined to establish agencies for the sale of his pianos in this new territory. Money had to be provided to meet the weekly payroll during his absence. He boldly went to his bank and asked for a credit of $20,000 for the term of six months. Considering the critical times, such a demand upon a bank in the city of Baltimore was almost preposterous, and when finally the banker asked Ernest what security he had to offer and the reply came, "Nothing but the name of Knabe," the banker shook his head and told the young man that he would submit the proposition to his board of directors. They decided that under existing conditions the loan could not be made. When delivering this ultimatum to young Ernest, the banker questioned him as to what he could or would do. Knabe answered promptly, " I shall go down to my factory and tell my employees that I am compelled to discharge them all because your bank refused a loan to which I am entitled," then took his hat and left the banker to his own contemplations. Before he reached his factory office a messenger from the bank had arrived there with a letter from the president, stating that the account of Knabe & Company had been credited with $20,000, to be drawn against as wanted.

Ernest did not go back to the bank, but packed his trunk and went on his journey. Within two months he had sold enough pianos and opened up sufficient connections to keep his factories busy to their limit, and when he returned home he called on his banker to thank him for the loan, of which his firm had not been obliged to use a single dollar. Ernest Knabe knew that just at that time the banks of Baltimore could not afford to have the doors of the city's greatest industrial establishment closed and hundreds of men thrown out of employment, for lack of funds, and he won out against the timid and shortsighted banker.

An era of great activity now commenced for the firm of Knabe & Company. A branch house was opened in New York, and later one in Washington. Ernest Knabe designed new scales for concert grands and upright pianos. Additional factories were built and equipped with the best of modern machinery, in order to produce pianos in keeping with the reputation of the firm as leaders in the industry. Wherever the Knabe pianos have been exhibited they were invariably awarded high prizes for superior construction and workmanship, notably so at the great Centennial Exposition in Philadelphia in 1876, where their large concert-grand piano was greatly admired. Leading virtuosos like D'Albert, Saint-Saëns and many others used the Knabe grand pianos in their concerts and were enthusiastic in their praise of the Knabe tone quality.

A princely entertainer, Ernest Knabe was an enthusiastic lover of music. He would often take the noon train from Baltimore to New York, consult with his New York manager while eating dinner, go to the opera to hear Sembrich, Lehmann or Niemann sing, or attend a Rosenthal or Joseffy concert, return by midnight train to Baltimore and appear the following morning bright and early at the factory or city warerooms to take up the every-day routine of work. He was an indefatigable worker and seemed never to tire. Of a most genial disposition, warm-hearted, helpful, he was adored by his workmen and beloved by all who knew him.

In the midst of the greatest developments misfortune came upon the house. William Knabe died suddenly in January, 1889, at the early age of 48. This sad event doubled the burdens of

Ernest and he succumbed to the inevitable result of over-exertion on April 16, 1894. Ernest Knabe had ever been one of the strong pillars of the piano industry, on intimate terms with his competitors, enjoying the close friendship of William Steinway, Albert Weber and other leaders. He left a gap which could not easily be filled. The great business was turned into a corporation which finally joined the American Piano Company, under whose care the traditions of the house are reverently safeguarded.

Among the historic Boston firms, the Hallet & Davis Piano Company can trace its origin to the year 1835, when Brown & Hallet started in business. Brown was a graduate of the Chickering factory and obtained several patents for improvements. He retired from the firm in 1843, and his place was taken by George H. Davis, the firm changing to Hallet, Davis & Company, under which title it continued with more or less success. After the death of George H. Davis on December 1, 1879, the business was incorporated. Under the management of E. N. Kimball as president, C. C. Conway, treasurer, and E. E. Conway as secretary, the concern has recovered its old-time prestige and is counted among the most progressive of the present day.

During the decade from 1830 to 1840 a coterie of piano makers lived at Albany, whose influence upon the piano industry of America has been of a lasting character. John Osborn came from Boston in 1829 and made pianos for Meacham & Company, dealers in musical instruments. F. P. Burns studied under Osborn in Meacham's shop, which probably was the first piano factory west of New York City. Henry Hazelton came from New York to work for Boardman & Gray. James H. Grovesteen, founder of Grovesteen, Fuller & Company of New York, came to Albany in 1839 and started to make pianos in 1840. A. C. James, later of James & Holmstrom, New York, learned piano making in Grovesteen's shop and, after working for Boardman & Gray, became a member of the firm of Marshall, James & Traver, later known as Marshall & Wendell. Myron A. Decker was also one of the Albany pioneers with George Gomph, P. Reed and others. F. Frickinger made pianos in 1837, but soon after started action making as a specialty. His business is continued by Grubb & Kosegarten Brothers at Nassau, N. Y.

Francis Putnam Burns, born at Galway, New York, on February 6, 1807, learned cabinetmaking and studied piano making under the

Francis Putnam Burns

genial John Osborn. In 1835 he commenced business on his own account. Of an artistic temperament and an excellent mechanic, he would never permit piecework in his shop, impressing his workmen with the idea that a piano is a work of art, requiring the most painstaking efforts, without regard to time consumed in its construction. While producing most elegant and durable pianos, Burns did not accumulate wealth, and when the Civil War prostrated business he could not stand the strain. His son Edward M. Burns, who was serving as a commissioned officer in the army, coming home disabled for further activity in the field, had to assume the management of the business. Although the United States Government retained him in military service for 18 months after peace was declared and desired his further service

Henry Hazelton

in the army, young Burns felt that filial duty demanded his devotion to his father's business. He picked up the remnants of the once flourishing business, injected new life and not only succeeded in maintaining the high reputation of the pianos, but had the great satisfaction of squaring all the old obligations in a most honorable manner. It was a loss to the piano industry of Albany when Edward M. Burns retired in 1869 to seek more remunerative activity in another field.

A man who for over 60 years can enjoy the respect and friendship of his competitors in business must be a strong character, with a lovable disposition. Such was Henry Hazelton, born in New York City in 1816. He served a seven years' apprenticeship with Dubois & Stodart, being released in 1831. Soon thereafter he joined the Albany colony, and in 1840 started the firm of Hazelton, Talbot & Lyon. Not fulfilling his expectations at Albany, Hazelton returned to New York and joined his brother Frederick, under the firm name of F. & H. Hazelton, in 1850. Later on a younger brother, John, was admitted to partnership and the firm name changed to Hazelton Brothers. All three brothers were artisans of high order, who eschewed commercial tactics, depending for ultimate success entirely upon the high quality of their product, and to this date the firm has a strong hold upon New York's Knickerbocker aristocracy as a clientèle, in whose circles grandmother's piano bears the name of Hazelton. After the death of the founders, the business came under sole control of Samuel Hazelton, who had enjoyed a thorough training with his uncles and was made a member of the firm in 1881. He is ably assisted by his son Halsey in maintaining the traditions of the respected firm.

Charles S. Fischer

Toward the close of the 18th century a Vienna piano maker in his wandering arrived at Naples, Italy. Somehow attracted by the place, he made it his home and began to make pianos, which found favor with the court, and young Fischer was appointed " Piano maker to King Ferdinand I, of Naples." He taught his art to his son, who afterward studied for a number of years with Vienna masters, and upon his return to Naples continued the father's business. His two sons, John U. and Charles S. Fischer, followed in the footsteps of father and grandfather, becoming expert piano makers. The inborn " wanderlust " of the Fischers landed these two young men in New York City in 1839. Taking at once employment with William Nunns, they became his partners soon thereafter under the firm name of Nunns & Fischer. Nunns

Frederick P. Stieff

retired in 1840, and the firm was changed to J. & C. Fischer. Building a reliable piano, they soon accumulated great wealth, and in 1873 John U. Fischer retired with a competency, to spend the rest of his days in his homeland, Italy. Charles S. then admitted his four sons, who had been thoroughly trained in all branches of the business, to partnership. The vigorous activity of the young men, under the wise guidance of their father, brought them rapidly to the front as great producers, increasing their yearly output to 5,000 pianos, at the same time studiously improving the quality. In 1907 the firm was changed to a corporation.

Hugh Hardman, who was born at Liverpool, England, in 1815, came to the United States and began to make pianos in New York City in 1840. His son John was admitted to partnership about 1874. This firm was among the first to manufacture good commercial upright pianos, and met with distinctive success. In 1880 Leopold Peck bought an interest in the firm, the name being changed to Hardman, Peck & Company. Under Peck's able management the firm has risen to a recognized position among the makers of high-grade pianos, their instruments ranking among the best in the market.

To change from teaching music and languages to dealing in pianos, and finally to become the founder of one of the largest and most respected piano manufacturing firms, was the career of Charles M. Stieff. Born in Wurtemburg on July 19, 1805, Stieff was educated at Stuttgart. In 1831 he emigrated to America and settled at Baltimore, where he took the chair in Haspert's school as professor of languages and also acted as leader of a church choir. In 1842 he imported his first

Jacob Gross

pianos from Germany, and opened regular piano warerooms on Liberty Street in 1843. Observing the success of the various piano manufacturers in Baltimore, Stieff undertook an extensive trip to Europe in 1852, studying the methods of the best piano manufacturers there. Upon his return he admitted his sons into partnership and started the manufacture of the " Stieff " piano, intrusting the management of the factory to Jacob Gross, an expert piano maker of the old school.

Born in Wurtemburg on July 26, 1819, Gross learned his trade in Stuttgart and afterward worked in some of the leading factories of Germany, Switzerland, Spain and Paris. Coming to America in 1848, he familiarized himself with the methods prevailing here and joined his brother-in-law, Stieff, in 1856. It was an excellent combination, the professional musician and business-

Christian Kurtzmann

man, Stieff, supported by the artistic piano maker and factory expert, Gross. The product of the firm was at once accepted as of superior merit and received distinguished awards wherever exhibited. The founder of the firm having passed to the unknown beyond, the business is carried on most successfully by his sons, Charles and Frederick P. Stieff, the technical management of the factories being in the hands of Charles J. Gross, who was educated by his father, the late Jacob Gross. It was remarkable that the great fire which destroyed nearly the entire business portion of the city of Baltimore in 1904 should stop short in its northward flight on the wall of the Stieff building, on North Liberty Street, just as if it had had respect for this landmark where the Stieffs had sold pianos for 63 years. The firm of Charles M. Stieff distributes its products almost entirely through its own stores, which are to be found in every prominent city of the southern States, as well as at Boston and elsewhere.

Following the chronological order, we find that Christian Kurtzmann established a piano factory in Buffalo in 1848. After his death in 1886, the business was taken over by a corporation.

William P. Emerson, who started in Boston in 1849, had perhaps more business acumen than mechanical talent and artistic inclinations. He started to make a low-priced instrument and built up a very large and profitable business within a few years. In 1854 he engaged C. C. Briggs, an expert piano maker of standing, to improve the piano, which was accomplished with such success that a reputation for superior quality was soon established and the name of Emerson became a valuable trademark. Emerson died in 1871, and the business came into possession of William Moore, who sold his interest

in 1879 to P. H. Powers, O. A. Kimball and J. Gramer. They organized the Emerson Piano Company, with Patrick H. Powers as president. Under his able management the business grew to commanding proportions. The product was continually improved to maintain its position as a high-class instrument, and the company enjoyed an enviable reputation for integrity and reliability.

P. H. Powers retired from active management in 1910, at the age of 84, after a most distinguished career as a business man, covering a period of 60 years. He is succeeded in the presidency by Edward S. Payson, who assisted Powers for many years as acting secretary of the company.

In the old town of Milton, where Crehore built his first piano, James Whiting Vose was born, on October 21, 1818. Learning the

Sincerely yours,

Patrick H. Power

cabinetmaker's trade, he soon became a piano maker, getting his experience in various Boston factories. In 1851 he made his first piano, and laid the foundation for a business which is counted among the leaders of the American piano industry. Educating his three sons in all branches of the business, he admitted them to partnership and changed the name to Vose & Sons. In 1889 the concern was incorporated, the stock being owned by the Vose family. James W. Vose served as first president of the Vose & Sons' Piano Company for a number of years. After his retirement his eldest son, Willard A. Vose, succeeded him as president and manager, with marked ability, maintaining and improving the distinguished standing of the Vose piano.

One of the most interesting characters in the history of American piano makers is Napoleon J. Haines. Born in London in 1824, he came to New York when eight years of age. He made the trip across the Atlantic alone with his younger brother Francis. His father, who had preceded the boys to New York, had paid the ship's steward thirty dollars to assure good meals for the youngsters. Napoleon, aware of that fact, objected to the poor coffee and " hard tack " with which the steward regaled the boys, throwing the stuff overboard and demanding " something fit to eat."

He caused such a disturbance that the captain was called, who promptly sided with the rebellious boy and admonished the steward to do his duty henceforth. It is said that young Haines after his arrival in New York, not from necessity, but from his desire to make headway, earned money as a bootblack after school hours. Whether that is true or not, young Napoleon certainly always demonstrated a restless disposition and a desire to advance. At the age of

James Whiting Vose

fifteen he apprenticed himself and brother to the New York Piano Manufacturing Company, learning all branches of the art. In 1851 he started in business with his brother under the firm name of Haines Brothers. Beginning with an output of two pianos per month, their business soon assumed large proportions, so that the erection of a factory, with a capacity of 20 pianos per week, became necessary in 1856.

Napoleon J. Haines was a thorough piano maker, whose name is also on record as an inventor in the United States Patent Office, but, besides that, he was a born financier and shrewd business man. One of the founders of the Union Dime Savings Bank of New York, he served as vice-president and president of that great institution for 21 years. Napoleon J. Haines died April 19, 1900. The business has been merged with that of the American Piano

Napoleon J. Haines

Company, under whose aus-
pices the Haines Brothers
piano is produced in larger
quantities than ever.

Real genius always leaves
an indelible mark in its
sphere of activity, and its
influence is as lasting as it
is permeating at the time
of its birth. To observe a
man rising from the lowest
rung of the ladder to the
height of a most promi-
nent manufacturer, educating himself meanwhile to
become a musician of ac-
knowledged talent and ver-
satility, handling complex financial problems with masterly
daring and withal acquiring a position of social influence, requires a combination of talents, an exercise of will-
power and self-denial seldom found. Albert Weber, born in
Bavaria July 8, 1828, landed in New York when 16 years of age.
Endowed with a liberal education, he had a good knowledge of
music, playing the organ efficiently. Attracted to the art of piano
making, he went through a regular apprenticeship with Master
Holden of New York, and later worked in the celebrated shop of
Van Winkle. To pay his board, young Weber gave music lessons
evenings, and played the organ at church on Sundays. When 23
years of age he started in business with a very small capital. Fire
destroyed his shop during the third year of his existence as a
piano manufacturer. Nothing daunted, he rented much larger

quarters and within a short time acquired a leading position among the piano firms of New York City. His energy and ambition knew no bounds. In 1869 he opened extensive warerooms at Fifth Avenue and Sixteenth Street, a move which astonished his competitors by its very boldness. Weber had invaded the abode of New York swelldom, with characteristic foresight, judging the future importance of this thoroughfare as a cen-

Albert Weber

ter of fashionable establishments. With this move his aggressive campaign for supremacy in the piano world commenced.

Although not given to inventing or creating anything new in piano construction, Weber was such a thorough piano maker, and perfect performer on the piano, that he knew how to utilize the best-proven methods of construction. He would engage at any cost the best workmen, the best talent to be found among piano makers, neither would he spare any expense or reckon the cost of any real improvement in the tone or general quality of his pianos. He inspired his men to take pride in their work. The result was that he produced pianos which were acknowledged second to none, and preferred by many leading virtuosos, especially by opera singers, for their sympathetic musical tone.

Because of his acute and musically trained hearing he succeeded in producing in his pianos, through his expert workmen, what he proudly called the " Weber tone." To listen to his playing for a prospective customer was a treat indeed, and seldom would an intending buyer leave his warerooms without having secured a piano. The man's enthusiasm, the real love for his piano was so intense, so genuine that he impressed the same on every person who would listen to his playing. Well read, a keen observer of men and things, Weber was a most interesting entertainer. His ready wit became proverbial and oftentimes served to clear unpleasant situations. For example, when during the strike of the journey-men for higher wages, shorter hours, etc., a committee of the work-men met with the assembled manufacturers, submitting their most unreasonable demands, the latter were dumbfounded by the bold-ness of the men. Weber broke the silence, complimented the men, arguing that it was their privilege to ask for all that they might want, but in his opinion they had not asked enough—they had for-gotten to ask for free Saturday afternoons with full pay, so that they could play tenpins, the bosses to pay for the beer and set up the pins for the men. With this remark he took his hat and left the conference. The strike was called off. With his timely sar-casm Weber had shown the men the ridiculousness of their de-mands and had turned the embarrassing conference into a merry laughter.

Many pertinent anecdotes could be cited to illustrate the quick-working mind of this remarkable man. He had one serious short-coming, however, which finally caused his untimely end. Cease-lessly planning to extend his business and enlarge his personal influence, Weber did not surround himself with sufficient competent assistants who could relieve him from dreary detail work, and con-sequently the management of his great factory, of the wholesale and retail departments, all of the financial affairs—in short, every detail of his great business—rested upon his shoulders. Working from morning until evening at his business, he would attend opera, theaters and clubs at night.   Being of a decidedly Bohemian temperament, he enjoyed the gay life of New York among brilliant men and women, but the everlasting strain was too much, even for this nervy man, and he succumbed, at the age of 50, on June 25, 1879, to the overtaxing of his brain and body.

The great business which he has founded, the great name which he made for his piano, are becomingly perpetuated by the Weber Piano Company, a corporation affiliated with the Aeolian Company of New York.   The fame of the Weber piano has extended to all the art centers of the globe to such an extent that the erection of a mammoth factory in London has become a necessity, in order to supply the ever-growing foreign trade.   The name of Albert Weber will live, as long as pianos are built in America, as one of the great leaders who believed in the artistic mission of the instrument and impressed this belief upon the mind of the public.

History teaches that hardships, adverse conditions and trying circumstances are the making of great men.   Henry Engelhardt Steinweg's career is a confirmation of this doctrine.   Born at Wolfshagen, Germany, as the twelfth child of a strong mother and a respectable father on February 5, 1797, he had to pass during his youth through all the miseries and privations brought upon a people by protracted warfare.   Napoleon's hordes devastated Germany, burned up the Steinweg home and killed several of his brothers in battle.   To fill his cup of misery he finally lost his father and remaining brothers in an accident, from which he alone escaped as by a miracle, and found himself an orphan at the age of 15, without home or shelter.

At 18 years of age he was drafted for the army and took part in the battle of Waterloo.   Returning from the field of battle, he found the soldier's life in the barracks very dreary, to coun-

H. Steinway Sr.

teract which he managed to build a zither, upon which he would play the patriotic songs of the time accompanied by the voices of his soldier comrades. Having never handled tools nor received even elementary instruction in music, his accomplishment in making and playing the zither clearly pointed to the road which he was to travel to achieve fame and wealth.

Having served his time in the army, he sought employment with a cabinetmaker, but being then 21 years of age, and engaged to a lovely girl, he did not cherish the idea of serving a five-year apprenticeship as the guild of cabinetmakers demanded. He wanted to learn the use of tools to build musical instruments, and we find him, therefore, soon in the shop of an organ builder at Seesen, where he also filled the place of organist in the village church. In 1825 he married the woman of his heart, and his wedding present was the first piano built by Steinweg's own hands. It was a fine instrument, which soon found a purchaser. Constructing pianos, earning his daily bread by repairing organs and all kinds of musical instruments, Steinweg prospered, and in 1839 exhibited at the fair of Brunswick one grand and two square pianos of his own make. The great composer, Albert Methfessel, played on these instruments and, as chairman of the jury, recommended that the highest prize, a gold medal, should be awarded to Steinweg for his superior instruments. It is said that the Duke of Brunswick bought the grand piano, paying therefor the large price of 3,000 marks.

Steinweg's reputation as a master piano builder was now established and he had to employ workmen to fill the orders which he received. His sons, Theodore, Charles and Henry, joined him in business as they grew to maturity and the prospects for the future looked very bright, when suddenly adversity came again through the political upheaval and revolution of 1848 and 1849, which paralyzed business all over Germany. The second son, Charles, had been during this excitement rather active in the ranks of the progressives, or revolutionists, and found himself compelled to flee as soon as the people's cause was lost. He escaped to Switzerland and went by way of Paris and London to New York, where he landed in May, 1849.

Charles sent such glowing reports regarding the possibilities for the family in the new world as compared with their homeland, and urged their coming to America so strongly and persistently that the entire Steinweg family, except Theodore, engaged passage on the steamer *Helene Sloman* from Hamburg, which landed them at New York on June 9, 1851. Instead of venturing into business at once, Henry E. Steinweg wisely chose first to gain practical knowledge of the language and business methods of the new world. He and his sons accepted employment in different piano factories. For two years the three men gathered experience, and on March 5, 1853, the firm of Steinway & Sons started on its brilliant career. The very first step in that direction, the changing of the name from Steinweg to Steinway, showed not only the business sagacity of Henry E. Steinway, but also the strong faith which he had in his ability to build a better piano than known at that time. Hence he wanted a distinct trade-mark, which could not be imitated, even if his pianos should be.

From the beginning the firm of Steinway & Sons was a happy combination of various talents, making success imperative. Henry E. Steinway was an experienced piano maker and careful business man. His son Charles managed the factory, for which he was eminently fitted. A fine mechanic, he possessed a highly developed sense for exactness and systematic organization, while the younger son Henry was a genius as an inventor, a good musician and a splendid mixer with artists, professionals and literary men.

At the Metropolitan Fair, held at Washington, D. C., March, 1854, Steinway & Sons exhibited a square piano and received a prize medal, but their great triumph came at the great fair of the American Institute in New York in 1855, where their overstrung square piano with full iron frame created a sensation in the piano world. As a result their business expanded so rapidly that in 1859 the erection of that mammoth factory on Fifty-third Street and Fourth Avenue, New York, became a necessity. Henry E. Steinway planned the factory and superintended its building. It is said that he would not permit a beam or rafter in the entire structure which contained a single knot or showed the least imperfection. The precision of the master builder dominated in whatever he did!

Gradually he permitted his sons to assume the responsibilities of managing the affairs of the great business. Successful beyond his fondest dreams in his enterprise, Henry E. Steinway had to bear the deep sorrow of losing his faithful co-workers and beloved sons, Charles and Henry, in the prime of their manhood. This great bereavement, together with the advancing years, began to bear upon that strong character, who had fought the battle of life so valiantly, and, after planning and superintending the erection of Steinway Hall in 1866, he retired more and more from active participation, going to his rest on February 7, 1871, at the age of 74. Beloved by all who knew him, respected by the community and famous as an inventor and manufacturer in the entire civilized world, a self-made man who had to wring success from fate's unwilling hand under most trying conditions, Henry Engelhardt Steinway's name will ever be revered.

His eldest son, C. F. Theodore Steinway, was one of those who show great brilliancy in their youth, but whose genius then lies dormant for a number of years, to break out with irresistible force after middle life, astonishing the world with their accomplishments. At the age of 14 Theodore was an accomplished pianist, so much so that he was given the task of showing off his father's pianos at the Brunswick Fair in 1839. Enjoying the advantages offered by the Jacobsohn College at Seesen, a celebrated institute of learning, he studied acoustics under Dr. Ginsberg, who took great interest in the brilliant boy, in return for which Theodore built the models needed by Dr. Ginsberg for demonstration in his lectures on acoustics. This intimate relation to the scientist in his youth prevented Theodore from ever becoming a mere empiric. It was the cause of the restless search he later so forcibly demonstrated for the scientific laws underlying the construction of the pianoforte. After going through college, he went to work at the bench in his father's shop, and, when the family sailed for New York in 1851, he was charged with winding up the affairs of business and following the family. Fate decreed otherwise. He met the only maid whom he would marry, stayed at Seesen and continued the business founded by his father. Success crowned his efforts, and seeking a larger field he removed his piano factory to Brunswick in 1859, where he built up a substantial business. However, when his brothers, Charles and Henry, died, filial duty demanded that he should assist his father in New York. He sold his business to three of his most able workmen and became a partner in the firm of Steinway & Sons, New York. Theodore took charge of the construction department, and commenced those revolutionary improvements which have made the Steinway a synonym of perfection in piano building.

Theodore's inventive and constructive genius had for all these years been tethered by the every-day care of managing all departments of his Brunswick factory. Freed now, with unlimited capital, an excellent factory organization and the most expert workmen at his command, Theodore Steinway had opportunity seldom offered. He made the best use of it. Step by step he invaded the fields of modern science, investigating and testing different kinds of wood in order to ascertain why one kind or another was best adapted for piano construction, then taking up the study of metallurgy, to find a proper alloy for casting iron plates which would stand the tremendous strain of 75,000 pounds of the new concert-grand piano that was already born in his mind, calling chemistry to his aid to establish the scientific basis for felts, glue, varnish, oils,—in short, nothing in the realm of science having any bearing on piano construction was overlooked. Having thus laid his foundation, he returned to Germany to be near Helmholtz and benefit by that great savant's epoch-making discoveries. It was but natural that in time he became an intimate friend of

Helmholtz, and the world was benefited by that friendship. Theodore made Brunswick his home again, going to New York at regular intervals to superintend the execution of his inventions. At his Tusculum in Brunswick he had one of the most complete collections of musical instruments of every character, ancient and modern, and he knew the characteristics of each so well that it was a treat to listen to him whenever he was in the mood to show and talk about his gems. To widen his horizon of knowledge, he traveled extensively, meeting the shining lights of science, art and literature wherever he went. Germany was just then in its greatest period of scientific, artistic and industrial Renaissance. Theodore profited greatly, being a keen observer, and he set to work to bring to life in his piano the discoveries of Helmholtz, Tyndall and others. The crowning result was his Centennial concert-grand piano, with the duplex scale, bent-rim case, cupola iron plate and improved action which would lift that heavy hammer made of 23-pound felt by the slightest touch of the key, setting the strings, which were of a length and thickness heretofore unknown, in vibration.

Theodore was an intense and enthusiastic worker. Once engaged upon a problem, he knew no limit of time. The author has often discussed problems of piano building with him, the experimental piano before us, until the early morning hours. Physically and mentally very forceful, imbued with quiet Teutonic strength, he aimed to create a piano which would respond to the demands of the modern dynamic compositions of a Liszt, Wagner or Rubinstein, and would, orchestra-like, fill the large modern concert hall to its remotest corners. He accomplished this object without sacrificing that desired nobility of singing tone quality.

While Theodore Steinway has not created anything positively new in piano construction, he revolutionized piano making and all auxiliary industries by forcing the acceptance of scientific

Charles Steinway

methods upon all who desired to stay in the progressive march. He demonstrated to what extent science can aid in the development of the piano by his own productions, and thus broke the path for the enormous development of the industry during the past 30 years. This is more than all the empirics have ever done. Theodore Steinway died at Brunswick, March 26, 1889.

Compensation is one of the inexorable laws of nature. Great results can only be achieved by great efforts and corresponding sacrifice. Steinway & Sons had to pay their tribute to the law of compensation!

Charles Steinway, born on January 1, 1829, was one of those silent workers who fill most important places in the world of activity. Of a modest and retiring disposition, wrapped up in his arduous duties of organizing and managing the ever-growing factories, Charles knew no bounds for his labors. He simply exhausted himself and died at the early age of 36 on March 31, 1865, leaving behind him as his monument the piano factory *par excellence,* a foundation for Theodore and William to build upon, without which neither one of these two great men could have achieved their triumphs.

Henry Steinway, Jr., born on March 27, 1831, also paid the penalty for too intense application to the furtherance of ambitious plans. Naturally of a highly artistic, nervous temperament, Henry devoted himself to the nerve-racking activity of inventing improvements, and the patent records speak loudly for his great achievements. Seeking food for his restless brain—enlightenment as to the demands of the artist—Henry was at night-time a studious citizen

Henry Steinway

of Bohemia, and during the day nervously at work on his drawing-board. Burning the candle of life thus brightly at both ends, it could not last long, and the talented young man died on March 11, 1865, aged only 34 years.

This great calamity of losing the two brothers within three weeks' time threw the entire burden of managing the great business upon young William, the aged father having gradually withdrawn from active assistance. William Steinway was born at Seesen on March 5, 1835, at a time when the Steinway family was enjoying prosperity and father and mother were in their prime. He was a strong, healthy boy, physically and mentally. Like his brother Theodore he attended the Jacobsohn College, but unlike Theodore devoted himself to the study of languages and music proper, rather than listening to dreary lectures on acoustics.

At the age of 14 he had a good command of English and French, played the piano acceptably and had such a musical ear that he could tune a three-stringed grand piano to perfection. When the family arrived in New York, William was offered the choice of studying music, for which he had shown pronounced talent, or learning piano making. He chose the latter and was at once apprenticed to William Nunns & Company, one of the best-known New York piano firms of that time. As soon as his father started in business William joined him, and worked for several years at the bench, until the commercial end of the business demanded closest attention. William was by unanimous agreement chosen as the head of the financial and commercial departments of the firm. It was his proper sphere and furnished another illustration of the keen judgment of Henry E. Steinway, Sr. He placed each of his sons where his particu'ar talents might produce the best results.

Being only 29 years of age when called upon to manage an establishment of enormous proportions, William did not waver. With the grit and determination inherited from his father, he began to plan greater extensions. Theodore was building pianos, William had to sell them. His pet scheme, a great concert hall, was soon carried out—Steinway Hall was opened in 1867 by Theodore Thomas' orchestra, with S. B. Mills as soloist at the piano. The opening of this hall was the inauguration of a new era in the musical life of America. Anton Rubinstein, Annette Essipoff, Teresa Carreno, Fannie Bloomfield-Zeisler, Rafael Joseffy, Eugene D'Albert, Leopold Damrosch and Anton Seidl made their bows to select audiences from the platform of Steinway Hall. William Steinway knew that the American people needed musical education. He provided it, and no one man has done as much for musical culture, or has inspired the love for art among the American people, as William Steinway.

Supporting Theodore Thomas' great orchestra, so that it might make its celebrated journeys through the entire country (and without the aid of Steinway this would have been impossible), William by most liberal offers induced leading European virtuosos to come on concert tours to America. He was the ever-helping friend to young students and teachers. His inborn liberality would often let the heart be master of better judgment, but he never regretted his acts of benevolence, even if sometimes repaid with base ingratitude.

To the astonishment and chagrin of the older and more conservative houses in the piano trade, William started an aggressive and heretofore unheard-of advertising campaign. As a competent judge he knew that his factories turned out the best pianos that could possibly be made, and he was bent not only on letting the world know it, but on making the world believe it, as he did. This was revolutionary, even shocking, but William persisted until he carried his point.

Having established the fame of his piano in America beyond dispute, William looked for other worlds to conquer, and opened a branch house in the city of London about the year 1875. Steinway Hall in London was formally opened in 1876. In 1880 the

Hamburg factories were started, to supply the ever-growing European trade.

While thus engaged in building up this great market for the products of the factories, William fostered ambitions in other directions. He wanted to see the name of Steinway on the map of New York; and with that end in view he bought 400 acres of land on the Long Island Sound in 1880, and there created the town of Steinway. Starting with the erection of a sawmill and iron foundry, in course of time the case and action factories were erected, and since 1910 the entire piano works of Steinway & Sons have been located at Steinway, L. I., New York.

William Steinway was a strong man in every sense of the word. As a young man he was counted among the invincible athletes of the German Turn Verein, and even in his later years it was one of his pleasantries to compare muscular strength with friends. To say that mentally he was a giant is no exaggeration. Whoever can contemplate the multitude of details, aside from the larger schemes, to which William Steinway paid closest attention, the complex financial problems which confronted him in times of business depression, the demands made upon his time by artists, members of the press, etc., must wonder how he could pay any attention to society or public affairs. Yet we find that he was often called upon to lead a movement in politics or municipal affairs, to which he would respond with unwonted energy and ability. For 14 years he acted as president of the Liederkranz, the leading German singing society of New York. He was director in several banks and an active member of leading clubs. Broadminded and liberal to a degree, William Steinway could always look far beyond Steinway Hall when danger threatened the piano industry or a helping hand could be extended for uplifting. It is unfortunate that history never will record his manly and heroic actions in the interest of the entire piano industry of

America during the dark days of the great panics of 1893 and 1896. He stood like the Rock of Gibraltar against the waves of destruction rampant in those days, and by his great influence in financial circles, his sound judgment and counsel, protected the credit and fair name of the industry, often by timely action preventing impending disaster to worthy firms. He applied himself with such intensity and abandon to his duties that even his won-

Albert Steinway

derfully robust constitution had to give way under the protracted strain and exertion. He died prematurely on November 30, 1896, a martyr of conscientious devotion to duty as he saw it. Carl Schurz delivered the funeral oration and New York was in mourning.

The youngest son of Henry Engelhardt, Albert Steinway, born on June 10, 1840, like his brothers had chosen piano making as his life work, and after the death of Charles assumed the management of the factories. He made the application of machinery for manufacturing, modern heating and lighting systems his special study and thus kept the Steinway factories in the front rank of progressive industrial establishments. The development of the village of Steinway was mainly his work, and the planning and erection of the sawmills, iron foundry, metal shops and case factory were entirely in his hands. With that restless zeal so characteristic of the Steinway family, urging him to accomplish in a given time more than his bodily strength would permit, he undermined his none too strong constitution and died at the age of 37 on May 14, 1877.

It is almost needless to say that in course of time honors were showered upon the house of Steinway, in recognition of its many valuable contributions to science, art and industry. Theodore and William were elected Members of the Societies of Art of Berlin, Paris and Stockholm, and William was decorated with the Cross of the Red Eagle by Emperor William of Germany. The highest prizes for meritorious products have invariably been awarded to the firm wherever their pianos have been exhibited, and the leading courts of Europe and Asia bestowed the honor of appointment as " special purveyors " to Steinway & Sons.

Charles H. Steinway, the president of the corporation, has been honored by the Sultan of Turkey with the Order of the Liakat; by the Republic of France with the Cross of the Legion of Honor; by the Shah of Persia with the Order of the Lion and Sun, and by the Emperor of Germany with the Order of the Red Eagle.

All of the founders of the great house having passed to the unknown beyond, their work is continued in most effectual manner by their scions, who, true to tradition, divide the manifold duties among themselves, according to their talents and training.

Charles H. Steinway, son of the late Charles, directs the commercial and financial policy of the corporation. His brother, Frederick T., is in charge of the factories, assisted by Theodore Cassebeer, grandson of Doretta Steinway-Ziegler.

Henry Ziegler, son of Doretta, and pupil of the late Theodore Steinway, is in charge of the construction department, assisted by the late William Steinway's son, Theodore F., whose elder brother, William R., is in charge of the European business.

Following their chosen leader cheerfully, just as Henry Engelhardt's sons acknowledged their father's authority under all conditions, the active members of the House of Steinway not only uphold the foremost position to which the founders had attained, but are adding new laurels to the illustrious name by constantly improving the quality of their instruments and extending their influence, as leaders of the industry, to all parts of the civilized world.

Theodore A. Heintzmann

Theodore A. Heintzmann is perhaps entitled to the name of father of the piano industry in Canada. Born at Berlin, Germany, on May 19, 1817, he started as a cabinetmaker, learned keymaking with Buchholtz and perfected himself as a piano maker under Grunow. After traveling extensively on the Continent of Europe, he landed in New York in 1850, where he found work in Lighte & Newton's factory. Charles Steinway had his work-bench in the same room with Heintzmann. In 1853 he went to Buffalo and started the Western Piano Company, which enterprise had to be abandoned during the panic of 1857. Moving to Toronto in 1860 he started a piano shop without any capital, but his instruments were of such a high order that he found purchasers for them quite easily. The business grew steadily under his energetic management and ranks to-day among the leading industrial establishments

Ernest Gabler

of the Dominion. Heintz-
mann died on July 25,
1899. The business has
been taken over by a cor-
poration, in the manage-
ment of which four sons
of the late Heintzmann
take active part.

Among the many Ger-
mans who left their fa-
therland after the failure
of the Revolution of 1848,
was Ernest Gabler. Born
in Glogau, Silesia, he
landed at New York in
1851, and started in business in 1854. Building a
substantial piano at a
moderate price, he met
with considerable financial success. He died February 27,
1883.

A peculiar character, with many strong traits, we find in Free-
born Garrettson Smith. Learning his trade in Baltimore, he worked
for some time in Chickering's factory. In 1861 he became superintendent for William B. Bradbury. Bradbury was a musician by
profession, who had bought an interest in the firm of Lighte &
Newton (established in 1848), and when he dissolved partnership
with Lighte, he found in Smith a good manager for his factory.
After Bradbury's death in 1867 Smith bought the business, continuing the name of Bradbury. Immediately the commercial in-
stincts of Smith came to the surface, and he developed greater

talents as a distributor of
pianos than as a maker.
Original in his methods, he
published for a long time a
testimonial of the well-
known preacher, T. DeWitt
Talmage, in which the latter
declared that if the angels
are using musical instru-
ments in heaven, the Bradbury piano would surely be
there, because of its sweet
tone.

F. G. Smith

Smith was among the
first who opened warerooms
in leading cities, selling his
product direct to the public rather than through dealers. He is
counted among the wealthiest of those men in the piano trade who
have accumulated their fortunes by thrift, energy and exceptional
business ability.

While working at the melodeon factory of George A. Prince
& Company of Buffalo, Emmons Hamlin made the important discovery of " voicing " organ reeds, so that a given reed could be
made to imitate a clarinet, violin or other instrument. He developed this discovery to perfection and in 1854 formed a partnership with Henry Mason under the firm name of Mason & Hamlin,
for the purpose of manufacturing a new musical instrument called
" organ harmonium." Hamlin was a painstaking, exact working
mechanic, with considerable genius as an inventor.

Henry Mason, reared under the best musical traditions of
Boston, and graduated from a German university, was imbued with

Bernhard Shoninger

that artistic devotion to music, which we find to this date expressed in the almost flawless instruments produced by the Mason & Hamlin Company.

Starting with a small capital, but determined to produce the very best instruments only, the firm met with almost instant success. Not content with the manufacture of their humble instrument, they soon developed what has become known as the American Cabinet Organ. This instrument won for the firm a world-wide reputation and the highest possible honors and awards were bestowed upon their products at all World's Expositions, wherever exhibited.

In 1881 the manufacture of pianos was added to their industries. The Mason & Hamlin piano advanced rapidly in popular favor and is accepted by the most eminent virtuosos and musicians of the day, as an artistic instrument of the highest order.

Among the pioneers of the melodeon and organ industry was Bernhard Shoninger, a native of Germany, who landed in America in 1847, and started his factory at New Haven, Conn., in 1850. Branching out to the making of pianos, he secured for his instruments the same enviable reputation which had been accorded to his organs. Bernhard Shoninger died on June 3, 1910. The business is continued under the able direction of his son, S. B. Shoninger.

Myron A. Decker, born at Manchester, N. Y., on January 2, 1823, served a four-year apprenticeship with Van Winkle at the time when Albert Weber was taking his post-graduate course in the same shop. He then went to work for Boardman & Gray at Albany, and started a factory in that city in 1856. At the State Fair held at Syracuse in 1858 Decker received a diploma for the best piano exhibited.

Myron A. Decker

In 1859 he removed to New York, occupying for many years the historic building on Third Avenue and Fourteenth Street, in which Osborn, and later Worcester, had made pianos many years before. In 1877 his son, Frank C. Decker, was admitted to partnership and the firm changed to Decker & Son.

Myron A. Decker died in 1901. He was one of the old school of master mechanics, more concerned in designing and building a thoroughly artistic piano than in accumulating wealth. The firm was changed to a corporation in 1909, with Frank C. Decker as president and manager. Frank C. Decker, Jr., grandson of the founder, is preparing himself, under the tutelage of his father, to perpetuate the well-earned fame of the name of Decker in the piano world.

George Steck

Among the few who devoted their lives to the one object, the improvement of the piano, especially its tonal qualities, George Steck's name will ever be mentioned as one of the first. Born near Cassel, Germany, on July 19, 1829, Steck studied with that celebrated master, Carl Scheel of Cassel. Coming to America in 1853, he started his factory in 1857 and met with such exceptional success that he was able to open Steck Hall on Clinton Place, New York City, in 1865, where his concert grand pianos were played by the leading artists of the day. Later on a larger hall was opened on Fourteenth Street to meet the demands of a steadily growing business.

Steck was one of those restless natures who are never satisfied with the best of their work. As a scale drawer he had no superior. His scales for both grand and upright pianos have been industriously copied by makers of commercial pianos, because of their exceptional merit for clear and large tone. His concert grands have been highly endorsed by Richard Wagner, Sophie Menter, Annette Essipoff, Sir Julius Benedict and many others. Because of the exceptional solidity of the Steck piano, it has been chosen for years by many schools and colleges all through the United States, and has become known as the " school piano."

Personally, George Steck was a most lovable character, who had no enemies, finding pleasure in the pursuit of his art, with no particular regard for the commercial end of the business. To assure for his co-workers proper compensation for faithful service, Steck incorporated his business in 1884, allotting shares of stock to his employees. Gradually shifting the responsibilities and cares upon younger shoulders, he retired from active participation in 1887. The last 10 years of

Henry Behning

his life were devoted entirely to his pet scheme of constructing a piano which would stand permanently in tune. His experiments in that direction were very interesting, but he could not see the fulfillment of his dream. He died on March 31, 1897. In 1904 the business was consolidated with the Aeolian Company of New York, under whose direction the manufacture of the Steck pianos is continued with great energy and ability. The business having outgrown the home facilities, large additional factories have been established at Gotha, Germany, to supply the foreign demand for these pianos.

One of the prominent piano manufacturers of the early days was Henry Behning. Born at Hanover, Germany, on November 3, 1832, he learned piano making with Julius Gercke and came to

Hugo Sohmer

America in 1856. He found employment in the shop of Lighte & Newton. At the outbreak of the Civil War he enlisted with the Union Army, taking part in the hostilities, but was soon honorably discharged for disability. In 1861 he started in business, making a good commercial piano. In 1880 he admitted his son Henry to partnership, under the firm name of Henry Behning & Son. He retired from business in 1894 and died on June 10, 1905. The firm was changed in 1894 to the Behning Piano Company, a corporation under the management of Henry Behning, Jr., and Gustav Behning.

Hugo Sohmer, born in the Black Forest, Germany, in 1846, had the benefit of a classical education, including a thorough study of music. He came to New York at the age of sixteen and served his apprenticeship with Schütze & Ludolff. Returning to Germany he studied piano making for two years in some of the leading factories there. In 1870 he founded the firm of Sohmer & Company, by taking over the business of Marshall & Mittauer. Sohmer is a thorough piano maker who has patented many improvements, enhancing the value of his product. With strongly developed artistic inclination, Sohmer has ever been satisfied to produce an artistic instrument, rather than to merely manufacture large quantities.

Among the firms that have succeeded in producing a high-grade piano and scoring at the same time a remarkable financial success, Jacob Brothers stand pre-eminent. Charles Jacob studied piano making with Calenberg & Vaupel, who stood high among the masters of their day, while his brother, John F. Jacob, worked for years with Hardman, Peck & Company, and Billings & Wheelock. They started in business in 1878. After the death of John F. in 1885,

Charles Jacob

the youngest brother, C. Albert, was admitted to the firm, and in 1902 the business was incorporated. Besides their own extensive factory, this corporation owns the Wellington Piano Case Company, the Abbott Piano Action Company and has also taken over the Mathushek & Son Piano Company, and the old established business of James & Holmstrom, all of which are continued with marked success under the presidency of Charles Jacob, assisted by his brother Albert.

One of the most interesting characters in the history of the piano industry was Frederick Mathushek, born at Mannheim on June 9, 1814. He learned piano making at Worms. After serving his apprenticeship, he traveled through Germany and Austria, and finally landed in Henri Pape's shop at Paris, where he became thoroughly infected with that inventor's bacteria. Returning to

Worms, he began to build freak pianos similar to those he had seen at Pape's. One of his octagon "table pianos," built at Worms, is among the collection of antique pianos at the Ibach Museum at Barmen. Although a splendid workman and particularly gifted tone specialist, which enabled him to build superior artistic pianos, his business was not a success financially.

In 1849 Mathushek landed in New York, and was immediately engaged by John B. Dunham to draw new scales and make other improvements. It is said that Mathushek drew a scale for overstrung square pianos in Dunham's shop in 1850. It has never been disputed that the reputation which the Dunham pianos enjoyed in their day was due to the work of Mathushek. It was here, also, that he constructed his piano hammer-covering machine, which has been used as a foundation for all later improvements in that line.

In 1852 Mathushek started again on his own account, continuing until 1857, when Spencer B. Driggs tempted him with most liberal offers to work out the vague, not to say wild, notions which Driggs had conceived of revolutionizing the construction of the piano. It was impossible for even so great and versatile a genius as Mathushek to achieve any practical results by following Driggs' ideas, and we find him in 1866 as head of the Mathushek Piano Company, at New Haven, Conn. It was here that he did his best work. His invention of the linear bridge and equalizing scale enabled him to produce in his small " Colibri " piano a tone richer and fuller than could be found in many a large square piano, while

Mathushek's " Table Piano," from the Ibach Collection

Frederick Mathushek

his orchestral square piano has never been excelled, if it ever had its peer. In volume and musical quality of tone these orchestral square pianos were far superior to many of the short grand pianos of the present time, possessing, especially in the middle register, an almost bewitching sweet mellowness of tone, reminding vividly of the cello tones. Unfortunately for Mathushek, the owners of the company soon commercialized the product, and his dream of some day building a concert grand piano such as he had in his mind was never realized.

He drew many grand piano scales for other manufacturers, but, strange as it may sound, Mathushek's scales were only a success when he could work out the entire piano as he conceived it in his own mind. It is no exaggeration to state that Mathushek could, as a voicer, produce a tone quality in his own pianos that no other man could imitate. The author had the privilege of working alongside Mathushek for a number of years at the New Haven factory and observed the radical transformation of tone quality after Mathushek had gone over the hammers with his tools. A good player of the piano, with a wonderfully sensitive and trained ear, he quickly detected an almost imperceptible shortcoming and usually knew how to correct it. His fault, if it is to be called so, was his irresistible restlessness in seeking for improvements, which often robbed him of his night's rest and prompted continual changes while a large number of pianos were in course of construction. Modern manufacturing methods do not permit of too much experimenting, and like his master, Pape, Mathushek died a poor man. In 1871 he left New Haven, and with his grandson started the firm of Mathushek & Son in New York. It was finally changed to a corporation and consolidated with Jacob Brothers, under whose able management the business has flourished.

It is impossible to discuss or even to enumerate the manifold inventions of Frederick Mathushek. He was even more prolific than Henri Pape, but differed from Pape in not being given to merely experiment with ideas for the sake of novelty.

Mathushek's whole existence was dominated by the desire to produce in a piano that *ideal* musical tone which he could hear mentally, just as the deaf Beethoven heard his symphonic poems when he wrote them. Mathushek never had an opportunity to develop what he had in mind and felt in his soul. He came near to it in his orchestral square piano, and almost accomplished his aim in his equilibre system. The piano industry of America is largely indebted for its wonderful development to the genius of Frederick Mathushek. He died November 9, 1891.

With hope and high ambition, William E. Wheelock entered the trade in 1873, at the age of twenty-one years, as a member of the firm of Billings & Wheelock. In 1877 the partnership was dissolved, and he began the manufacture of the Wheelock piano. In 1880 the firm name became William E. Wheelock & Co. The demand for the Wheelock piano had increased so rapidly that better facilities became necessary, and a large factory with grounds comprising 21 city lots on 149th Street, New York, was acquired. In 1886 the Stuyvesant Piano Company was started to meet the de-

William E Wheelock

mand for a medium-priced piano, and in 1892 control of the business of the late Albert Weber was obtained. Wheelock and his partners, Charles B. Lawson and John W. Mason, organized the Weber Piano Company and thus became the first manufacturers who could offer to the trade a full line of the most merchantable grades: the Weber, a piano of the highest reputation and qualities; the Wheelock, as a first-class instrument, and the medium-priced Stuyvesant—all made in separate factories, but practically under one control and management. This idea, later on, was successfully followed by many of the leading concerns in the United States. When the opportunity to consolidate his three companies with the Aeolian interests presented itself in 1903, Wheelock saw the greater possibility for the future of his enterprise in such a combination and entered into the arrangement whereby he became treasurer of the new and larger corporation then formed, while remaining president of the several piano companies of which for many years he had been the head.

Educated as a musician, becoming a violinist and orchestra conductor of note, Simon Krakauer, born at Kissingen, Germany, in 1816, came to America in 1854 and started manufacturing pianos in 1869, with his son David, who had learned the trade in A. H. Gale's shop and later on worked for Haines Brothers and other New York makers.

It was but natural that the thorough musician, Krakauer, should strive to build an artistic piano, making quality the dominant effort, seeking to obtain musical tone quality. In 1867 Julius and Daniel Krakauer joined, and the firm was changed to Krakauer Brothers. In

Simon Krakauer

1903 the concern was incorporated. David Krakauer died in 1900, and his father in 1905.

William B. Tremaine, born in 1840, entered the piano business in 1868 as a member of the firm of Tremaine Brothers. A man of restless disposition, cultured and versatile, he seized upon opportunities whenever presented. When Mason J. Mathews had his orguinette ready for the market, Tremaine organized in 1878 the "Mechanical Orguinette Company," and marketed these automatic instruments by the thousands. Later on the "Celestina" (an enlarged orguinette) was introduced with considerable success, and in 1883 the Aeolian organ was brought out. Acquiring in 1888 the patents and stock in trade of the Automatic Music Paper Company of Boston, Tremaine organized the Aeolian Organ & Music Company, manufacturing automatic organs and music

William B. Tremaine

rolls. Success crowning his efforts, he purchased in 1892 all the patents owned by the Monroe Organ Reed Company of Worcester, and in 1895 introduced the " Aeriol " self-playing piano.

W. B. Tremaine was the founder of the business of manufacturing automatic playing musical instruments. Before the advent of the " Pianola " there was neither competition nor encouragement from the piano trade, and it required a man of keen foresight and courage to meet these conditions and make a success of the business, as he did, up to the time of his relinquishing it to his son.

Many writers point to the fact that a large number of our captains of industry have been born on a farm, have lacked higher education and had to " make themselves," inferring, if not positively asserting, that greatness in man can only originate on the soil or in the dwelling of the poor. In 1866 a boy was born in the city of Brooklyn who was christened Harry B. Tremaine. The father and mother, highly educated people of culture and refinement, brought up their boy with all the advantages which a large city offers. Unlike the country lad, young Tremaine saw the sky-scraping office buildings of New York go up, saw the traffic on its thoroughfares, the ships in the harbor, loading and unloading merchandise to and from all quarters of the globe. He was not awe-struck. It looked natural to him. He saw it every day when he went to school, but he observed and absorbed. Contrary to the old prescription according to which the great men of the future had to leave the schoolroom at the age of 13 or 14 to learn a trade, young Tremaine wanted to go to the high school. Instinctively, he felt that there must be a big story back of all this commotion on Broadway and in

Harry B. Tremaine

Wall Street, there must be laws and system behind all of it, and he wanted to know them before he would attempt to take his place on the stage as one of the actors. That he would play a leading rôle was beyond question for him, but he wanted to be well prepared to know his lines and what they meant.

In Harry B. Tremaine we meet the new element in the business world. The thorough education which he had enjoyed had trained his mind in logical reasoning, supporting his large vision for utilization of modern inventions and discoveries on a large scale. Tremaine had the great advantage that he had nothing to forget. He also knew how to apply all that he had learned in relation to modern economics. When he, in 1898, took charge of the business of the Aeolian Company as president, he surveyed the situation as

Edward R. Perkins

it presented itself. His father had laid a good foundation. Votey had perfected his Pianola. How to exploit what he found, to its fullest extent, was the problem for Tremaine to solve. Believing with the enthusiasm of youth in the almost boundless commercial possibilities of the new automatic appliances for musical instruments, he knew that success was only obtainable if adequate capital could be combined with the manufacturing and selling organization then at his command. So strong was his faith, so plausible the plans which he had worked out that he did succeed in interesting men of affairs, and obtained capital by the millions for the furtherance of his ambitious plans. Backed by this abundant capital, he lost no time in setting his machinery in motion. The advertising campaign for the Pianola, which he inaugurated immediately, stunned the old-timers in the piano trade. Dire disaster was prophesied by many, but Tremaine knew his cards, his carefully laid plans did not miscarry and no one to-day denies him the credit of having blasted and paved the way for the popularity of the player piano. Like all great leaders, Tremaine has the talent to pick the right man for the right place. He found an able assistant in Edward R. Perkins, who joined the Aeolian forces in 1893 at the age of 24. Perkins exhibited such ability and strength that he was intrusted with the responsible position of vice-president and general manager when the greater organization was completed.

William E. Wheelock came into the fold as president of the Weber Piano Company in 1903, and is now in charge of the financial department as treasurer of the corporation.

Edwin S. Votey

Tremaine understands the economy of high-priced labor. When he wanted to build the best player pianos he secured the services of Pain, Votey, Kelly and others of ability. Just as soon as he was ready to enter the piano field proper, he associated with the Weber and Steck piano, and finally made a combination with the house of Steinway for the exclusive use of the Pianola in their instruments. Knowing that large capital can be economically applied only under conditions of increasing returns, which again are only possible with relatively large markets, he branched out and went into the markets of Europe, Asia, South America and Australia. For the stimulus of the home market bidding for the patronage of the wealthy, Tremaine built Aeolian Hall, in the very heart of New York's fashionable quarters, engaging the best artists to demon-

George B. Kelly

strate the value of his products at the elegant auditorium. In 1903 he organized the Aeolian, Weber Piano & Pianola Company, capitalized at $10,000,000 and controlling the following subsidiary companies: The Aeolian Company, the Orchestrelle Company (London), The Choralion Company (Berlin), The Aeolian Company, Ltd. (Paris), The Pianola Company Proprietary, Ltd. (Melbourne and Sydney), the Weber Piano Company, George Steck & Company, Wheelock Piano Company, Stuyvesant Piano Company, Chilton Piano Company, Technola Piano Company, Votey Organ Company, Vocalian Organ Company and the Universal Music Company. These companies give employment to about 5,000 people, scattered all over the world. Aside from the extensive piano factories in New York City, and the player factories at Garwood and Meriden, there is a Steck piano factory at Gotha, Germany, producing 3,500 pianos annually, and a large factory for the Weber Piano Company is in course of construction at Hayes, near London. Operating as independent concerns, these companies are capitalized at about $4,000,000. The total capital employed under the direction of Harry B. Tremaine amounts to $15,500,000, which is more than the capital invested in the entire piano and organ industry of the United States in 1890.

The remarkable results achieved by Tremaine within so short a time can be accounted for by the fact that he learned from history what others had to learn in the dreary school of experience. As an observant student, he saw the potentialities of mechanical appliances for musical instruments and knew how to develop them. A genius as an organizer, he believes in combination of capital and brains, division of labor and responsibilities, and adequate compensation for all. He has proven that a higher education is not an hindrance for advancement, but a necessity for progress in industrial, commercial or financial pursuits. He has made his record in breaking the path for the new school of industrial revolutionists in the piano industry. A pioneer of the most forceful, aggressive type, he is withal of a gentlemanly and most retiring disposition, shunning publicity to an unwarranted degree.

William B. Tremaine died in 1907, having seen his work bear fruit a thousand-fold under the magic wand of his gifted son.

How rapidly the player piano is forging to the front, with almost irresistible force, is clearly demonstrated by the tremendous growth of such factories as seem to know how to serve the public best.

Among those the Autopiano Company has made its mark by producing a player piano of distinctly original construction and quality.

The demand for their player has always been ahead of the capacity to supply, and artists of the highest standing are praising the dominant features which distinguish this instrument from many others. Although established only 8 years (1903) the Autopiano Company, under the aggressive management of President R. W. Lawrence, has risen to a position of one of the largest producers of player pianos. Manufacturing thoroughly reliable instruments and employing comprehensive, modern business methods the Autopiano Company is rendering valuable service for the introduction of the player piano.

Because of the impetus given to the player-piano industry by the extensive advertising of the Aeolian Company, Wilcox & White Company and others, a demand for a reliable player action made itself forcibly felt. Charles Kohler seized upon the opportunity and established the Auto-Pneumatic Action Company in 1900. He secured the active assistance of W. J. Keeley, Thomas Danquard and other experts. Danquard obtained a patent in 1904 for a device called the " flexible finger," by means of which the wippen of the piano action is attached direct to the player mechanism, thus eliminating the harshness of contact and imparting elasticity without interfering with the function of the piano action.

Because of their excellent quality a large number of piano manufacturers have adopted these actions for their player pianos. The Auto-Pneumatic Action Company is perhaps the largest producer of player mechanism at the present time.

The Standard Pneumatic Action Company, the Amphion Company, Ariston Company, Gulbransen-Dickinson Company, Chase & Baker Company and Simplex Piano-Player Company are also making history for the player piano.

Among the phenomenal successes of latter days, the firm of Kohler & Campbell stands pre-eminent. Beginning with a small capital in 1896, this firm has placed over 120,000 pianos on the market within 14 years.

John Calvin Campbell, born at Newark, N. J., in 1864, was a mechanical genius. After serving his apprenticeship as a machinist, he turned to construction, and invented several useful wood and iron working machines. In 1890 he took up piano making and made a scientific study of piano construction. He was so successful that his pianos were at once accepted by the wholesale trade as of splendid commercial value, and he saw his firm rise to unexpected magnitude. He died in 1908.

To his surviving partner, Charles Kohler, the credit is due of organizing the great business in such a manner as to keep pace with the demand for their pianos. Born at Newark, N. J., in 1868, he attended the public school and studied for one year at Princeton College. At the age of 20 he turned to piano making. Establishing the firm of Kohler & Campbell, he found opportunity to display his remarkable talent as a factory organizer and business man. Supplementing Campbell's ingenious construction with thorough workmanship in all details of the piano, he made advantageous use of modern methods in manufac-

John C. Campbell

turing and produced a fine piano, which he could offer at tempting prices to large distributors. The remarkable fact is to be recorded that among his largest customers are piano manufacturers of note who carry the Kohler & Campbell pianos in their various retail warerooms.

Naturally modest and of a retiring disposition, Kohler has not been active in any of the general trade movements, but that he will be called upon to take his part in time to come is warranted by the record which he has made.

The American Piano Company of New York, incorporated in June, 1908, is another of the modern combinations of large establishments. Capitalized at $12,000,000, it controls the factories of Chickering & Sons, in Boston; William Knabe & Company, in Baltimore; Haines Brothers, Marshall & Wendell, Foster & Com-

pany, Armstrong, Brewster and J. B. Cook companies, located at
Rochester, N. Y.   C. H. W. Foster of Chickering & Sons is president of this company, with George C. Foster, George L. Eaton,
Charles H. Eddy and William B. Armstrong as vice-presidents.
While maintaining retail warerooms at New York, Boston, Baltimore and Washington, this company distributes its products elsewhere through dealers exclusively.

The house of Wing & Son, New York, was founded in 1868 by
Luman B. Wing, as partner in the firm of Doane, Wing & Cushing.
Luman B. Wing died in 1873, and was succeeded by his son, Frank
L. Wing, who admitted R. Delano Wing (his son) to partnership in
1905.   This firm is probably the pioneer of the mail-order business in pianos.   Building a reliable instrument, the concern has
met with uninterrupted success during the 43 years of its
existence.

New York is proud of such names as Kranich & Bach, Strich &
Zeidler, Mehlin & Sons, Behr Brothers, Lauter (of Newark),
Wissner, Stultz & Bauer, Ludwig & Company, Pease Piano Company, Winter & Company and others who are making history as
manufacturers of meritorious pianos.

Philadelphia has, besides the time-honored Schomacker, the
Blasius, the Lester and the Cunningham Piano companies—all of
whom are as true to the traditions of honest values in pianos as
any the old Quaker City has ever produced.

Among the firms who have done much to keep Boston to the
front is the Henry F. Miller & Sons Piano Company.   Henry F.
Miller, born at Providence, R. I., on September 25, 1825, was educated as a musician and acquired a reputation especially as an
organist.   His commercial inclination prompted him, however, to
accept an offer of the Boston piano makers, Brown & Allen, to join
their forces in 1850.   After studying with this concern for seven

years, he accepted a more promising position with enterprising Emerson, and in 1863 started, in connection with J. H. Gibson, who was an expert scale draughtsman and constructor, to make the " Miller " piano. Success followed his efforts, and in course of time he admitted his five sons to partnership, incorporating finally under the name of Henry F. Miller & Sons Piano Company. He died on August 4, 1884, at Wakefield. His sons took up the work

Henry F. Miller

of their father under the leadership of Henry F. Miller, Jr., continually improving their product so that many of the greatest virtuosos are using the Miller grand pianos in their concert work. Besides paying proper attention to the development of the musical character of their instruments, Miller & Sons were among the first and most persistent advocates of architecturally correct designs for piano cases, and achieved marked success in that direction as well.

Aside from the many illustrious names founded many years ago, Boston can proudly point to younger firms, who by superior merit of their production are adding new luster to its fame as a piano-producing center of the highest order. It was in 1883 that Frank A. Lee joined the John Church Company of Cincinnati, and in November of that year the Everett Piano Company was

started in Boston through his efforts. The name Everett was chosen by Church because of its euphonious clearness, which makes it as easy to remember as it is easy to spell. John Church and the other associates of Lee, having been piano dealers for many years, started out to build a commercial piano, but as soon as Lee became president of the Everett Piano Company he changed that policy and began to make pianos of the highest order. It took years of perseverance, and often discouraging trials, to obtain for the Everett piano that recognition as an artistic piano which it deserved. Lee never lost faith in its ultimate success, and through his determination, ably assisted by the artistry of his superintendent, John Anderson, he finally had the satisfaction of seeing his concert grands used by Reisenauer, Dr. Neitzel, Chaminade, Carreno and other leading virtuosos, and the Everett pianos admitted among the selected leaders of the world's pianodom.

The John Church Company also controls the Harvard Piano Company of Dayton, Ky., and, with its large catalogue as music publishers, is a great factor in the music world. Frank A. Lee, as president, has guided the destiny of this great company since 1894.

The Ivers & Pond, Briggs, Merrill, Hume, Jewett and Poole Companies, Theodore J. Kraft and others are maintaining the tradi-

tions of famous Boston makers and assisting creditably
in making history for the
future.

Turning to the West, we
encounter a galaxy of brilliant men to whose excep-
tional talents, business acumen, shrewdness and cour-
ageous farsightedness the
unparalleled development of
the industry in that part of
the country must be ascribed.
The most prominent figure
was William Wallace Kim-
ball. Descending from good
old English stock, Kimball
was born on a farm in Oxford

County, Maine, in 1828. After passing through the high school
he practiced teaching for a while, but soon became a commercial
traveler. In his wanderings he came to Chicago, and was so
impressed with the future possibilities of the little city that he
made it his home and established himself as a piano dealer in
1857. He sold the Chickering, Hallet & Davis and Emerson pianos
largely in his early days. When Joseph P. Hale introduced his
commercial piano, Kimball took hold of it with such energy that
he soon became the largest piano dealer in the West. The great
Chicago fire of 1871 did not spare Kimball's warerooms, which
were entirely destroyed. Kimball immediately ordered a new stock
of pianos from his manufacturers, turning his home into an office
and the barn into a piano wareroom until he could find new quar-

ters in the business center of the city. In what high esteem Kimball was held by the people of whom he bought is shown by the fact that Hale, of New York, telegraphed him on the day of the fire, " You can draw on me at once for $100,000." Hale appreciated the good customer and demonstrated unlimited faith in Kimball's integrity.

A born organizer, Kimball outgrew the limited sphere of the local piano dealer. He branched out and became a jobber on a large scale. Among his first employees was a lank and lean farmer's boy from Wisconsin, who showed such aptness for the business that he soon became Kimball's right-hand man. Edwin Stapleton Conway was just the man to carry out Kimball's far-reaching plans. The west being sparsely settled in those days, but rapidly filling up with a splendid class of wealth-producing farmers, pianos were not in great demand. Kimball resolved to bring the pianos to the farmer's door. He made Conway the general field organizer, whose duty it was to travel from place to place and select in each town the brightest young fellow who could be trusted with consignments of organs and pianos, which he was to sell to the farmers of his neighborhood. Conway's personality, his energy, power of persuasion and convincing manners fitted him excellently for that work, and many a prosperous dealer of the middle west proudly calls himself to-day a " Conway Boy," meaning that he was induced by Conway to enter the field and profited by Conway's coaching. Pretty soon Kimball had a net of agencies covering the entire western country and the proceeds of his yearly sales of pianos and organs ran into the millions of dollars.

Bright and early, on a spring morning, Conway blew into the author's office, in New York, explaining in a

Edwin S. Conway

few words that he had finally convinced the " Governor " of the necessity of making his own organs at Chicago, and now wanted all the information he could get, in order to buy material. Kimball had resolved to climb a step higher and become a manufacturer. Success was a foregone conclusion, because he controlled the outlet of thousands of organs, and even his piano sales at that time exceeded the imposing number of 4,000 per year. When the organ manufacturing was well under way, he started in 1882 his piano factory. At stated before, Kimball was a born organizer. With unerring eye he always understood how to pick the right man for the right place and to keep him there. When his manufacturing department assumed greater proportions he sent for

W. Lufkin

his nephew, W. Lufkin, and charged him with the management thereof, although Lufkin had, up to that time, never been inside of a piano or organ factory. Kimball was original in all that he did. He reasoned that, for the management of such big factories as he contemplated, a man brought up at the work-bench or at an office desk would have too narrow a vision. He wanted a man who would just as readily plan to make 30,000 instruments a year as 5,000. Lufkin was that man. He made the first 5,000 pianos, and is turning out 30,000 instruments per year now, including most imposing church organs. Without a doubt, the Kimball factories stand without a parallel. Not only are they producing all parts of the piano, from the case up, including iron plates, actions and keys, but since 1904 the entire mechanism of the player piano has been also made there, including the music rolls. To the small parlor organ, the building of church organs was added in 1890. Kimball reversed the order of things. Two hundred years ago the church-organ builders made pianos as a side issue. Kimball, evolving from a small retail dealer to the largest piano manufacturer in the world, became a church-organ builder as well.

Kimball, not so bold as Conway, listened carefully to the latter's aggressive plans, worked them down to the line of safe possibility and then charged Lufkin with making the goods which Conway had to sell. A splendid trio, with a most able leader, and hence the unparalleled success. Kimball saw his business grow to an institution with a turnover of over $4,000,000 per annum. He died on December 15, 1904. The corporation is continued with C. N. Kimball as president, E. S. Conway, vice-president, and W. Lufkin, treasurer.

H. D. Cable, born at Walton, N. Y., in 1849, spent his early days on a farm. After

attending the Walton Academy, he turned to teaching, with such success that at the age of 17 he was elected principal of the schools at Easton, Pa., and a year later appointed superintendent of schools at Williamsport, Pa. In 1869 the publishing house of Barnes & Company sent him to Chicago as manager of their western department, and for 11 years Cable filled that responsible position with great success and fidelity. In 1880 he formed a partnership with the organ builder, F. R. Wolfinger, organizing the Wolfinger Organ Company, which was changed to the Western Cottage Organ Company, and later on to the Chicago Cottage Organ Company.

Cable applied the methods used in selling books, as far as possible, to the organ and piano business, with amazing success. Like

J. Frank Conover

Kimball, he was a born ·organizer and an excellent judge of men and their abilities. The training which he had enjoyed in the bookselling business impelled him to introduce system in his manufacturing and selling organization, with all that this word implies in modern business management, and perhaps he was the first in the piano industry to profit by the application of scientific accounting. At all events, his success was so rapid, and his business assumed such immense proportions, that it became the wonder of his contemporaries.

Of an exceedingly nervous temperament, Cable was not only a rapid thinker, but also a worker of extraordinary capacity. Himself the soul of honor and integrity, he treated everybody on that basis, and his keen judgment assisted his intuition in making bold moves on the chessboard of trade with advantageous results. Starting out in his enterprises by catering to the demands of the masses, he aimed for the highest in his piano production, and in 1890 he consolidated the business of Conover Brothers, of New York, with his own, securing at the same time the valuable assistance of that eminent piano constructor, J. Frank Conover, for the manufacture of the Conover piano. As his business assumed larger proportions, he called his brothers, Hobart M. and Fayette

S. Cable, to his aid, and, although he had surrounded
himself with a number of
able men, his close personal
application to the complex-
ities of his large business
finally undermined his constitution and he died prematurely on March 2, 1899,
at the age of 50.

The business, having
been incorporated, has been
continued, but the name of
the company was changed to
the Cable Company, in
honor of the founder. F. S.
Cable served as president
until 1903, when he started

in business on his own account. He was succeeded by F. S.
Shaw, under whose able management the company largely extended its activities, adding a department for player pianos,
and paying careful attention to the development of the artistic
Conover piano, preparing for the introduction of the same on the
concert platform. In the short space of 20 years the Cable Company has attained a position as one of the great leaders of the
western continent, and the genius of H. D. Cable has shown to
contemporaries the great possibilities of the piano business in its
legitimate channels.

Lucien Wulsin, born in Louisiana in 1845, came with his father's family to Cincinnati in his early childhood. He went
through the Cincinnati public school and part of the high school.
At the age of 19 he enlisted with the Union army, at first serving

in a Kentucky infantry battalion, and from January, 1864, until the end of the war, in the Fourth Ohio Cavalry. In March, 1866, he entered the employ of D. H. Baldwin, a music teacher, who was selling the Decker Brothers' pianos in Cincinnati. Wulsin started in as a clerk, bookkeeper and general factotum, and made himself so useful that he was admitted to partnership in 1873, the firm name becoming D. H. Baldwin & Company.

An era of expansion and larger activity was inaugurated. As the first move, a branch store was opened at Indianapolis. In 1878 the Louisville branch was started under the management of R. A. Johnston, who was made a partner in 1880. After Johnston's death in 1882, George W. Armstrong, Jr., Clarence Wulsin and A. A. Van Buren, who had been employed by the firm for a number of years, became partners. With the growth of the business the necessity of manufacturing became more and more apparent, and in 1889 the Hamilton Organ Company was organized as a subsidiary concern for the making of organs—the Baldwin Piano Company, Valley Gem Piano Company and Ellington Piano Company soon following. Later on the Hamilton Piano Company was formed, and the firm of D. H. Baldwin & Company changed into a corporation under the title of The Baldwin Company, the latter controlling all the above subsidiary companies.

D. H. Baldwin died in 1899, leaving the bulk of his estate for missionary purposes. Ordinarily this would have meant the winding up of the business, in order to pay out the large amount which represented Baldwin's interest, but Wulsin did not propose to have the work of his life destroyed through an act of the man whom he had made wealthy by his 33 years of faithful devotion. Together with Armstrong he arranged to buy all the stock of the Baldwin estate and of the only remaining partner, A. A. Van Buren.

Freed from all interference, the two partners set to work to develop the business to its fullest possibilities. They were an excellent team. Wulsin, the man of ideas and business foresight, enthusiastically believing in the progress of the American people and the perpetual growth of the nation, planned the ultimate expansion. Armstrong, the mathematician and man of figures, worked out the details of the plans to never-failing exactness. As a matter of good business policy, stress was laid in the beginning upon the commercial—the money-making—part of the business, with proper regard for the building up of a reputation for reliable goods, but just as soon as an efficient number of artisans had been trained, under the guidance of Superintendent Macy, the development of the artistic Baldwin piano was taken in hand with avidity and with corresponding success.

Lucien Wulsin's inborn love for the noble and beautiful is stamped upon every part of the great institution. The factories, located opposite beautiful Eden Park, at Cincinnati, are models of decorative architecture. Instead of imprisoning his men between four plain brick walls, Wulsin engaged an architect to design his factories, with orders to combine the beautiful with the practical, paying attention to hygienic improvements. Always kept scrupulously clean, the workrooms in the Baldwin factory impress the visitor much more as artists' ateliers than as piano makers' workshops. The walls of the spacious offices are decorated with pictures of Greek and Roman structures of architectural beauty, to train the eyes of the workman for proper and correct forms; flower-beds surround the factories and living flowers are to be found at the factory windows. An air of refinement permeates the entire establishment and gentlemanly behavior is a characteristic of the Baldwin employees.

The sound policy underlying the management of this great business is best described in Wulsin's own words, which he used

Benjamin Starr

in a letter to the author: "I realize that the welfare of our company and the success of its people will come from a fair treatment of all our men and the awakening in them of the ideals and enthusiasm which, after all, do exist in the average human being."

It is not to be wondered at that the Baldwin pianos carried off the highest prizes, wherever exhibited, gaining even that much-coveted distinction, the Grand Prix at the Paris Exposition of 1900. Nor does it require an explanation why Pugno exclaims, "The Baldwin tone is boundless; you can't get to the bottom of it—can't pound it out," and when, on the other hand, æsthetic de Pachmann whispers his enchanting Chopin pianissimo passages on that same piano. The Baldwin piano is an art product, made by artists who are living and working in an artistic atmosphere, because the man who created the Baldwin institution is an idealist. Lucien Wulsin was decorated with the Cross of the Legion of Honor at the Paris Exposition of 1900.

As far back as 1849 an Alsatian by the name of Trayser made pianos and melodeons in Indianapolis. Drifting about the country, he came to Ripley, Ohio, in 1869, where he started a piano factory, which was removed to Richmond, Ind., in 1872, when James S. and Benjamin Starr acquired an interest in the concern. In 1878

Trayser retired, and Milo J. Chase entered the firm, the name of which was changed to the Chase Piano Company. In 1884 the Starr Brothers obtained control of the business and changed the name to the Starr Piano Company, with Benjamin Starr as manager. Upon the retirement of James Starr, Henry Gennett and associates obtained control of the company and began a campaign of expansion which has made the concern one of the leaders of the

Henry Gennett

middle west. Gennett assumed the business management and opened distributing warerooms in many leading cities of the western and southern States. Benjamin Starr superintended the factories, ably assisted by Harry Gennett. The business assumed immense proportions under the guidance of Henry Gennett, while his son Harry developed into a good piano constructor, who has done excellent work in improving the Starr piano and promises more as a piano maker for the future. Benjamin Starr died in 1903, having had the satisfaction of seeing the small factory with which he started grow to an establishment producing annually about 18,000 pianos of a quality above the ordinary market instrument. It is the laudable ambition of Harry Gennett to see in the near future the Starr concert grand, designed and constructed by him, used by artists of note in their public concerts.

In the romantic vales of Bunifort, County of Cork, Ireland, a boy was born on March 17, 1840, to farmer Healy, the thirteenth child of a poor but happy family. The boy was christened Patrick Joseph. When the good " ould sod " would not yield enough to support the growing family, Healy senior packed up his worldly goods and took his family to the land of promise and possibilities. Patrick Joseph was 10 years of age when he landed in Boston. Attending the public schools, he had an eye for earning money, and we find him working the bellows of a great church organ for the organist, Bancroft. This man became interested in the Irish lad, and when Healy had finished his school course Bancroft secured for him a position as errand boy with the music dealer, George P. Reed. The errand boy soon advanced to be a clerk, and we next find him in a responsible position in the great music publishing house of Oliver Ditson & Company.

Ditson had a keen perception of the possibilities in the rapidly developing cities of the west and planned the establishment of branch houses at Cincinnati, St. Louis, Chicago and San Francisco. He gave Healy the choice of either of the three last named. After visiting St. Louis and Chicago, Healy wisely decided for the latter, and in 1864 the firm of Lyon & Healy was established under the protection of the parent house of Oliver Ditson & Company. To encourage the young men, Ditson predicted that they would do a business of $100,000 per year within 10 years. Healy reported sales of over that amount before the first 12 months had passed! The piano trade of America has produced a large number of "great workers," but it is the opinion of all who knew him that Healy outworked them all. The great results achieved by him are, however, due not only to the amount of work which he performed, but largely to the systematic methods he applied.

The author will ever remember Healy's first visit to his New York office. After the usual greeting, and every-day question, "How is business with you?" Healy pulled out of his pocket a small black note-book and read off statistics as to how many letters had been received daily by his firm during the past month as compared to the same month of one, two and three years before. The methodical statistician, the mind which from the small detail could construct a prognostication of the future, was thus displayed. It was the key to Healy's great achievements. Nervously working at the store during the daytime, he would take memoranda of the day's doings to his home and there work out statistics to guide him in his bold undertakings. Those who wondered at Healy's positive, unfaltering aggressiveness did not know how well he had fortified himself with unfailing figures and facts, gathered from his comparative statistics, proving the correctness of his conclusions. Thus Healy was able to accomplish more in one lifetime than would ordinarily be possible for the combined efforts of several business men.

However, searching for the main cause of the success of the man who built the greatest music house in the world, we find it in the character of P. J. Healy. Although exacting to a degree, his sympathetic character enabled him to draw from his employees the best that was within them in a manner which made all of his

young men enthusiastic workers for the success of the firm. Just and fair under all conditions, he displayed a sincere solicitude for all who worked with him. Like all leaders, he had the faculty of picking the right man and putting him into the right place. As Kimball found his Conway, so Healy discovered in another Wisconsin farmer's boy the qualities which only need opportunity for developing into the making of a strong man. Charles N. Post entered the employ of Lyon & Healy as a bookkeeper in 1864, when 16 years of age. He grew up to be Healy's right-hand man, and when the business had outgrown the sphere of merely dealing in musical merchandise, and the manufacturing of instruments became a necessity, young Post was charged with the responsibility of managing that department.

After success was secured in the making of guitars, mandolins, etc., Healy's ambition was to build an instrument of the higher order. Although the Erard harp was at that time considered to be perfection, Healy knew from experience that even that renowned make was not satisfactory, and he charged Post with the work of producing a harp which would be acceptable to the artists as superior to the Erard. Post engaged the services of George B. Durkee, an inventor of note, and the two men set to work to construct a

Lyon & Healy Harp

harp which made the name of Lyon & Healy famous wherever orchestra music is played. Durkee went at his problem with a well-trained scientific mind and succeeded in constructing a mechanism which did away with the irritating " buzzing " so common to the ordinary harp. He further developed a scale so perfect as to make the playing of the instrument much easier. By enlarging the soundboard he furthermore increased the volume of tone perceptibly. The first harp was turned out in 1886, and Healy had the satisfaction of seeing his instruments accepted by the Gewandhaus orchestra of Leipsic, and by nearly all the leading orchestras of Berlin, Vienna, Stuttgart, St. Petersburg, New York, Boston, Chicago, etc.

The building of church organs was the next addition to the manufacturing department, which had grown to such magnitude that in the year 1890 over 100,000 instruments were turned out. The business, started in 1864 in a modest manner, had steadily grown until it was known all over the globe as the greatest establishment of its kind. When Lyon retired from the firm in 1890, the corporate form was adopted, with P. J. Healy as president, Charles N. Post, vice-president, and Robert B. Gregory, treasurer. The concern continued in its onward march under Healy's inspiring leadership, extending its influence in all directions, but Healy had to pay the penalty for drawing to excess on nature's limitations. He died on April 5, 1905, at the age of 65, mourned by all who knew him, honored by the members of the trade with the sobriquet, " The grand old man of the music trade," leaving his footprints behind as an example to coming generations that honesty of purpose, application to duty and fairness in all dealings with fellow-men make life worth living to a much greater degree than the mere accumulation of wealth.

Charles N. Post succeeded Healy in the presidency until 1908, when he retired to the pleasant life of a gentleman farmer, on his

Rudolph Wurlitzer

ranch in Southern California. Healy's fourth son, Paul, has since been the active head of the great corporation, and upon his instigation the manufacture of pianos has been added. The factories are in charge of his brother, Mark Healy, who is studiously preparing himself for the career of a master builder of the Lyon & Healy piano.

Coming from a family of musical-instrument makers who pursued that art for generations in the little town of Schöneck, Saxony, Rudolph Wurlitzer landed in New York about 1854. His career was such as usually falls to the lot of young German emigrants who land here without means, but endowed with a thorough education and expert knowledge of their profession. Struggling for the first few years to earn a living, he finally found his bearings in Cincinnati, where he established himself as an importer of musical instruments in 1856. With the enthusiasm and optimism of youth, he overcame the many obstacles and difficulties facing a young business man who has to earn his capital, and gradually climbed up the ladder until he was recognized as a power by his contemporaries. In 1890 his eldest son Howard was admitted to partnership. By studying the musical-instrument business in all its phases for several years in Europe, young Howard was well prepared for his work and soon made his presence felt, and the rise of the house of Wurlitzer to its pre-eminent position dates from that time.   Incorporating in 1890 with a capital of $200,000, as the Rudolph Wurlitzer Company, it has now increased its capital to $1,000,000, and owns the Rudolph Wurlitzer Manufacturing Company, also with a capital of $1,000,000.   In the course of time two other sons, Rudolph H. and Farney Wurlitzer, joined the concern, each taking charge of a department, so that at the fiftieth anniversary, in 1906, Rudolph Wurlitzer, Sr., was able to retire from active participation and enjoy the well-merited rest of private life.   The Wurlitzer Company at present is perhaps the largest manufacturer of mechanical instruments, including player pianos, its business connections covering all parts of the globe.

Among the many remarkable men who have made their mark in the development of the piano industry of the west, William H. Bush stands out as one of those sturdy characters whom misfortune only spurs on to greater efforts.

Coming from good old Holland stock, William Henry Bush was born in 1829 on a farm near Baltimore, Md.   One of the first railroads built in the United States ran through the Bush farm to the City of Baltimore, and we find William as a lad of 14, with remarkable enterprise, contracting for the use of the steam engine and the one freight car of which the railroad could boast to carry his vegetables to Baltimore, so as to be the first in the marketplace. In 1854 he landed at Chicago and soon engaged in the lumber business, accumulating a fortune.   The great fire of 1871 burned up his lumber yard and reduced him again to the point where he had started 17 years before.   Success was his, and in 1886 he started in partnership with his son, William Lincoln Bush, and John Gerts, under the firm name of W. H. Bush & Company, for the manufacturing of pianos.

William H. Bush

William L. Bush, born in 1861, had served his apprenticeship with Geo. H. Woods & Company as an organ and piano maker, and from 1881 to 1883 as salesman for the W. W. Kimball Company. John Gerts had learned piano making in Germany, thoroughly mastering all branches of the art.

With W. H. Bush at the head as financier, the concern prospered from the very start, and was changed to a corporation in 1891 with a paid-up capital of $400,000.

Philanthropically inclined, the elder Bush planned to create for Chicago an institution which should serve music and the arts, but before his well-conceived plans materialized he passed away in 1901 at the age of 74.

The Bush Temple of Music was started in 1902 and completed in 1903, and stands as a monument to the enterprise, energy and liberality of the Maryland farmer boy, as one of Chicago's landmarks.

The Conservatory of Music connected with the Bush Temple was founded by William Lincoln Bush in 1901, with Kenneth M. Bradley as Director and Mme. Fannie Bloomfield-Zeisler at the head of the piano department, the position now being occupied by Mme. Julie Rivé King. Among the teachers of note who have given luster to this school, the great violinist, Ovide Musin, may be mentioned.

William L. Bush, a talented musician himself, is very solicitous for the lasting success of this music school, which has achieved a far-reaching reputation. He also established similar institutions at Dallas, Tex., and Memphis, Tenn., thus assisting in the propaganda for musical development not only as a manufacturer of excellent pianos, but also as a lover of the art for art's sake.

Albert Krell, Sr.

The Bush & Gerts Piano Company is known for its zeal in upholding and defending the ethics of the piano trade. William L. Bush is using his forceful pen with telling results in the warfare against the illegitimate stencil and dishonest methods of selling, insisting that the maker's name should be on every piano and a fixed selling price established by the maker.

Albert Krell, born at Gelbra, Germany, on September 10, 1833, came to America in 1848 and settled at Cincinnati in 1849. Coming from a family of musical-instrument makers, he was an expert violin builder, and started in business at the age of 16, renting a small shop in the rear of a drug store. He established a reputation as a repairer of old violins, and built altogether about 300 new instruments, which he sold at prices ranging from $150 to $300 apiece. In 1889 he, in conjunction with his sons, Albert and Alexander, who had studied piano making with George Steck,

started a piano factory ˙under the name of the Krell Piano Company. Alexander died in 1895, and Albert Krell, Sr., in 1900.

After his brother's death, Albert, Jr., retired from the company and organized the Krell-French Piano Company of Springfield, Ohio. This concern, after a disastrous fire, moved to New Castle. Albert Krell resigned from this company in 1905 and started the Auto Grand Piano Company of America in Connersville, Ind., making the manufacture of player pianos a specialty.

Among the successful pioneer piano makers of the west Braton S. Chase has made his mark. Tracing his connection with the trade back to 1869 when his father started the Chase Piano Company at Richmond, Ind., Braton acquired a thorough and practical knowledge of the art under his father's tutelage.

In 1889 he formed a connection with C. H. Hackley, the philanthropic lumber king of Muskegon, Mich., and started the Chase-Hackley Piano Company, for which enterprise he soon secured recognition as one of the leading piano producers of the west, fully realizing Hackley's desire to bring fame to the City of Muskegon as the home of the Chase Brothers and Chase-Hackley pianos.

Among the many sturdy and thrifty German emigrants who have done so much in the development of the great middle west,

Mathias Schulz was one of those typical characters whose will-power could not be downed by adversity or obstacles. Born at War- burg, Germany, in 1842, his mother being left a widow at the time of his birth, the child had of necessity to be placed with relatives until he reached the age of 11, when he became entitled to the privileges of the military orphan asylum at Potsdam because of his late father's services as a soldier. At the age of 14 he was apprenticed

Mathias Schulz

to a cabinetmaker. Just as soon as he had served his time he took to " wandern " and started to visit his dear mother. Arriving at his home town, he learned that his mother had been buried two weeks previous. Broken-hearted, he started on his journey again, leaving it to fate where he might land.

Sentimentally inclined, young Schulz felt his lonesomeness in- tensely and resolved to enlist as a soldier, just to get comrades and companionship, to find someone who would take an interest in him and for whom he could care. But, fortunately for him, fate intervened. The day before his physical examination by the mili- tary authorities he broke his shoulder-blade and was not accepted. With no prospect for a military career, he longed to go to America, and started for London, where he expected to earn enough money to pay his passage to New York. He found work in a piano factory

Otto Schulz

and learned the art as it had then been developed. After a two years' stay in London he sailed for New York in 1868 and made his home in Chicago. The piano industry being then in its infancy in America, Schulz returned to cabinetmaking and, in partnership with two colleagues, started a shop at Chicago in 1869. In 1876 Schulz bought out his partners. With remarkable energy he overcame all the difficulties which beset a young manufacturer who lacks experience as well as capital, and his superior craftsmanship, extraordinary capacity for work, together with his inborn honesty and integrity, soon brought prosperity and his business grew steadily. In 1889 it had assumed such large proportions that it was incorporated under the name of M. Schulz Company, with his son, Otto Schulz, as vice-president. The manufacturing of organs and pianos was now made a specialty.

Like many pioneers, Schulz had overtaxed himself in the attempt to satisfy ambition and passed away in 1899 at the age of 57.

His son, Otto Schulz, succeeded him as president. Under his aggressive leadership the company has forced its way to the front rank of large producers in the piano industry. The business started by the German orphan boy has grown to imposing proportions, with splendid prospects for future development.

Born in Suavia about 60 years ago, John V. Steger inherited all the characteristics peculiar to the scions of the Bajuvarian tribe. Energetic, shrewd and tenacious, they are known to make their way, irrespective of surroundings or conditions.

At the age of 17 Steger landed at Chicago and found employment in a brass foundry. Having accumulated a small capital, he formed a partnership with a piano tuner and opened a piano store. It was but a short time after, when Steger became sole owner of the business, in which he prospered beyond his fondest dreams.

Observing how other piano dealers had drifted into piano manufacturing with great success, Steger bought out a small concern which owned a factory near Chicago, and following the example set by J. P. Hale, commenced to manufacture a commercial piano for the wholesale trade. Satisfied with a comparatively small margin he soon created a large demand for his product. Around the permanently increasing factory buildings in the prairie, the town of Steger grew up. Ambitious to be counted among the leaders of the industry, he made use of every opportunity to enlarge his business. A shrewd financier and one of the boldest manipulators in the piano trade, Steger accumulated great wealth in a comparatively short period and is at present counted among the

Julius Bauer

largest producers of pianos in the west.

Among the pioneers of the western piano trade, Julius Bauer & Company have always maintained a reputation for producing a high-grade piano of merit. Founded in 1857 by Julius Bauer, the business, since the death of the founder in 1884, has been under the able management of his son, William M. Bauer.

History is made for the west by such names as Chickering Brothers, Bush & Lane, George P. Bent, Newman Brothers, the Melville Clark Piano Company, Schumann Piano Company, Gram-Richtsteig, Grinnell Brothers, the Farrand Company—famous for the manufacture of high-grade instruments.

The fact that Chicago has, during the past decade, become the greatest piano market in the world is largely due to the energy and enterprise of firms like Smith, Barnes & Strohber Company, Price & Teeple, Hobart M. Cable Company, Schaeffer Piano Mfg. Company, Cable-Nelson Piano Company, Adam Schaaf, Schiller Piano Company, the Haddorff Piano Company, the Straube Piano Company, P. A. Starck Company, Arthur P. King, H. P. Nelson Company, and others, who manufacture pianos in quantities of from 3,000 to 15,000 per year in their modern establishments. It is claimed that the large western factories are at present able to give the greatest value in the market, which accounts to some extent for the unprecedented growth. Although scarcely 25 years old, the western factories supply to-day fully half the pianos sold in the United States.

All the pioneers in the organ trade of the United States have eventually turned to piano making, in most instances discarding the organ altogether.

Farming in New Hamp-

shire has ever been a most precarious occupation, the rocky soil and long winters seldom enabling even a hard-working and intelligent farmer to support his family. Jacob Estey was born on such a farm near Hinsdale, N. H., on September 30, 1814. When only four years of age he had to leave his parents' home to be supported by a neighboring farmer. The boy had to work very hard for his meals and scant clothing, but, being made of the right stuff, he ran away when 13 years of age and escaped to Worcester, Mass., where he was apprenticed to a plumber. After serving his apprenticeship he took to traveling, following his profession, and landed in 1834 at Brattleboro, Vt., the town which was to become famous all over the world because of the organs which Estey, later on, made there and sent to all parts of the globe.

In 1835 he established his own plumbing shop. Thrift and economy brought him wealth, so that in 1848 he could erect a large building on Main Street. The upper part of this building he rented to a melodeon maker by the name of Greene. Having surplus money to invest, Estey bought an interest in the melodeon business, continuing, however, his profitable plumbing establishment. Fire destroyed the building in 1857, and Estey found himself almost a poor man once more, as all his money had finally been invested in the melodeon factory. With the grit of the Yankee, Estey did not give up. He had observed the possibilities of the organ business, and within a year he started again to build parlor organs.

In 1860 he engaged Levi K. Fuller as engineer. Fuller was then only 19 years of age, but had studied mechanics so thoroughly that he became most valuable to Estey. The business grew by leaps and bounds. Superior quality was the watchword all through the factory. Fuller was admitted to partnership together with Estey's son Julius in 1866, when the Estey Organ Company was organized with Jacob Estey as president, Levi K. Fuller, vice-president, and Julius Estey, secretary and treasurer. From its small beginning the production of the Estey factories rose to an output of 1,800 organs per month. The Estey factory became the alma mater of a number of young students who later on made names for themselves in the organ world. Joseph Warren, of Clough & Warren; the four Whites, father and sons, of Wilcox & White fame; Stevens, of the Stevens Organ Company; Putnam, of the Putnam Organ Company, Wright, of Mason & Hamlin, and last, but not least, Votey, of the Aeolian Company, are all graduates of the Estey school of organ building. In 1885 the Estey Piano Company was organized, establishing a large factory in New York City. Branch stores had been

established in New York, St.
Louis, Philadelphia, Boston,
Chicago, London (England),
and elsewhere. Wherever
exhibited, the Estey pianos
and organs carried off highest awards for superior construction and workman-
ship.

Jacob Estey was a man
of firm character, molded in
the school of adversity from
his earliest childhood, but,
perhaps because of his own
sufferings, he became a very
sympathetic employer and
enjoyed the respect and love
of his employees. He died
on April 15, 1890.

Levi K. Fuller was a born scientist and did valuable service in
the improvement of the Estey organ. A great reader and student,
he was well versed in acoustics, and his collection of tuning-forks
and acoustic apparatus exhibited at the World's Fair, Chicago, in
1893, was honored with a special award by the judges. Fuller
served as Governor of the State of Vermont, and received numerous other public honors in recognition of his ability. Ambitious
and conscientious to an exalted degree, Fuller would often over-
work himself in a manner which finally caused his untimely demise
on October 10, 1896, at the age of 55.

Julius Estey, like his father, was an enterprising but careful
business man. After the death of his two senior partners, the

Julius Estey

management of the business rested upon him, and with the inborn Estey spirit he sought for new fields in which to expand the business and spread the fame of the name of Estey. He commenced the building of large church organs in 1901, erecting a special factory with the most modern equipment for that purpose. It was not for him to see the full development of this new enterprise. He died on March 7, 1902, aged 57. His sons, Jacob Gray Estey and J. Harry Estey, succeeded him as managers, enjoying the services of their trusted office manager, L. W. Hawley, who has been in the continued service of the Estey Company for over 50 years.

John Boulton Simpson acquired control of the Arion Piano in 1869, and manufactured high grade pianos until 1885, when he formed a combination with the Esteys, by which the name was changed from Arion Piano Company to Estey Piano Company.

A large factory with modern appliances was erected in New York, and the Estey grand and upright pianos soon became a dominant factor in the piano trade. John Boulton Simpson is still president of the company, assisted by Jacob Gray Estey and J. Harry Estey as active business managers, maintaining the prestige of the Estey reputation for high-class products.

Every now and then we hear of a genius, born on the rocky soil of New England, who has music in his soul. Being the exception, this trait, when existing, is usually so forceful that such a man's life will be entirely wrapped up in it, in contra-distinction to his fellow-Yankee, who as a rule is shrewd and practical, but cannot whistle a simple tune correctly. Henry Kirk White was born and raised on a farm near Hartford, Conn. His family dates back to the good old English stock

Henry Kirk White

of the early settlers who landed at Nantasket, Mass., in 1630. Supposed to spend his life on the " home place," Henry thought more of music than of farming. With no opportunity for musical education, his natural ability made him a teacher of singing and leader of choruses at the age of twenty. He learned the art of tuning pianos and organs, and traveled from place to place following that profession, acquiring valuable knowl-edge as to the various constructions of these instruments. In 1845 he began to make musical instruments and two years later manu-factured melodeons at New London. In 1853 he removed his fac-tory to Washington, N. J. The Civil War compelled him to abandon his enterprise and take up his abode at Philadelphia, where he found a rich field as a tuner and repairer of pianos and organs.

James H. White

He established a reputation as an expert tuner, and in 1865 the great Estey Organ Company called him to Brattleboro, Vt., as superintendent of their tuning department. He worked with the Estey Company twelve years, and during that time taught his three sons the art of organ making.

When in 1877 that great captain of industry, H. C. Wilcox of Meriden, made White and his sons a tempting offer to start an organ factory, the family packed up their belongings and moved to Meriden, Conn. The Wilcox & White Organ Company, capitalized at $100,000, was organized, and the White family began to make their imprint on the history of organ and piano building in the United States.

The oldest son, James H. White, born on September 26, 1847, had served for a number of years in the Wanamaker house at Philadelphia, studying commercial usages and merchandising, before he learned organ building at Estey's. It was but natural, therefore, that he should be intrusted with the business management of the new concern. Like his father, born with considerable talent and love for music, we find him as a young man playing the organ in his church at Brattleboro, Vt.

Having acquired a thorough knowledge of the works of the great composers, and being an expert judge of tone and tone quality,

James H. White would ever search for the highest in tone production, and, together with his brothers, supplemented the inventions of his father. The records of the United States Patent Office speak volumes of the valuable contributions which the White family has made to the industry, but his greatest service to the company was the courage and energy which he displayed in times of stress and danger, steering the ship clear of breakers and advancing the prosperity of the con-

Edward H. White

cern in the face of apparent adversity. Strong as his father and brothers were as inventors and technicians, without the artistic and commercial genius of James Henry, the company would hardly have reached that dominant position which it occupies to-day.

Edward H. White, born April 5, 1855, inherited the inventive genius of his father and made his mark, especially by inventing the Angelus piano player, which at once brought that company to the front in the industry of piano-playing mechanism. He died September 16, 1899, at the age of forty-four years.

Howard White, the youngest of the three talented brothers, was born on September 9, 1856. After he had mastered all branches of the art he was intrusted with the management of the large factories, which in the course of time had grown to a huge establish-

Howard White

ment. He applied himself so zealously to his manifold duties that he passed away on December 9, 1897, aged only forty-one years. The founder, Henry Kirk White, died January 13, 1907. James H. White, the only surviving member of the founders, still guides the destiny of the great corporation, which now employs a capital of $450,000.

After the decease of Edward and Howard White, Frank C. White, son of James Henry, was placed in charge of the mechanical department of the factory. He was always of a very decidedly inventive turn of mind, and to him are due many valuable improvements and devices that have made the Angelus world renowned.

As a commercial enterprise the Sterling Company of Derby, Conn., is one of the earliest successes in history. Taking over the assets of what was known as the Birmingham Organ Company in 1871, Charles A. Sterling organized in 1873 the Sterling Organ Company with a capital of $30,000. The manufacturing of pianos was commenced in 1885. Shortly after, J. R. Mason joined the company, acting as secretary and treasurer until 1901, when he was elected to the presidency. A thorough piano-man, with many years of experience in the west, where he was born in 1847, Mason developed the business of the company to its present magnitude, improving the quality of the instruments in every respect, being particularly successful in producing a satisfactory player piano. The company is now counted among the largest producers of pianos, and the capital stock has been increased from $30,000, in 1873, to $1,000,000.

A number of workingmen skilled in the art of organ building, started the Detroit Organ Company on a co-operative plan in 1881.

Chas A Sterling

Like all such Utopian undertakings, the enterprise did not succeed, and in 1883 C. J. Whitney, a prominent music dealer, and E. S. Votey, a practical organ maker, bought the business and incorporated the Whitney Organ Company. In the same year W. R. Farrand joined the corporation, assuming the financial management, the manufacturing being in charge of Votey. In 1887 Whitney retired and the name was changed to the Farrand & Votey Company. Ambitious to extend its business, the company commenced to manufacture church organs in 1888. Consummating an advantageous deal for all the patents of the renowned organ builder, Frank Roosevelt of New York, the company was in a position to build most excellent instruments, and scored a decided success at the Chicago Exposition of 1893, where Guilmant and

J. R. Mason

Clarence Eddy gave memorable concerts upon the immense pipe organ erected by the Farrand & Votey Company.

E. S. Votey displayed his ingenuity as an inventor by devising many improvements in church-organ mechanism, and more especially in his work on piano players. He had such implicit faith in the future of the piano player that he joined the Aeolian Company in 1897, buying the pipe-organ and player-piano departments of the Farrand & Votey Company, and building his first thousand of Pianolas in the Detroit shops. The company's name was now changed to "The Farrand Company," and special attention was given to its own creation, the Cecilian player piano, an instrument of merit and high quality. The company has also put upon the market a metallic piano-player action.

An expert reed-organ builder, Isaac T. Packard interested a number of capitalists to start an organ factory at Fort Wayne, Ind., in 1871. Packard was a fine mechanic and inventor, producing an instrument of superior quality. Under the conservative guidance of S. B. Bond, as president of the company, steady progress was made, the concern depending more upon the superior quality of its product than upon the ordinary business propaganda.

S. B. Bond, born at Lock-
port, N. Y., October 17, 1833,
came with his father's family
as pioneers to Fort Wayne
in 1842.   At the age of 13
young Bond went to work
as porter and assistant clerk
for the State Bank of In-
diana, which at that time was
under the management of
Hugh McCulloch, who later
on acquired fame as Lin-
coln's   Secretary   of   the
Treasury.   In 1874 Bond
was elected president of the
Fort Wayne National Bank.
He remained in the presiden-
tial chair until December,

1904, when he resigned in order to devote his whole time to the
growing business of the Packard Company.

Although identified with banking from boyhood, Bond was in
love with the inspiring atmosphere of the organ and piano factory, which he always preferred to the cold walls of the banking house, though he made his mark in both.   He died July 20,
1907.

His son, Albert S. Bond, entered the service of the Packard
Company as an apprentice at the age of 16, in 1879.   After five
years' experience on the bench, young Albert spent two years
traveling as salesman for the Company and was elected general
manager in 1886.   Under the guidance of his father he soon expanded the business.   Well educated, with distinct artistic inclinations and full of progressive enthusiasm, he added the manufacture

Calvin Whitney

of pianos in 1893. Maintaining the high standard of the Packard name, the pianos were readily accepted by the trade as high-class instruments, and since the successful introduction of the Packard Player Piano the business of the corporation has assumed commanding proportions. The Packard products are valued for musical quality of tone and most exquisite workmanship in all details.

Another concern which has strongly assisted in establishing the reputation for the highest quality of western-made pianos is the A. B. Chase Company of Norwalk, Ohio. Starting in 1875 to manufacture organs, it began the making of pianos in 1885. A. B. Chase died in 1877, when Calvin Whitney assumed the management. Whitney was a strong character, who impressed his personality indelibly upon the enterprise. Born at Townsend, Ohio, on September 25, 1846, he started in business at the age of 19 with a capital of $400, which he had saved from his earnings as a store clerk. A man of lofty ideals, he aimed in whatever he undertook for the highest and purest. With unfaltering faith he conquered all the difficulties which the western pioneer manufacturers had to encounter and had the satisfaction of seeing his company rank in the lead of high-class piano manufacturers. He was among the first to take up the player piano earnestly, and in 1905 produced the Aristano grand player piano. Whitney died on June 6, 1909, having lived a strenuous but very useful life. L. L. Doud has served the company as secretary since its start in 1875, and still fills his position with zeal and ability. W. C. Whitney, son of Calvin, educated in the factory and office of the Chase Company, is preparing himself for greater work in the future, acting at present as vice-president of the company.

Among the pioneers of the music trade in the west, Hampton L. Story's name stands foremost. Born at Cambridge, Vt., June 17, 1835, he showed an inborn talent for music, and his first employment was in a music store at Burlington, Vt., at the princely salary of $50 per month and board. Having saved a small capital from his wages as schoolteacher, he bought out his principal in 1859. Not satisfied to be merely a dealer, he joined a piano maker by name of Powers, manufacturing the Story & Powers piano in 1862. This was perhaps the first piano factory in the State of Vermont.

The business prospered, but the field was too limited for enterprising Story, and when in 1867 Jacob Estey offered him the agency for the Estey organs, in the western states, Story closed out

E. H. Story

his business at Burlington and established himself at Chicago. In 1868 he admitted Isaac N. Camp as partner. The firm of Story & Camp soon became one of the leaders in the piano and organ trade of the west, having stores at Chicago and St. Louis, controlling a large wholesale and retail trade through the entire west.

With his characteristic keenness and foresight, Story observed that the west would eventually manufacture its own musical instruments, and he therefore retired from the firm of Story & Camp and in 1884, with Melville Clark and his son, Edward H. Story, founded the firm of Story & Clark, for the manufacture of reed organs.

Melville Clark was known as an expert reed-organ builder, who had patented many improvements. The business was successful from the start, and in 1888 the Story & Clark Organ Company was incorporated, with E. H. Story, son of the founder, as president, and Melville Clark, vice-president. The foreign trade grew so rapidly that a factory was erected at London, England, in 1892, under the management of Charles H. Wagener, and another in 1893 at Berlin, Germany.

The organs designed and made under the supervision of Melville Clark were of the highest order in quality and tone, and, when in 1895 the making of pianos was commenced, the same high standard was maintained. Melville Clark severed his connection with the company in 1900, to start the Melville Clark Company, and the management has since been in the hands of Edward H. Story. The demand for pianos increased at such a rate that the erection of larger factories became necessary, and in 1901 the company erected its model plants at Grand Haven, Mich. Counted among the largest producers

Melville Clark

of high-grade pianos, the company is its own distributor, controlling a chain of warerooms in the principal cities of the United States.

Melville Clark's name will forever be printed upon the pages of the organ and piano industry as one of the most prolific inventors. Born in Oneida County, New York, he inherited a love for music and became an enthusiastic student. Desirous to learn all about the construction of pianos and organs, he served an apprenticeship as a tuner and took to traveling. Landing finally in California, he started a factory for the production of high-grade organs. The enterprise was a success, but the market for the product was limited, and in 1877 he sold out his interest. After a short stay in Quincy, Ill., we find him in 1880 at Chicago making organs under the firm name of Clark & Rich.

In 1884 he joined H. L. Story under the firm name of Story & Clark. Desirous of devoting himself entirely to the development of the piano-player mechanism, Clark severed his connection with the Story & Clark Piano and Organ Company in 1900, after 16 years of zealous activity, and started the Melville Clark Piano Company with a capital of $500,000, erecting modern factory buildings at De Kalb, Ill. The patent records tell the story of Clark's activity and success in his efforts in that direction. Clark produced his first 88-note cabinet player in January, 1901, and his 88-note interior player piano in 1902, while his first grand player piano was completed in 1904. He had the satisfaction of seeing his self-playing grand piano used in a public concert at New Orleans in December, 1906, under the auspices of L. Grunewald & Company. Among the many improvements in player mechanism for which Clark obtained patents may be mentioned the application of the downward touch of the key and his transposing device, the latter having been adopted by other player-piano makers under Clark's patent.

The career of Frederick Engelhardt, senior partner of Engelhardt & Sons, is interesting. Born in Germany, he came with his parents to New York at the age of 10. Having gone through the public school, he was apprenticed to a cabinetmaker. After serving his apprenticeship, desirous of seeing something of the life of the "Wild West," he enlisted as a cavalryman in the United States Army, and took part in many of the early battles with Indians on the far-western plains, narrowly escaping the massacre of Custer's force by Sitting Bull. After his discharge from the army he entered the employ of the author, and was soon advanced to the position of superintendent of the soundboard department at the Dolgeville, N. Y., factories. He designed and executed the exhibit of that department for the Paris exhibition of 1879, for which the highest award was granted by the jury.

Ambitious to be more than a mere soundboard maker, Engelhardt sought a position in a piano-action factory. He finally found employment with Steinway & Sons, where for seven years he had charge of the action department as fore- man. In January, 1889, he formed a partnership with A. P. Roth, who had acquired a thorough business training in the author's store and general offices in New York, and the firm of Roth & En- gelhardt began business as makers of piano actions. In

1898 the firm placed their first player piano on the market. It was known as the " Peerless " self-playing piano. This was soon followed by the " Harmonist " player piano, and later on by the coin-operated automatic player piano with endless tune sheet.

A. P. Roth retired from the firm on January 1, 1908, and Engel- hardt admitted his sons, Alfred D. and Walter L., to partnership under the firm name of F. Engelhardt & Sons. Still in the prime of life, Engelhardt has seen his enterprise grow from the smallest beginning to one of the largest establishments of its kind, with the prospect that its future is guaranteed by the activity of his sons.

Another firm which graduated from the Steinway school is Wessell, Nickel & Gross, action makers. Otto Wessell, born in

Otto Wessell

Holstein, Germany, in 1845, came to America with his parents in 1847. Graduating from the New York public school, he was apprenticed to a cabinetmaker, and improved upon that by learning the piano trade afterward. While in the employment of Steinway & Sons he advanced to a position of trust and responsibility. In 1875 he started in business, forming a partnership with his colleagues, Nickel and Gross, who were also employed as action makers by Steinway & Sons. Because of their practical experience in producing the highest class of work, the business was a success from the start and the firm has ever since maintained the leading position for quality.

Otto Wessell was a self-made man. With few opportunities in his youth, he achieved his prominent position in the business world by force of character, unimpeachable integrity and that peculiar *noblesse* and liberality which is usually acquired only by those who have to commence at the bottom rung of the ladder. The writer often met Otto Wessell, in his early days, at piano factories loaded with two upright actions, which he had carried from his shop, partly to save the expense of hiring an expressman, but also to see whether his customer was satisfied, and a broad smile would run over his genial face when the actions were accepted without criticism.

From those small beginnings Wessell saw his firm rise to prominence second to none in America, employing over 500 hands and counting among his customers the foremost makers of high-class pianos. An indefatigable worker, Wessell, like others of his kind, drew too rapidly on nature's bounty and passed away on May 25, 1899, at the age of 54. The business is con-

John Frederick Schmidt

tinued by his partner, Adam Nickel, with Henry Nickel, Jr., and Arthur and Fernando Wessell, sons of the founder, as junior partners.

Among the old-time hammer coverers, John Frederick Schmidt stood in the front rank during the period of his activity. Born at Marburg, Germany, in 1823, he learned the trade of cabinet-making. He went in partnership with Peter De Witt Lydecker in 1864, succeeding Ole Syverson, who had founded the business in 1856. In 1877 Lydecker retired, and Schmidt continued until 1886, when ill health compelled him to seek the quietude of private life. His firm has ever enjoyed an enviable reputation for excellent workmanship in hammer making. He died on September 26, 1906. His son, David H. Schmidt, is carrying on the business as a corporation with marked ability and success.

Charles Pfriemer

Charles Pfriemer is another Steinway graduate who made his mark.

Born in 1842, under the shadow of the romantic old castle Hohenzollern, where the forefathers of the Emperor of Germany dwelt, Pfriemer performed his duty as a soldier during the Austro-Prussian War and came to America in the latter part of 1866.

A cabinetmaker by trade, he learned hammer making in Steinway's shop, and later on assumed charge of the hammer department in Albert Weber's factory. In 1874 he started in business on his own account, and was among the first to use iron hammer-covering machines. Achieving an enviable reputation for making a peculiarly pear-shaped hammer, Pfriemer built up a large and lucrative business. He died in 1908. The business is carried on by his two sons.

PART FOUR

Influence of Piano Virtuosos upon the Industry

CHAPTER I

Bach, Mozart, Chopin, Liszt, Rubinstein, Bülow, Joseffy, Rosenthal, Carreno, de Pachmann, Busoni, Paderewski, Hofmann.

PART FOUR

CHAPTER I

INFLUENCE OF PIANO VIRTUOSOS UPON THE INDUSTRY

THE great virtuosos and teachers of the piano have ever been valuable helpmates of the piano maker. He receives his inspirations from their playing on the one hand, and is continually spurred to greater efforts by their never-ceasing demands for a perfect action, greater and purer tone.

In contrast to the violin, which was almost perfect from its first appearance, the piano required more than 200 years for develop-

Johann Sebastian Bach

ment, and the last word has not yet been said. Handel, Haydn, and even Mozart, with their sweet, heavenly music, could

Wolfgang Amadeus Mozart

be satisfied with the clavichord and harpsichord. In their days music was the entertainment of the privileged higher classes, who assembled in salons to play chamber music of a pleasing and enchanting, but not soul-stirring, character. Johann Sebastian Bach, that titan of the organ, felt the need of something stronger, more positive and powerful than the clavichord, and it was he who aroused Silbermann to greater efforts in piano building, when he condemned his first pianos in unmeasured terms.

Bach must have had a divine inspiration as to the ultimate development of the piano when he wrote his immortal compositions for that instrument, which was then in its infancy. It is questionable whether Silbermann, the organ builder, would have striven to improve his piano but for Bach's criticism, which hurt the feelings of the proud and sensitive artisan and made him resolve to construct a piano which would compel Bach's favorable comment and approval. And it was the great cantor of the Thomas School of Leipsic who gave the first testimonial to a piano maker, when he played upon and praised the improved Silbermann pianos at the New Palace at Potsdam in the presence of Frederick the Great.

Old Gewandhaus, Leipsic

Old Gewandhaus Saal, Leipsic

Bach's son, Johann Christian Bach, did not hesitate to serve as demonstrator of the piano, with the avowed purpose of making propaganda for the piano as a musical instrument. He went to London, taking several German pianos along, and there gave a number of piano recitals. His first concert in June, 1763, was a revelation to the music lovers of London. Never before had they listened to such brilliant playing, nor had they heard such tones, so much more forceful than

Ludwig von Beethoven

the clavichord and equally more musical than the harpsichord tone. Bach aroused the London harpsichord makers to the study of the new instrument.

Then came young Wolfgang Amadeus Mozart, who discarded the clavichord and was most happy to discover at Augsburg the Stein piano with an action which " did not block." He wrote to his mother an enthusiastic testimonial for the Stein piano, praising Stein as an artisan who did not build pianos to make money, but for the love of his art. Stein always tried to meet Mozart's demands, and finally presented to Beethoven a grand piano of six octaves and for years it served the master for his composing. But Beethoven wanted still more. Six octaves were too small a compass for the symphonic tone pictures which raved in his soul,

Frederic Chopin

and his admiring friend Nannette Stein-Streicher, had to build for him a six and one-half octave grand piano.

We of the present day, used to iron-frame construction, the aid of machinery, etc., can scarcely conceive what difficulties that ingenious woman piano builder encountered when she attempted to meet Beethoven's desire for extended compass and greater tone, but she succeeded, and Beethoven wrote many letters to her, every one of them a grand testimonial for the Nannette Stein-Streicher piano.

Like Bach, Beethoven was powerful, titanic. He admired the strong, the mighty, the forceful, and when John Broadwood sent him one of his improved grand pianos from far-away London, Beethoven, in spite of his sincere friendship for Nannette, wrote to London regarding the piano, '' I shall regard it as an altar upon which I shall place the most beautiful offerings of my spirit to the divine Apollo.''

Chopin, that most poetic of all composers, and, in his day, boldest of all performers, allowed his admiration for the Pleyel piano and his personal friendship for the maker to control him to such an extent that he would not play on any other piano if he could obtain a Pleyel.

New Gewandhaus, Leipsic

New Gewandhaus Saal, Leipsic

Franz Liszt in his early days was a "holy terror" for piano manufacturers. His colossal technique and powerful stroke demanded an action of superlative construction and workmanship. It is said that at his first concert at the Leipsic Gewandhaus in 1840, being in an ugly mood because he could not have his favorite French piano to play upon, he smashed a number of hammers off the action with his very first chords, so that another piano had to be provided.

Franz Liszt

Perhaps no other virtuoso has forced the piano makers so persistently to never-ceasing efforts to improve the strength and pliability of the action as Liszt, who almost invariably required two grand pianos for an evening concert. His forceful touch and rapid execution, after one hour's playing, would put most of the pianos made in that early period out of tune, hence we can understand later on, when the iron-frame construction and the modern action came into universal use, why Liszt did not spare his approving testimonials for the creations of Steinway, Bösendorfer, Ibach and others. All of the master builders aimed to construct grand pianos which would meet the taxing demands of Liszt so that they could obtain his testimonial, the highest possible indorsement of piano quality.

Anton Rubinstein

Next to Liszt, Anton Rubinstein will perhaps be recorded as the greatest piano virtuoso—Rubinstein's art developed with the piano. In 1840, as a boy of 10, he played on the delicate pianos then made in Paris, but later on Becker as well as Schröder, of St. Petersburg, built for him modern grand pianos, playing which he could allow his genius free rein, fearless of consequences to the piano.

Whoever has heard Rubinstein, while he was in his prime, knows that he surpassed even Liszt in forceful attacks on the piano, and, next to Liszt, Rubinstein has made greater propaganda for the piano than any other virtuoso. His testimonials were sought for, and he gave them freely and willingly to the many makers of meritorious grand pianos.

That scholarly genius, Hans von Bülow, was hard to please in his choice of pianos. Not of that storming temperament of a Liszt or Rubinstein, Bülow rather discouraged great volume of tone, demanding a sensuous mellowness, which he could at will, if necessary, raise to thundering chords by that wonderful control which he had over his technique. How adverse Bülow was to being considered a demonstrator of piano quality is illustrated by an incident which happened on his American journey in 1875 and

Steinway Hall, New York

Chickering Hall, New York

1876. As is the custom in all American concerts, a large sign, bearing the name of the maker of the piano, was placed on the side of the piano toward the audience. When Bülow came out on the platform he noticed the sign, and, in a rage, tore it from the piano, threw it onto the floor and, tramping upon it, cried loudly to the audience, " I am not an advertising agent," after which he sat down and played as inspiringly as ever, and finally gave the

Hans von Bülow

piano maker a strong testimonial, praising the superior qualities of the piano.

Who has not listened to Rafael Joseffy's wonderful pianissimo passages and wondered how the same piano upon which Liszt and Rubinstein had thundered could sing like music from heavenly spheres under Joseffy's wonderful touch. To satisfy Joseffy's demands for elasticity of touch and pure tone quality is a master's task, yet we find that a great many piano builders proudly point to Joseffy's indorsement.

Josef Hofmann, who astonished the world as a " wonder child " and now, in his manhood, is considered the reincarnation of Liszt and Rubinstein combined, is not only a great pianist and musician but also a genius as a mechanician, capable of appreciating the difficulties confronting the piano maker in his efforts to satisfy the virtuoso's demands, and therefore does not hesitate to express his

Rafael Joseffy

satisfaction with the piano he plays upon.

Moriz Rosenthal is another of the virtuosos who demands much of the piano maker. Sensitive to an extraordinary degree, Rosenthal insists upon an evenness of scale, singing quality, but also powerful tone, in order to exhibit his masterly control of phrasing, which makes his rendering of Liszt's Don Juan paraphrase so captivating.

And what of the dreaming Paderewski, the lyric de Pachmann, the versatile Busoni, or captivating Carreno? Do they not call for extraordinary display of genius on the part of the piano makers, and are our present-day master builders not equal to their demands? The many testimonials, clothed in phraseology which does not permit of doubt or misinterpretation, prove that they do satisfy all the demands made upon them, and thus the influence of these exacting virtuosos becomes of immeasurable benefit to the industry of the day, as it has been from the beginning.

Many virtuosos, like Clementi, Cramer, Kalkbrenner, Pleyel, Herz and others, took such intense interest in the development of the piano that they invested their money earned on the concert platform in piano factories and took an active part, trying to construct such instruments as they desired for their art. Many an improvement can be traced to these virtuoso-piano makers, notably the Herz-Erard grand piano action.

The erection of concert halls by piano manufacturers is entirely due to the influence of the virtuosos. Very few cities had concert halls possessing the necessary acoustic qualifications for piano recitals, consequently Broadwood built his recital hall in London; at Paris the Salles Erard, Pleyel and Herz appeared; in New York, Steinway,

Moriz Rosenthal

Chickering and Steck halls were erected; Vienna has its Saal Bösendorfer and the Saal Ehrbar, and in Berlin we find the Saal Blüthner—all of them built for the purpose of permitting the player's virtuosity and the piano's tonal qualities to be heard under most favorable conditions.

PART FOUR

CHAPTER II

Value of Testimonials

PART FOUR

CHAPTER II

VALUE OF TESTIMONIALS

THE impression prevails, more or less, that testimonials of artists are bought by the piano manufacturers, a misapprehension equally unjust to the artist and the piano maker. No virtuoso who is accepted by the music-loving public as an artist will give a testimonial praising the quality of any piano unless he has thoroughly satisfied himself by a severe test that it meets his most exacting requirements.

De Pachmann

When Franz Liszt, who admired the Erard, wrote to Bösendorfer, "The perfection of your grand piano surpasses my most idealistic expectations,"

Teresa Carreno

and then wrote to Steinway, "Your grand piano is a glorious masterpiece in power, sonority, singing quality and perfect harmonic effects," he used forcible language to express his conviction.

Rubinstein is on record for unstinted praise of the Ehrbar, Pleyel, Blüthner and many other pianos. After using the Steinway in 215 consecutive concerts " with eminent satisfaction and effect," he so stated. Rafael Joseffy used the Bösendorfer, Blüthner, Erard and Chickering pianos and expressed his admiration for all of them because they merited such, and now plays the Steinway. De Pachmann dreams his Chopin interpretations upon all celebrated pianos and goes into ecstasies over the Baldwin. Exacting Bülow, averse to anything smacking of advertising, gave tone and character to the opening of the Saal Bösendorfer at Vienna and of Chickering Hall in New York, but did not overlook the merits of the Irmler nor the Broadwood and many others. Teresa Carreno finds great pleasure in playing the Blüthner, Schiedmayer, Weber and Steinway, and indorses the Everett as " a distinct achievement in piano construction." Ossip Gabrilowitsch admires Becker, lauds the power and brilliancy of the Everett and praises " the phenomenal carrying and singing quality " of the Mason & Hamlin. Moriz Rosenthal is " enchanted " with

Salle Erard, Paris

Salle Pleyel, Paris

Bösendorfer, uses the Steinway with great satisfaction
and considers the Weber
" sublime." Sofie Menter
plays the Erard, describes
the volume of tone in the
Steinway as " tremendous,"
and tells Bösendorfer that
" nothing gives her greater
pleasure than to play on his
pianos." Paderewski made
his reputation with the Steinway, and has words of praise
for the Erard and Weber.
Josef Hofmann, who played
the Weber on his first American tour and the Schröder

I. J. Paderewski

while studying with Rubinstein, says, " I use the Steinway because
I know it is the best."

And so forth *ad infinitum!* All of which goes to prove that the
leaders in the piano industry keep abreast of the times and know
how to build pianos to satisfy the great exponents of the art of
piano playing. Why should a piano virtuoso confine himself to
one make of piano? The violin virtuoso plays on a Stradivarius,
Amati, Guarnerius, a Vuillaume, Bausch or Gemünder—all of them
master builders.

It is true that in some instances, and especially in America, the
piano maker has to assume the rôle of financial backer of a piano
virtuoso's concert journey, because the artist must have a guar-
antee, but that does not involve dishonest public expression of
opinion regarding the value of the piano used by the virtuoso. If

Josef Hofmann

the piano is not of the highest order, the artist cannot afford to use it, no matter what financial consideration might be offered, because, if he should use a poor piano in his concerts, his own reputation as a performer might be ruined.

Since the piano manufacturer craves the indorsement of leading performers, he naturally is exceedingly liberal in his treatment of artists. He willingly assumes all the risks of a concert journey, sends his pianos for the use of the artist wherever he may require them and is solicitous for the artist's personal comfort, just as Nannette Stein-Streicher cared for Beethoven 170 years ago. Modern piano makers go beyond that. They assume all the risk, willingly granting to the artist all possible benefits. It is of record that not many years ago a piano house made a contract with a pianist, guaranteeing him $30,000 for a season's concert journey, no matter what the proceeds might be. It was a gamble, because the artist was entirely unknown in America. The guaranteed sum was more than the artist had earned in his entire career, and he was, of course, elated over his good fortune. Then, how surprised was he when, at the end of his journey, the piano maker handed him his check for an additional $15,000, because the concerts had drawn full houses, for which fact the in-

Saal Blüthner, Berlin

Saal Bösendorfer, Vienna

telligent and bold advertising of the piano house, to a large extent, deserved the credit. The artist's name, fame and fortune were made in his first American season.

The virtuoso who plays the piano is the expert, capable of rendering judgment as to quality and volume of tone, touch, etc. His favorable testimonial is desirable and becomes valuable through its influence upon the piano-buying public. The fact that every virtuoso willingly gives his indorsement to many pianos, all of which he has tested in his concert work, does not detract from the value of the testimonial. On the contrary, it enhances the same, to the interest of the industry. The value of artists' testimonials has ever been an incentive to progressive piano makers to improve their instruments so that the greatest virtuoso cannot well refuse to play upon them.

PART FIVE

CHAPTER I

National Associations of Manufacturers and Dealers in Europe and America.

PART FIVE

CHAPTER I

NATIONAL ASSOCIATIONS OF MANUFACTURERS AND DEALERS

WHEN, through the advance of the factory system, the guilds of the various trades disappeared, no other organization took their place for a long time, and, instead of the old-time harmony of the members of an industry, the rivalry became so intense that competitors in business looked upon each other as enemies. Once in a while a strike on the part of the workingmen would bring the bosses together for a consultation, but even those meetings usually lacked harmony. However, the evident solidarity of interests finally forced a closer connection and we learn of the organization of the " Chambre Syndicale of Manufacturers of Pianos " and the " Chambre Syndicale of Manufacturers of Musical Instruments," of Paris in 1853. Both chambers were merged into one organization in 1889 under the name of " Chambre Syndicale of Manufacturers of Musical Instruments." This organization was presided over by Mons. Thibouville-Lamy until 1896, since which time Mons. Gustave Lyon of Pleyel, Lyon & Company has been acting as president.

The object and purpose of this association is defined in its constitution as follows:

Gustave Lyon

(1) To strengthen the relations between all the members of the industry.

(2) To facilitate the development of their prosperity.

(3) To support all claims and requests regarding duties, taxes, railroad and insurance rates, etc.

(4) To furnish members information regarding the financial standing of clients, and finally to maintain loyalty and dignity in their commercial relations. The annual dues are 20 francs for each member. No foreign manufacturer can belong to the chamber until he has been established in France 10 years and the majority of his products are manufactured in France. The officers are: a president, two vice-presidents, a secretary-general, a keeper of records, a treasurer and an assistant secretary. The election of officers is held annually. The organization is divided into five groups, as follows:

(1) Piano Industry (pianos and organs).

(2) Wind Instruments (wood and brass).

(3) String Instruments (violins, etc.).

(4) Supplies.

(5) Automatic Instruments.

Each group has its own organization, with a president and secretary.

In case of differences among members, with each other or with outsiders in connection with the industry, the president appoints a committee of arbitration, whose members shall act as friendly advisers to the disputing parties. All decisions of the chamber are subject to the vote of the majority. Every member must pay special dues of 12 francs annually to meet extraordinary expenses and strengthen the treasury.

Adolf Schiedmayer

Austria has no national organization of the music trades, but a number of local associations, of which the " Association of Musical Instrument Makers of Grasslitz " is the oldest. It was founded in 1883, has over 300 members and supports a school in which young men are taught the technical and practical making of instruments.

The Vienna piano and organ makers formed an association in 1905. Its aims and purposes are similar to those of the " Paris Chambre Syndicale." Franz Schmidt is acting president and Friedrich Ehrbar, one of the directors. Ludwig Bösendorfer is the only honorary member of the body.

Germany has a large number of associations for the various branches of the music industries. The " Association of Piano Manufacturers " was organized at Leipsic in 1893 with Adolf

Carl André

Schiedmayer as president. The " Church Organ Builders " followed in 1895, " Musical Instrument Makers " in 1897 and the " Piano Dealers " in 1899. The " National Association of Piano Manufacturers " pursues the same objects as its Paris contemporary, but in addition thereto has entered upon an effective policy of practical aid to its members. It is, for instance, compulsory for each manufacturer to educate a number of apprentices proportionate to the number of men employed in his factory. The energetic president of the association, Privy Commercial Counselor Adolf Schiedmayer of Stuttgart, is organizing a trade school for piano makers in that city, to assure the education of young men in the scientific theories and practice of piano building. This is the first institution of its kind, and when fully established will be of great service to the industry at large. The school is mainly supported by contributions from members of the associations and enjoys the protection and aid of the royal government of Wurtemburg.

The " National Association of Piano Dealers," with headquarters at Leipsic, has, from its inception, under the able leadership of President Carl André of Frankfort, a./M., inaugurated and carried on a most energetic campaign against fraudulent advertising, sham sales and all dishonest or disreputable methods prevalent in the piano trade, with excellent results. The association has 344 active members and maintains a bureau of information, publishing periodically confidential circulars containing records of objectionable people dealing in pianos and other trade notices.

In October, 1908, the various organizations formed the " National Association of Musical Instrument Industries," without, however, disturbing the existing organizations. This national association has its headquarters at Leipsic and is subdivided territorially into three sections, with bureaus at Leipsic, Berlin and Stuttgart. The management is in the hands of a president, Adolf Schiedmayer of Stuttgart; a vice-president and treasurer, Hermann Feurich of Leipsic, and a vice-president and secretary, Max Blüthner of Leipsic. The main purpose of this association is to represent the entire industries as a body in matters of tariff laws, transportation, factory regulations, etc., seeking to harmonize the needs and wants of the various special organizations of the German Empire.

The " Music Trade Association of Great Britain " was organized in March, 1886, with Sir Herbert Marshall as president. The principal object of this association is " to extend a watchful regard over all matters affecting the retail trade and to give timely information to the members," and, further, " to hold conferences for the interchange of views on questions of general trade interest, and generally to co-operate and take such combined action in defense of the just interests of the retail trade as may be found needful."

The " Pianoforte Manufacturers' Association " of London, founded in 1887—George D. Rose, president—has as its object: " To promote and protect the various interests of the music trade generally, to promote and support or oppose legislative or other measures affecting the aforesaid interests; to secure the more economical and effectual winding up of the estates of bankrupts or insolvent debtors; to endeavor to secure prosecution of fraudulent debtors, and to undertake, if requested by both parties, settlement by arbitration.''

In the United States the piano manufacturers of New York organized the first association in the fall of 1890. William E. Wheelock was elected first president and served until 1893. Later on a number of local associations of piano manufacturers and dealers were organized who combined in August, 1897, to form the '' National Piano Manufacturers' Association of America.'' Its object is the furtherance of:

(1) A better acquaintance among the members of the trade, good-fellowship and interchange of views on topics of mutual concern.

(2) The ethics of the piano trade.

(3) Territorial rights of manufacturers and dealers in regard to selling pianos.

(4) A uniform warranty.

(5) The products of supply houses: i.e., the question of stamping the manufacturer's name upon piano parts furnished by the supply houses to the trade.

(6) The relation of the manufacturers to the music-trade press.

(7 and 8) To obtain reductions in insurance and transportation rates.

(9) The establishment of a bureau of credits.

(10) Legislation by united action; that more uniform laws shall be enacted in several States regarding conditional sales, and such other matters of importance to the piano trade as may come up from time to time.

Presidents of the National Association of Piano Manufacturers of America from
1897 to 1911

Presidents of the National Association of Piano Dealers of America from 1902 to 1911

The association is governed by a president, two vice-presidents, a treasurer, secretary and assistant secretary. Contrary to the European system, where officers, once elected, are regularly re-elected as long as they are able to attend to their duties with efficiency, this association changes its governing board (with the exception of the assistant secretary) annually.

The " National Association of Piano Dealers of America " was organized in May, 1902. Its object is tersely stated in its constitution, as follows:

" The object of this association shall be the mutual elevation of trade interests." Its by-laws provide for the following board: a president, four vice-presidents, a commissioner for each State and Territory (to be known as state commissioners), a secretary, a treasurer, and an executive board consisting of the president, secretary, treasurer and four members of the association. The officers are elected at the annual meeting and usually a new set is chosen each year. The membership is divided into active and associate members. The latter class takes in any one engaged in any branch of the musical industry not otherwise eligible. The annual dues are $10 for active and $5 for associate members. The association has a membership of over 1,000, and has done very effective work in guarding the ethics of the piano trade, and is making strenuous efforts for the general introduction of the one-price system.

National piano exhibitions have lately been held in connection with the annual dealers' conventions, apparently to the benefit of both dealers and manufacturers.

PART FIVE

CHAPTER II

The Trade Press—Its Value to the Industry.

PART FIVE

CHAPTER II

THE TRADE PRESS—ITS VALUE TO THE INDUSTRY

IN America the piano-trade press evolved slowly and, after many interruptions from so-called musical journals, the first of which, the " American Musical Journal," was founded in 1835. It carried some advertisements of piano manufacturers and would publish, off and on, items which at that time were considered trade news.

In 1843 Henry C. Watson established his " Musical Chronicle " in New York. Watson was a most remarkable man, equally gifted and learned as a musician as he was as a writer, and withal a man of business. He saw the necessity of enlisting the active support of the piano manufacturers for his journal and endeavored honestly to render value for such support. Thus Watson became the founder of piano-trade journalism. It is to be regretted that space does not permit a complete record of the brilliant career of this interesting character.

Born in London on November 4, 1818, he appeared at Covent Garden in " Oberon " at the age of nine, singing the part of a " fairy." In 1841 he came to New York, welcomed by such men as William Cullen Bryant, Horace Greeley and others of like standing. He was immediately engaged as a musical critic for the " New World," then edited by Greeley. Besides his duties as a critic and also writing lyrics and composing songs, Watson man-

Henry C. Watson

aged to publish the " Broadway Journal," enlisting Edgar Allan Poe as editor. He found, however, his real field of usefulness in his " Musical Chronicle," in which he interested Jonas Chickering as well as the leaders among the New York piano manufacturers. He had discovered that the interests of musical art and the interests of the piano industry were interdependent and that the one must support the other for mutual benefit. He, therefore, devoted considerable energy to the propaganda of the piano. In course of time he changed the title of his publication to " Musical Times," " Philharmonic Journal " and finally to " The American Art Journal." He was one of the founders of the Philharmonic Society and also organized the Mendelssohn Union of New York.

As musical critic of the " New York Tribune " and editor-in-chief of " Frank Leslie's Illustrated Newspaper," Watson was for many years one of the pillars of musical life in America. He died on December 4, 1875, at the age of 57. " The American Art Journal " was continued by Watson's pupil, William M. Thoms, until his retirement in 1906.

The " Music Trade Review," founded in November, 1875, by John C. Freund, appeared for about two years; it was followed in 1878 by the " Musical Times," which soon changed to " Musical and Dramatic Times." In 1881 Freund started a journal called " Music," which title was changed to " Music and Drama." " Freund's Weekly " appeared in 1884. Soon changed to " Music and Drama." In 1887 Freund joined J. Travis Quigg in publishing the " American Musician," and in 1893 he started, with Milton Weil, " Music Trades."

Charles Avery Wells established the " Music Trade Journal " in 1876, which he changed to the " Musical Critic and Trade Review " in 1879. In January, 1888, Edward Lyman Bill bought an interest in the journal and soon became sole owner. He changed it from a fortnightly to a weekly, under the title of " Music Trades Review," making it the first trade paper published in America devoted exclusively to the music industries. He has also published several valuable treatises on piano construction, in book form, which are enumerated elsewhere.

In 1880 Harry E. Freund began to conduct a journal called " Music and Drama," which title he later changed to " Musical Age."

William E. Nickerson started the " Musical and Dramatic News " in 1877. It went into the hands of the Lockwood Press, who sold the same to Marc A. Blumenberg in 1881, and the name was changed to " Musical Courier." In 1897 Blumenberg separated the musical and industrial departments, publishing the " Musical Courier Extra " strictly as a trade edition.

" The Indicator," established by Orrin L. Fox at Chicago in 1880, devoted to the liberal arts and art industries, was changed into an organ for musical industries exclusively, being the first in the field to make effective propaganda for the piano industry of the west.

" The Presto " was founded at Chicago by Frank A. Abbott in

1883. The " Presto Year Book " is a very valuable, historical compendium of trade events. Abbott associated himself in 1894 with C. A. Daniell, who holds the responsible position as editor-in-chief of the various Presto publications.

The " Chicago Musical Times " was started by William E. Nickerson in 1885, and has been developed to its present commanding position by C. B. Harger, who acquired control in 1895.

George B. Armstrong established his dignified monthly journal, " The Piano Trade," at Chicago in 1903.

In 1910 C. A. Daniell assumed the management of the " Piano Magazine," an illustrated monthly published in New York City. This publication treats mainly of the historical, musical and technical aspects of the piano and allied musical industries in an entertaining manner, thus differing from the trade journals which deal mainly with the news of the day.

The " Zeitschrift für Instrumentenbau " was established by Paul de Wit at Leipsic in 1880 and has a wide circulation all over Europe.

The " Welt-Adressbuch " of musical industries, compiled and published by Paul de Wit, is a most valuable reference book. It contains the names of all the firms connected in any way with musical industries in all parts of the world.

The " Musik Instrumenten-Zeitung," published in Berlin, was started in 1890.

In England the " London and Provincial Music Trades Review " was established in London in 1877; " Musical Opinion and Music Trade Review," also a monthly publication, often contains valuable contributions of interest to the piano trade. " The Piano Journal " is a monthly devoted entirely to the interests of piano makers and dealers. The monthly journal, " Music," also makes reference to trade topics.

The Importance and Value of the Trade Press to the Piano Industry

As the government of a nation is only the reflex of the individuals composing the nation, so is the trade press the reflex of the individuals composing an industry. The character of a trade press is stamped upon it by its patrons. The earlier piano-trade papers, after Watson's time, allowed themselves to be used by a group of firms, from which they received liberal financial support. This tended to demoralization, and the cry of blackmail was heard. The papers depending on this one-sided support had a precarious existence, and had to go to the wall whenever the extra subsidy was withheld. Questionable methods were resorted to, off and on, to compel more liberal financial support from the piano makers.

The conditions existing in the piano trade some 30 years ago were such as really to infect part of the trade press with the bacillus of coercion. But, after all, the papers which did pursue a policy of coercion became unconsciously " ein theil von jener kraft, die böses will und gutes schafft." Repeated failures of the most aggressive papers of that character proved the error of playing champion for one or more firms, and the various later publications started out with the pronounced policy of aiding the entire industry and injuring none. Success followed this policy, and the piano trade of to-day has in its trade press a great helpmate which is worthy of the support it enjoys.

It is altogether wrong to consider the support of a clean trade paper as a tax. Every laborer is worthy of his hire, and the more liberally the trade press is supported the better service it can render, a service needed by the trade and obtainable only through a well-organized press.

That music-trade journalism is an honorable profession has

been demonstrated by its founder, Henry C. Watson, who enjoyed the respect and warm friendship of his supporters as well as that of the community at large. The value of an honest and able trade press is almost unmeasurable in the coin of the realm. From year to year the piano-trade press has grown in dignity and usefulness, and, just as soon as the industry itself gets entirely upon the plane of legitimate business methods, whatever may be objectionable in the trade press of to-day will then of necessity die its natural death.

PART FIVE

CHAPTER III

Literature on the Pianoforte

PART FIVE

CHAPTER III

LITERATURE ON THE PIANOFORTE

THE first attempt to write a history of the pianoforte was made in 1830 by M. Fetis, " Sketch of the History of the Pianoforte and the Pianists," a laborious effort by a brilliant writer, but of little value to the piano maker.

Kusting's " Practisches Handbuch der Pianoforte Baukunst," Berne, 1844, is a more practical treatise than Fetis' attempt, but antiquated and only of interest to the historian. The same may be said of the interesting work of Professor Fischhof, " Versuch einer Geschichte des Clavierbaues," Vienna, 1853.

Welcker von Gontershausen published in 1860 " Der Clavierbau in seiner Theorie, Technik und Geschichte," a fourth edition of which was printed in 1870 by Christian Winter, Frankfurt a./M.

As a practical piano maker, fairly well posted on the laws of acoustics and thoroughly acquainted with the characteristics of all known musical instruments, Welcker has given a work of interest and value. It is to be regretted that his extreme patriotism and rather biased opinion do not permit him to do full justice to pianos made in other countries than Germany. Aside from this fault, his book is to be recommended to the studious piano maker as well as the student of musical-instrument lore.

Dr. Ed. F. Rimbault published in 1860, in London, his ambitious work, " The Pianoforte." Written at the time when the English piano industry was at its height, it is pardonable that the author laid his emphasis on English efforts and achievements rather at the expense of the French, German and Austrian schools. It must be assumed that the achievements of the latter were not known to him in their entirety and importance. Especial credit is, however, due to Rimbault for having produced documentary evidence of Christofori's priority as inventor of the pianoforte.

G. F. Sievers of Naples, an able piano maker, published in 1868 his "Il Pianoforte Guida Practica," with a special atlas showing piano actions in natural size and therefore of great value to the piano student.

Dr. Oscar Paul, a professor at the Conservatory of Music in Leipsic, wrote in 1868, "Geschichte des Claviers." The learned professor of music failed to do justice to the title of his book. Entirely unacquainted with the practical art of piano making, he assumes an authority which is amusing to the knowing reader. Like Welckers, Dr. Paul suffers too much from German egotism. All through the book the effort of ascribing all progress in piano construction to his countrymen is painfully palpable, he even going so far as to imply that Christofori had copied Schröter's invention, an effort which demonstrates Paul's ignorance of action construction. However, the book contains sufficient good matter to repay reading it. Published by A. H. Payne, Leipsic.

For the practical piano maker who reads German, the "Lehrbuch des Pianofortebaues," by Julius Blüthner and Heinrich Gretschel, published in 1872 and revised by Robert Hannemann in 1909, Leipsic, Bernh. Friedr. Voigt, offers much valuable information, treating with great care the construction of the piano and the materials, tools and machinery used in the manufacturing of the instrument. It also has a short essay on acoustics written by Dr. Walter Niemann, who furthermore contributes a history of the piano up to the time of the general introduction of the iron frame.

Edgar Brinsmead's " History of the Pianoforte," London, 1889, dwells too much upon the achievements of the firm of Brinsmead & Sons and loses all importance when compared to A. J. Hipkins' " Description and History of the Pianoforte," published by Novello & Company, London, 1896. An earnest scholar and careful writer, Hipkins successfully avoids the many pitfalls of the lexicographers and gives a clear and succinct description of the development of the piano from its earliest stages to the modern concert grand. The book is well worth careful perusal by anyone interested in the piano industry.

Daniel Spillane's " History of the American Pianoforte," New York, 1890, is an interesting compendium showing the development of the piano industry in the new world, with sidelights upon the men who have been most prominent in that sphere.

Edward Quincy Norton, a piano maker of long and manifold experience, wrote his " Construction and Care of the Pianoforte " in 1892. This book, published by Oliver Ditson & Company of Boston, contains valuable suggestions for tuners and repairers, and is still meeting with a ready sale.

The more modern books, " Piano Saving and How to Accomplish It," by Edward Lyman Bill, and " The Piano, or Tuner's Guide," by Spillane, also William B. White's books, " Theory and Practice of Pianoforte Building," " A Technical Treatise on Piano Player Mechanism," " Regulation and Repair of Piano and Player Mechanism, Together with Tuning as Science and Art " and " The Player Pianist," all published by Edward Lyman Bill, New York, have found wide circulation among practical piano makers because of their popular treatment of intricate subjects. All of these books are almost indispensable for a conscientious tuner and repairer.

Among the strictly scientific works, John Tyndall's treatise on " Sound " and Helmholtz' " Sensation of Tone " offer much food

for thought to the student of acoustics, although Helmholtz's originally much-lauded " Tone Wave Theory," as well as his so-called discovery of the " Ear Harp," have been vigorously attacked by Henry A. Mott in his book, " The Fallacy of the Present Theory of Sound " (New York, John Wiley & Sons), and by Siegfried Hansing in " Das Pianoforte in seinen akustischen Anlagen," New York, 1888, revised edition, Schwerin i./M., 1909.

Hansing's work is beyond question the most important, so far written, on the construction of the pianoforte. His studies in the realm of acoustics disclose a most penetrating mind capable of exact logical reasoning. He bases his conclusions on exhaustive studies, without regard to the accepted theories of earlier scientists. As a thoroughly practical piano maker and master of his art, Hansing studied cause and effect in its application to the piano, and his book is a rich mine of information for the prospective piano designer and constructor. Free from any business affiliations, he treats his subject with an impartial and unbiased keenness of perception which is at once impressive and convincing.

Dr. Walter Niemann's " Das Klavierbuch," C. F. Kahnt Nachfolger, Leipsic, is an entertaining little book on the piano, its music, composers and virtuosos, containing many illustrations of rare and valuable pictures of noted artists playing the piano.

Henry Edward Krehbiel's more pretentious and serious work, "The Pianoforte and Its Music," Scribner, New York, 1911, is a valuable work of interest to the student of the piano, the musician and music lover.

Of special interest to the studious piano maker are the catalogues of old instruments collected by Morris Steinert of New Haven and Paul de Wit of Leipsic. "M. Steinert's Collection of Keyed and Stringed Instruments" is the title of a book published by Charles F. Tretbar, Steinway Hall, New York. It contains excellent illustrations of the clavichords, spinets, harpsichords and claviers which Steinert has discovered in his searches covering a period of 40 years. The illustrations are supplemented by a minute description of each instrument. A concise history of the development of the piano and illustrations with explanatory text of Steinert's collection of violins, etc., complete the volume.

In "Reminiscences of Morris Steinert," compiled by Jane Martin, G. P. Putnam's Sons, New York, 1900, Steinert gives interesting and amusing accounts of his experiences hunting old instruments in America and foreign countries. Steinert, a gifted and many-sided musician by profession, became a dealer in musical instruments, especially pianos, and founded the great house of M. Steinert & Sons, with headquarters at Boston and branch stores in leading cities of New England. The firm also controls the Hume and the Jewett piano factories.

The "Katalog des Musikhistorischen Museums von Paul de Wit, Leipsic," published by Paul de Wit, 1904, is the most complete compendium in existence, describing old instruments of all kinds, their origin and makers. Although this catalogue is profusely illustrated, De Wit published in addition a most artistic album, "Perlen aus der Instrumenten Sammlung," von Paul de Wit,

Morris Steinert at the Clavichord

Paul de Wit tuning the Clavichord

Leipsic, 1892. This album contain 16 illustrations printed in colors, each plate a master work of the color-printer's art. For the connoisseur, this album is a desirable and valuable addition to the library.

Paul de Wit has devoted his life to advance the interests of the piano industry. A sketch of his career is, therefore, only an acknowledgment of his valuable services. Born at Maastricht, Holland, on January 4, 1852, de Wit studied the cello under Massart at the conservatory of Luettich and showed decided talent. His parents objected to an artistic career and forced the young man to conduct a wholesale wine business at Aachen. Since the cello had a much more magnetic attraction for him than wine, he did not make a success of the wine business, and sold his interest in 1878. He went to Leipsic and became connected with the music publisher, C. F. Kahnt, where he made the acquaintance of Liszt, von Bülow, Carl Riedel, etc., and also the versatile Oscar Laffert. In partnership with the latter, he started in 1880 '' Die Zeitschrift für Instrumentenbau,'' a dignified journal, devoted to the interests of the music trades of Germany. Laffert retired in 1886, and de Wit became sole proprietor of the publication, which to-day ranks among the most influential of trade journals in Germany and circulates in all civilized countries.

An artist, enthusiast and born collector, de Wit was not satisfied with his success as an editor and publisher, but set to work collecting ancient instruments of all kinds. He started a workshop with Hermann Seyffarth, the well-known repairer of violins and other musical instruments, in charge. Seyffarth rejuvenated the battered relics which de Wit had discovered during his travels, in storehouses, barns, garrets and cellars. De Wit virtually searched the Continent for old instruments, and many valuable discoveries stand to his credit. Whenever he heard that an old spinet, violin, bass drum or flute had been unearthed somewhere, de Wit would take the next train, no matter how great the distance or expense, to satisfy himself whether the relic was worthy of a place in his collection. As a result he assembled three collections, which are unrivaled. His first, containing 450 instruments, was bought in 1889 by the Government of Prussia for the Academy at Berlin. It was supplemented in 1891 by an addition of the grand piano used by Johann Sebastian Bach. His second collection of nearly 1,200 instruments was bought by Wilhelm Heyer of Cologne, who erected a special building to house his gems.

The industry owes to de Wit and Steinert a debt of gratitude for their unselfish labors in bringing to light the works of the old masters. Their efforts to again create a taste for the enchanting tone quality of the clavichord will bear fruit, by inducing the piano constructor of the future to search for a more pronounced combination of the liquid with the powerful tone than we find in the piano of the present.

Notable collections of ancient instruments are also to be found at the South Kensington Museum at London, in the Germanische Museum at Nuremberg, and in the Metropolitan Museum of Art, New York, which latter has a genuine Christofori piano e forte. The most complete of all, however, is the unexcelled collection of Wilhelm Heyer at Cologne.

PART FIVE

CHAPTER IV

Conclusions.

PART FIVE

CHAPTER IV

CONCLUSIONS

ORIGINATING in Italy during the inspiring period of the Renaissance as a strictly art product, a musical instrument whose outer form was designed by architects, decorated and embellished by painters and sculptors, the piano received its first development in strength and fullness of tone under the hands of the Teutonic master builders of Austria and Germany. The latter brought it to England, where the Anglo-Saxon imprint was impressed by the first efforts of manufacturing pianos, calling factory organization and machinery to its aid. This Anglicizing was furthermore marked by the invention of a more forceful action.

After this the piano was taken in hand by Paris builders, who, in harmony with the French taste, took off the rough edges of the English construction and went back to the more dainty Italian design of case, and invented actions which permitted of a more delicate execution. However, the French builders did not quite follow the dynamical assault of the new school of music, which demanded more tone power to fill large concert halls, and America took the field with its full iron frame, enlarged scales and heavy hammers. Germany was first to adopt this innovation from America and again took the lead in Europe.

These various schools can be traced most distinctly from their beginning to the time when they reached the point of highest development and were superseded by another school. Italy reached its height with Christofori in 1720, and has never since been a factor. Germany took hold of Italy's heritage, and the German school prospered from 1720 to about 1800, when England stepped in, wrested the laurels from Germany and developed its mammoth factories from 1800 to about 1860. France in the meantime (1803-1855) became the successful rival of England because of more artistic designs and refined tone qualities. After 1855, however, both England and France were out-classed by America, which has been able to maintain its supremacy ever since. Germany, having more or less rested upon its laurels up to 1855, took the cue from America and after 1860 out-rivaled England and France in the production of pianos.

While no accurate statistics are obtainable, a reasonable estimate of the number of pianos produced in the various countries, based on careful computations made by manufacturers of piano supplies, indicates the following annual production at the present time:

America	350,000
Germany	170,000
England	75,000
France	25,000
Austria and Switzerland	12,000
Russia	10,000
Netherlands and Scandinavia	4,000
Spain	2,500
Italy	1,500
Grand Total	650,000

The piano born in Italy required Teutonic force for development, French taste for refinement, English matter-of-fact industrialism and commercialism for better introduction and finally American enterprise and wealth for general adoption as an indispensable part of home furnishing. The history of the piano shows that in its present-day finality it represents the activity of many minds in the constructive, artistic, industrial and commercial fields. The industry has now reached a point where the genius of the born organizer on modern lines will be next heard from in any further progress. Combinations of large firms are inevitable. Competition forces greater economies in production as well as distribution. America is leading in the new movement, and will adopt it more generally than any of the other nations, because nowhere is a general standardization so crying a necessity as in the United States. The product has to be standardized to bring the business of distribution out of its slough of disreputable tactics and practices. This standardization was the aim of the American trust movements of 1892-99. While these attempts were premature, the correctness of the underlying philosophy has been proven by the subsequent successful amalgamation of large concerns into harmonious entities.

When we search for the cause or reason why the piano industry has been so slow in developing along commercial and industrial lines, in comparison with other leading industries, we find it in the fact that nearly all the founders of successful firms were graduates of the cabinetmaker's work-bench. They were primarily mechanics with a strong inclination to the artistic, both of which qualities are the antithesis of industrialism and commercialism. Their very occupation of designing pianos, inventing improvements, dreaming of tone quality, etc., totally unfitted them for the cold, exact calculation of the economic factory organizer and the liberal distributor of the finished product, not to mention the reasoning of the financier, who never has an eye for anything else but cold figures and algebraic reductions.

We find, therefore, that England, where commercial tactics dominated when the piano appeared there, was the first of the nations to manufacture them in large numbers. The English knew how to sell and how to distribute them after they were made. The astonishing growth in America came when the kings of merchandising in the piano business became manufacturers and supplemented the factory methods, started in England, with the science of wholesale distribution. It must not be overlooked here that the piano industry in all countries, with exception of England, has always suffered as a whole from lack of sufficient working capital. In Germany, France and America capital was never attracted to the piano industry, simply because it lacked a solid foundation and apparently had no stability. In many instances a business of magnitude would die with the death of its founder, because its main asset was the name and the individuality of its owner.

When we analyze the characters of all the leaders in this industry, from its beginning to the present day,—barring a few notable exceptions of latter days,—we find that all were exceptionally strong men who had to fight their way from poverty and misery by sheer will-power, supported by decided talent or genius. Nearly all of them were without early education. They had to pick up whatever they acquired in knowledge in their spare hours, and we must admire these men for their great accomplishments, considering the conditions under which they worked. Even their petty jealousies must be pardoned. If we look back to the days in which they lived, we need not wonder that Pleyel and Broadwood were intimate friends and made front against Erard, nor that Chickering opposed the overstrung system for years because Steinway advocated it. All of these men thought more of their instruments, the children of their brain, than of making profits on broad lines of industrial and commercial development.

Modern organization, to be successful in the piano industry, requires a division of labor and duties, which will enable the constructor to follow his thoughts irrespective of factory, selling, or financial conditions and requirements. Indeed, the managers of each of these departments must be adepts and experts in their particular calling, and must be so situated that they can work out their plans on the basis which their coadjutors furnish from their respective departments. We have now establishments which turn out 30,000 instruments per year under one management. The time is not far off when we shall see organizations whose output will surpass 100,000 pianos per year, and those large organizations will set the pace, will create the standard, which every competitor must follow.

The piano factory of the future has not even been sketched out as yet, but it will come, just as the town of Gary has been built for the steel industry. The laws of evolution are at work in the piano industry as strongly as elsewhere, and the avoidable economic waste, the trifling away of fortunes in the present cumbersome, unscientific way of making pianos and much more so in the kindergarten methods of distributing the products,—methods which often make the cost of selling larger than the cost of production,—must come to an end for the good of everybody connected with the industry. Some of the money saved by such modern methods should be expended for the support of high-grade trade schools, where the art of piano making would be taught, and part of the increased profits coming from the economic savings should go to a labor pension fund, in order to attract to the industry the best class of wage-workers obtainable.

Even when, by proper factory organization, the piano shall come to the level of an every-day commodity, it will, after all, remain an art product; and, since we can form no conception as to its further development, talented young men must be brought into the field to continually inject that vigor and enterprise which is indispensable to progress. Adequate compensation and assurance of a competency for old age are the only means of attracting ability and energy.

The piano industry should be as attractive as any to the young man of to-day. All we lack is proper training schools, which may easily be supplied by donations from the leading manufacturers of each nation. Germany is making an effort in that direction, and England, France and America ought not to delay the foundation of such schools. The day of the apprentice has passed forever. We know how to impart to a properly schooled young man more knowledge of a craft in one year than he could acquire, under the apprentice system, in five years. The university for the physician and lawyer, the college for the farmer, must be supplemented by the college for the craftsman, so that he may perfect himself in his chosen profession after he leaves the manual training school.

While for the past 100 years all the efforts of inventors and piano constructors had but one aim—to augment the tone of the piano—the labors of de Wit, Steinert and Dolmetsch in creating an interest in the clavichords, furthermore the tenacity of the Vienna and French schools in clinging to the more limpid though smaller tone, are arousing the interest of piano constructors to seek for more soulful, expressive tone quality, without, however, curtailing the carrying capacity—a problem, no doubt, very difficult to solve, but, therefore, so much more inviting to the thinking piano maker.

The factory manager, the sales manager and the financial director will have problems continually looming up before them, to solve which a clear understanding of the past history, the present conditions and the trend of events in the near future becomes imperative. If this book shall serve as a guide and inspiration to the younger element in the various branches of our art and craft, it will have fulfilled its intended mission.

APPENDIX

List of Firms Manufacturing Pianos and Supplies at the Present
Time

APPENDIX

APPENDIX

List of Firms Manufacturing Pianos and Supplies at the Present Time

ITALY

PIANO MANUFACTURERS

	Established		
Griffini & Co., R.	Established	—	Milano
Coppi, Federico	"	—	Napoli
Rick, Giuseppe	"	—	"
Lachin, Nicoló	"	1830	Padua
Berzioli, Fratelli	"	1836	Parma
Agmonino, Giacinto	"	1850	Turin
Berra, Ing. Cesare	"	1850	"
Colombo, Federico	"	—	"
Fea, Fratelli	"	1900	"
Fea, Giovanni	"	1880	"
Forneris, Fratelli	"	—	"
Lacchio & Co	"	—	"
Migliano & Borello	"	—	"
Mola, Cav. Giuseppe	"	1862	"
Olivotto, B	"	—	"
Perotti, Cav. Carlo	"	1870	"
Quartero, Vittorio Felice	"	—	"
Roeseler Cav. Carlo	"	—	"
Savi & Co., Rod	"	1905	"

GERMANY

PIANO MANUFACTURERS

	Established		
Hilger, Eduard	Established	—	Aachen
Haegele, Heinrich	"	1846	Aalen
Gebauer, Jr., Gg. Dietr.	"	1819	Alsfeld
Maass, W.	"	1891	Altona
Möller, Ernst	"	1819	"
Dittmer, A.	"	—	Anklam
Neupert, J. C.	"	1868	Bamberg
Ibach Sohn, Rud.	"	1794	Barmen
Lehmann, Arthur	"	1898	
Steingräber & Söhne	"	1852	Bayreuth
Andrä & Co., Robert	"	—	Berlin
Anghöfer's Pianofabrik	"	—	"
Bartel & Co., Ernst	"	—	"
Barthol, R.	"	1871	"
Bechstein, C.	"	1853	"
Beer & Co.	"	—	"
Becker, Aloys	"	—	"
Biese, W.	"	1851	"
Blasendorff, Carl	"	1898	"
Böger & Sohn, Wilh.	"	1860	"

443

Name	Established	Year	Location
Bogs & Voigt	Established	1905	Berlin
Bönecke, Hermann	"	1906	"
Borkenhagen, M	"	1892	"
Brandes, Erich	"	——	"
Compagnie Concordia	"	1869	"
Dassel, Aug	"	1859	"
Donadoni & Pohl	"	1880	"
Dreyer & Co., Max	"	1896	"
Duysen, I. L.	"	1860	"
Ecke, Carl	"	1873	"
Emmer, Wilhelm	"	——	"
Engelmann & Günthermann	"	1888	"
Euphonie	"	1906	"
Excelsior Pianofabrik	"	——	"
Fehn & Co., A.	"	1903	"
Felschow, A.	"	1875	"
Fröhlich & Kemmler	"	——	"
Gawenda, Franz	"	1888	"
Geil & Co., Friederich	"	1904	"
Giese, Reineke & Co.	"	1888	"
Görs & Kallmann	"	1877	"
Goetze & Co.	"	1866	"
Grabau, M.	"	1880	"
Grand Nachf., A.	"	1869	"
Gude, Moritz	"	1886	"
Günther, Otto	"	——	"
Günther, Robert	"	1880	"
Hahmann, Gustav	"	1884	"
Haucke, Carl	"	1890	"
Hanne, Paul	"	1861	"
Hansen, H.	"	1871	"
Harmonie	"	——	"
Hartmann, W.	"	1839	"
Hauschulz, Jul.	"	——	"
Heidrich, Hermann	"	1881	"
Heilbrunn Söhne, K.	"	1875	"
Heinke, Carl	"	——	"
Hedke, Wilh.	"	1890	"
Heindorff, A.	"	1892	"
Hepperle, Otto	"	1872	"
Heyse, E. H.	"	1872	"
Hillgärtner, Heinrich	"	1901	"
Hilse, C.	"	——	"
Hilse Nachf., W.	"	1876	"
Hinke, Alfred	"	1901	"
Hintze, Carl H.	"	——	"
Hohne & Sell	"	1885	"
Hoffmann Pianos	"	——	"
Hooff & Co.	"	1873	"
Horn, Alfred	"	1905	"
Janowsky, M.	"	——	"
Jaschinsky, A.	"	1880	"
Kewitsch, Johannes	"	1878	"
Klimes, Schwitalla & Co.	"	1905	"
Klingmann & Co., G.	"	1869	"
Knöchel, Ad.	"	1876	"
Koch & Co., Ernst	"	1896	"
Krause, Conrad	"	1868	"
Krause, Hermann	"	1860	"
Krause & Dress	"	——	"
Krengel & Co., H.	"	1906	"

Kriebel, H.	Established 1863		Berlin
Kuhla, Fritz	"	1872	"
Kuhl & Klatt	"	——	"
Lämmerhirt, Emil	"	1880	"
Langfritz, L.	"	1889	"
Lehmann & Co., Adolf	"	1890	"
Laurinat & Co.	"	1879	"
Lenz, A.	"	1876	"
Liedcke, W.	"	1872	"
Linke, Godenschweger & Co.	"	1890	"
List, Ernst	"	1888	"
Lubitz, H.	"	1875	"
Lüdecke, M.	"	——	"
Machalet, T.	"	1862	"
Manthey, Ferd.	"	1868	"
Marquardt & Co., Otto	"	1905	"
Matz & Co., H.	"	1869	"
Menzel, Wilhelm	"	1890	"
Meyer, Richard	"	1881	"
Möbes & Co.	"	1869	"
Mörs & Co., L.	"	1869	"
Müller, Max	"	1905	"
Nesener & Segert	"	1903	"
Neufeind, R.	"	1888	"
Neumeyer, Ernst	"	1905	"
Neufeld, L.	"	1872	"
Neugebauer Nachf., C.	"	1878	"
Neumeyer, Max	"	1906	"
Neumeyer, Gebr.	"	1905	"
Nieber & Co., A.	"	1885	"
Noeske & Co.	"	1888	"
Oppermann, Albert	"	——	"
Otto, Carol	"	1866	"
Paul & Co., Ernst	"	1899	"
Paul & Co.	"	——	"
Pechmann & Co.	"	——	"
Pfaffe, Julius	"	1860	"
Pfeiffer, J.	"	1880	"
Pianofabrik A. Lüddemann	"	——	"
Pianofortefabrik "Euterpe"	"	1886	"
" Ottomar Fiedler	"	——	"
" "Opera"	"	——	"
" W. Hoffmann	"	1888	"
Plösch & Co.	"	——	"
Pöschel, A.	"	——	"
Quandt, C. J.	"	1854	"
Roesener, F.	"	1839	"
Schiemann & Madsen	"	1870	"
Schiller, J.	"	1884	"
Schleip, Benedictus	"	1816	"
Schmeckel & Co.	"	——	"
Schmidt, L.	"	1865	"
Schmidt, Rudolf	"	1887	"
Schmidt & John	"	——	"
Schönlein, Ernst	"	1895	"
Schötz & Co., Heinrich	"	1907	"
Schübbe & Co.	"	1894	"
Schulz, W.	"	1862	"
Schütze, Heinrich	"	1877	"
Schütze & Schmidt	"	——	"

Schwechten, G.	Established 1853	Berlin
Seidel Nachf., Rob.	" ——	"
Siewert, C.	" ——	"
Skibbe, Max	" 1905	"
Sommer, Mathias	" ——	"
Steuer, Wilhelm	" 1894	"
Steinberg & Co.	" 1908	"
Stoessel, Gertler & Co.	" 1880	"
Tempe, Reinhold	" 1868	"
Tietze, R.	" 1890	"
Ulbrich, R.	" 1888	"
Vierling, Rudolph	" 1879	"
Vieritz & Werner	" ——	"
Wahren, Carl	" 1902	"
Weber, F.	" 1860	"
Werner, Ed.	" 1881	"
Westermayer, Ed.	" 1863	"
Westphal, Robert	" 1894	"
Wittenburg & Hermann	" 1900	"
Wittig, Ernst	" 1863	"
Wöhler Nachf., Adolf	" 1885	"
Zahn, F. H.	" 1885	Bernburg
Mann & Co., Th.	" 1836	Bielefeld
Grotrian, Steinweg Nachf.	" 1835	Braunschweig
Wechsung, G.	" 1857	"
Zeitter & Winkelmann	" 1837	"
Palven, Jr., P.	" 1901	Bremen
Berndt, Traugott	" 1837	Breslau
Hüttner, Alfred	" 1896	"
Welzel, P. F.	" 1835	"
Hauck, J. B.	" 1865	Bruchsal
Lipczinski, Max	" 1890	Danzig
Arnold, Karl	" 1830	Darmstadt
Werner, F. W.	" 1845	Döbeln
Beyer-Rahnefeld, Otto	" 1852	Dresden
Gerold, F.	" 1875	"
Goetze, Franz	" 1874	"
Hagspiel & Comp.	" 1851	"
Hoffmann & Kühne	" 1899	"
Kuhse, Johann	" 1874	"
Kulb, Jos.	" 1873	"
Mannsfeldt & Notni	" 1867	"
Müller, Clemens H.	" 1877	"
Rönisch, Carl	" 1845	"
Rosenkranz, Ernst	" 1797	"
Ullrich, H.	" 1876	"
Urbas, Johann	" 1894	"
Urbas & Reisshauer	" 1894	"
Vogel, F. E.	" 1845	"
Wolfframm, H.	" 1872	"
Werner, Paul	" 1810	"
Zimmermann, Gebr.	" 1904	Leipzig Mölkau
Erbe, J.	" 1881	Eisenach
Finger, Alb.	" 1887	Eisenberg
Geyer Nachf., Adolph	" 1877	"
Kluge & Treydel	" ——	"
Vogel, Robert	" ——	"
Weber & Fuchs	" 1905	"
Weissbrod, R.	" 1884	"
Winkelmann & Co.	" 1908	"
Tetsch & May	" 1867	Emmerich a. Rhein

Hansen, Julius	Established	1838	Flensburg
Philipp, G.	"	1872	Forst
Andrè, C. A.	"	1828	Frankfurt a. M.
Baldur Pianofortefabrik	"	1872	"
Philipps & Söhne, J. D.	"	1877	"
Welte & Söhne, M.	"	1833	Freiburg i. Br.
Glück, Carl	"	1843	Friedberg
Spaethe, Wilh.	"	1859	Gera
Maetzke, Eduard	"	1862	Görlitz
Steck Piano Co.	"	1857	Gotha
Ritmüller & Sohn, W.	"	1795	Goettingen
Ritter, C. Rich.	"	1828	Halle a. S.
Behnken, Gebr. N. & E. H.	"	1873	Hamburg
Buschmann, Gustav Adolf	"	1805	"
Kohl, H.	"	1855	"
Neumann, F. L.	"	1854	"
Rachals & Co., M. F.	"	1832	"
Schnell, H.	"	1872	"
Steinway & Sons	"	1880	"
Stapel, G.	"	1848	"
Gertz, Wilh.	"	1873	Hanover
Haake, Karl	"	1836	"
Helmholz, Fr.	"	1851	"
Rissmann, C. C.	"	1846	"
Glass & Co., C. F.	"	1879	Heilbronn
Nagel, G. L.	"	1828	"
Uebel & Lechleiter	"	1871	"
Sprunck, Fr.	"	1839	Hettstedt
Glaser, F.	"	——	Jena
Weidig, C.	"	1843	"
Neuhaus Söhne, W.	"	1840	Kalkar
Beckmann, W.	"	1806	Kassel
Scheel, Carl	"	1846	"
Günther & Söhne	"	1819	Kirchheim, u. Teck
Kaim & Sohn	"	1819	"
Arnold, Heinrich	"	1830	Klein-Umstadt
Rowold & Söhne, Ernst	"	1793	Kleve a. Rhein
Mand, C.	"	1832	Koblenz
Prein, Friedr.	"	1857	Köln
Gebauhr, C. J.	"	1834	Koenigsberg
Schusterius, C. A.	"	1869	"
Stockfisch, H.	"	——	Kottbus
Adam, F.	"	1864	Krefeld
Hain, Stephan	"	1892	"
Blüthner, Julius	"	1853	Leipzig
Feurich, Julius	"	1851	"
Fiedler, Gustav	"	1871	"
Förster & Co.	"	1840	"
Francke & Co., A. H.	"	1865	"
Irmler, I. G.	"	1818	"
Kreutzbach, Julius	"	1874	"
Schimmel & Co., Wilh.	"	1885	"
Schumann, Carl	"	1857	"
Stichel, F.	"	1877	"
Zierold, Gustav	"	1882	"
Freytag, Andreas	"	1889	Liegnitz
Geister & Schwabe	"	1871	"
Gerstenberger, J.	"	1864	"
Liehr, Franz	"	1871	"
Neumann, Carl	"	1897	"
Pätzold, Gottl.	"	——	"

Schneider, Albin	Established 1907	....	Liegnitz
Schuppe & Neumann	" 1897	....	"
Seiler, Eduard	" 1849	....	"
Sponnagel, Eduard	" 1866	....	"
Förster, August	" 1859	....	Löbau
Crasselt & Rähse	" 1881	....	"
Niendorf, Gebr	" 1897	....	Luckenwalde
Pabst & Schneider	" 1905	....	"
Scharf & Hauk	" 1870	....	Mannheim
Thürmer, Ferd	" 1834	....	Meissen
Brinkmann, Emilie	" 1879	.... Minden, Westfalen	
Selle, Gebr	" 1828	.... Mühlhausen, Thüringen	
Berdux, V	" 1871	....	München
Mayer & Co., J	" 1826	....	"
Knake, Gebrüder	" 1808	....	Münster
Samson & Bennemann	" —	....	"
Boekh, Hermann	" 1866	....	Nördlingen
Hegeler & Ehlers	" 1895	....	Oldenburg
Rohlfing, Gebr	" 1790	....	Osnabrück
Vogel & Sohn	" 1828	....	Plauen
Courtois, Hermann	" —	....	Prenzlau
Weidig, Georg	" 1890	....	Regensburg
Bock & Hinrichsen	" 1869	....	Rendsburg
Deesz, Julius	" 1820	....	Saarbrücken
Hermann, Alexander	" 1835	....	Sangerhausen
Held, H	" 1867	....	Schleswig
Soph & Sohn, F	" 1902	....	Schmölln
Perzina, Gebr	" 1871	....	Schwerin i. M.
Sauter, C	" 1846	....	Spaichingen
Hoof, Ludwig	" 1882	....	Sprottau
Siegel, R	" 1849	....	Stade
Wolkenhauer, G	" 1853	....	Stettin
Lindner Sohn, I. P	" 1825	....	Stralsund
Prestel, Anton	" 1820	....	Strassburg
Lochow & Zimmermann	" 1900	....	Strausberg
Ackermann, F. J	" 1882	....	Stuttgart
Dörner & Sohn, F.	" 1830	....	"
Elias, G	" 1875	....	"
Gschwind, I. G	" 1858	....	"
Hardt, Carl	" 1855	....	"
Krauss, E	" 1870	....	"
Krumm, Jacob	" 1900	....	"
Lipp & Sohn, Rich	" 1831	....	"
Müdler, G	" 1857	....	"
Matthaes, Theodor	" 1888	....	"
Oehler, C	" 1857	....	"
Pfeiffer, Carl A	" 1862	....	"
Sauer & Sohn, I. P	" 1863	....	"
Schiedmayer Pianofabrik	" 1853	....	"
Schiedmayer & Soehne	" 1809	....	"
Schilling. Fr	" 1871	....	"
Wagner, Herm	" 1844	....	"
Eigelbaum & Hoffmann	" 1907	....	Torgau
Simon, L	" 1880	....	Ulm
Imhof & Muckle	" 1848	.... Vöhrenbach, Baden	
Ketnath, Friedrich	" 1836	....	Weiden
Römhildt Pianofortefabrik	" 1845	....	Weimar
Adam, Gerhard	" 1828	....	Wesel
Biehl, Joh. Heinr	" 1868	....	Wittgendorf
Müller-Schiedmayer, Erwin	" 1874	....	Würzburg
Pfister, N	" 1800	....	"

Fahr, Albert	Established 1887		Zeitz
Geissler, F.	"	1878	"
Gerbstädt, Oscar	"	1888	"
Hoelling & Spangenberg, C.	"	—	"
Hupfer & Co.	"	1874	"
Krietzsch, Hermann	"	1847	"
Morenz, Bruno	"	1891	"
Schemelli & Co., R.	"	1900	"
Schmidt & Sohn Nachf., P.	"	1876	"
Donath, Max	"	1882	Zittau

PIANO SUPPLY MANUFACTURERS

Name	Product	Year	City
Bühl, W. G.	Keys	1894	Barmen
Burk & Bastian	"	1905	"
Kluge, Hermann	"	1876	"
Aichele & Bachmann	Iron Frames	—	Berlin
Allisath & Müller	Hammers	—	"
Bartsch, A.	"	—	"
Beetz, H.	Actions	—	"
Bellin, W.	Hammers	1890	"
Bohn & Co., C.	Keys	1871	"
Berliner Gussstahl Fabrik	Iron Frames	—	"
Beyer, A.	Hammers	—	"
Buchholtz, Heinrich	Keys	1866	"
Eggersdorfer Filz Fabrik	Felts	—	"
Wolff & Co., L.	Iron Frames	—	"
Fulte, Georg	Hammers	—	"
Gallowsky, H.	"	1863	"
Jacob, Ernst	Actions	—	"
Johst, W.	Hammers	—	"
Kaselow, Hermann	"	1900	"
Klaviaturfabrik Union	Keys	—	"
Köhler, Oscar	Actions	1883	"
Langer & Co.	"	1882	"
Laurisch, Ferdinand	Hammers	—	"
Leonhardt, M.	"	1896	"
Leonhardt, Max	Keys	—	"
Leonhardt, Richard	Hammers	—	"
Leuschner, Carl	"	1880	"
Lexow, Ad	Actions	1854	"
Loepke, W.	Hammers	—	"
Walter, Adolf	Keys	—	"
Wehrmeier, Franz	Hammers	1876	"
Weisner, Gustav	Actions	1880	"
Dittersdorfer Fils Fabrik	Felts	1881	Dittersdorf
Kutter, Alfred W.	Keys	—	Dresden
Kutter, E. G. Robert	"	—	"
Patzak, Adalbert	Hammers	—	"
Syhre, Edmund	"	1879	"
Dornheim & Sohn, F. W.	Keys	1874	Eichfeldt
Schlessiger, Herm	Soundboards	1853	Gera
Eicken & Co.	Wire	—	Hagen
Merckel, Wilh.	Hammers	1845	Hamburg
Weidner, W.	Keys	—	"
Boecker, Heinr. Wilh.	Wire	—	Hohenlimburg
Bongardt & Co., Gebr.	"	1832	"
Weber & Giese	"	—	"

Kissing & Möllmann	Soundboards	——	Iserlohn
Rysse & Co., Oscar	Keys	1905	Langenberg b. Gera
Beier, Adolf	Hammers	1894	Leipzig
Dethleffs & Co.	Keys	1874	"
Driver & Toepfer	Actions	1882	"
Fleming, H. F.	"	1874	"
Matkowitz, Carl	Hammers	1906	"
Morgenstern & Kotrade	Actions	1846	"
Polenz & Lange	Hammers	1899	"
Thieme, Carl	Soundboards	1843	"
Tränkner, Hugo	Keys	1843	"
Weickert, I. D.	Felts	1847	"
Gustav Meurer	"	1878	Liebenzell
Jentzsch & Co.	Keys and Actions	1882	Liegnitz
Stammitz, Hermann	Keys	1894	"
Thelocke & Kluge	"	1859	"
Scherdel, Siegmund	Wire	1889	Markt Redwitz
Julius Klinke	Pins	1847	Neuenrade
Schürmann & Hillecke	"	1879	"
Beck, Georg Joh.	Wire	1642	Nürnberg
Fuchs, Joh. Wolfg.	"	1787	"
Poehlmann, Moritz	"	1850	"
Marthaus, Ambrosius	Felts	1834	Oschatz
Kaiser, J.	Pins	1864	Plettenberg
Schulte, D. W.	"	1840	"
Wagner, jun., W.	"	——	"
Zimmermann, Paul	Keys	1898	Radis
Stahl & Drahtwirk Roeslau	Wire	1832	Roeslau
Sempert, Carl	Keys	——	Rudolstadt
Bösch, Franz	Hammers	1872	Stuttgart
Düschler, Friederich	"	——	"
Fritz & Mayer	Actions	1857	"
Kanhäuser, G. & E.	Hammers	1844	"
Keller & Co., J.	Actions	1857	"
Koch & Co.	Keys	1879	"
Pape, Paul	"	1877	"
Renner, Louis	Hammers and Actions	1882	"
Schäuffele Wwe, Gg.	Keys	1846	"
Schäuffele, Wilhelm	"	1882	"
Wörner, G. F.	Hammers	1865	"
Dunker, J. W.	Pins	1847	Werdohl
Giese, I. H. Rud	Wire	1883	Westig
Grunert, Emil	Keys	——	Zeitz
Kummer, Adolf	Actions and Hammers	1890	"
Tischendorf, Franz	Keys	1888	"
Tischendorf, Karl	"	——	"
Zugehör, Oscar	Hammers	——	"

ENGLAND

PIANO MANUFACTURERS

Ajello & Sons, G.	Established 1863		London
Albion Pianoforte Co.	"	1871	"
Allen & Caunter	"	1894	"
Allison & Co., Arthur	"	1840	"
Allison & Sons, Ralph	"	——	"
Ambridge & Son, Henry	"	1890	"
Arnall & Co., H. B.	"	——	"

Arnold & Co., J.	Established 1880		London
Bansall & Sons	"	1883	"
Barnett & Sons, Samuel	"	1832	"
Barber & Co.	"	1892	"
Barratt & Robinson	"	1877	"
Beadle & Langbein	"	—	"
Beckhardt & Sons	"	—	"
Berry, Nathaniel	"	1866	"
Bishop & Co., Joseph	"	1877	"
Brasted, H. F. & R. A.	"	—	"
Brinsmead & Sons, John	"	1836	"
Brinsmead, E. G. S.	"	—	"
British Piano Manufacturing Co.	"	—	"
Broadwood & Son, John	"	1723	"
Brock, Bernard	"	1890	"
Brock & Vincent	"	1897	"
Browne, Justin	"	—	"
Burling & Mansfield	"	—	"
Byers, Walter Charles	"	1896	"
Carleton Piano Works	"	—	"
Challen & Son	"	1804	"
Challenger & Co , George	"	—	"
Chappell & Co.	"	1812	"
Child, E.	"	—	"
Cohen & Co., Philip	"	1893	"
Collard & Collard	"	1760	"
Cons & Cons	"	1884	"
Cramer & Co., J. B.	"	1824	"
Danemann & Co., W.	"	—	"
Dodson, William	"	1867	"
Dunno, Ellis & Hill	"	—	"
Dunckley, William	"	1865	"
Eavestaff & Sons	"	1823	"
Edwards & Searle	"	—	"
Ellis, John	"	1888	"
Empire Piano Co.	"	1892	"
Eungblut, C. & J.	"	—	"
Feord, Garrett	"	—	"
Fitzsimmons, Robert	"	1879	"
Fleming & Barker	"	—	"
Forrester, J	"	—	"
Fox, T. G.	"	—	"
Gautier, Jules	"	1866	"
Gilbert, Thomas, John	"	1880	"
Grantone Piano Co.	"	—	"
Green & Savage	"	1876	"
Grover & Grover	"	1830	"
Grover & Deare	"	1879	"
Hardcastle, J.	"	—	"
Harland, Alfred, Joseph	"	1879	"
Harold & Denson	"	1883	"
Harper, Thomas W.	"	1880	"
Harrison, Thomas	"	1890	"
Harvey & Son, G.	"	—	"
Hawkins, R.	"	—	"
Healy & Richards	"	1889	"
Hickey & Co., T. J.	"	1901	"
Hicks & Son, Henry	"	1845	"
Hillier Piano & Organ Co.	"	1855	"
Hopkinson, J. & J.	"	1835	"
Hulbert & Jones	"	1883	"

Humphreys, A. & E.	Established 1883		London
Imperial Organ & Piano Co.	"	——	"
James & Son, Henry	"	1878	"
Jarrett & Goudge	"	1871	"
Jenn Bros.	"	1874	"
Keith, Prowse & Co.	"	1862	"
Kelly & Co.	"	1824	"
King Bros.	"	——	"
Knapton & Co.	"	1896	"
Lambert, F. B.	"	1881	"
Lawrence & Co.	"	——	"
Little, Charles Edwin	"	1878	"
Livingstone & Cook	"	1897	"
Lyon, Louis George	"	1875	"
McRill & Sons	"	——	"
McVay Piano Mfg. Co.	"	——	"
Merrington Bros.	"	——	"
Monington & Weston	"	1858	"
Moore & Moore	"	1837	"
Munt Bros.	"	1873	"
Murdoch, John G.	"	1862	"
Murray & Co.	"	——	"
Payne, T. & G.	"	1892	"
Pinnell & Co., E. J.	"	——	"
Pugh & Son, Joseph	"	——	"
Pull & Field	"	——	"
Pyrke, C. H.	"	1895	"
Rayner, S.	"	——	"
Reed & Sons, J. W.	"	1868	"
Reeve & Co., W.	"	1881	"
Regester & Sons	"	——	"
Rintoul & Sons, John	"	1858	"
Robertson & Co.	"	——	"
Rogers & Sons	"	1843	"
Rudd & Co., A.	"	1837	"
Russell & Co., Geo.	"	1842	"
Samson Piano Works	"	——	"
Sandon & Steedmann	"	——	"
Seager Bros.	"	1897	"
Shenstone & Son	"	——	"
Shipmann & Shipmann	"	1877	"
Smith, Andrew	"	——	"
Snell, Harry	"	——	"
Southam, Cooper	"	——	"
Spencer & Co., John	"	1883	"
Spiller, Boult & Co.	"	——	"
Squire, Jr., William	"	1881	"
Squire & Son, B.	"	1829	"
Strohmenger & Son, J.	"	1835	"
Strong & Sons, John	"	1851	"
Taylor & Co., A.	"	1890	"
Taylor & Co., C. R.	"	——	"
Tucker & Co.	"	——	"
Wallis & Son, Joseph	"	1848	"
Watkins. T. & G.	"	——	"
West Green Piano Works	"	——	"
White, Broadwood & Co.	"	1879	"
White, T.	"	1895	"
Whiteley, William	"	——	"
Willcocks & Co.	"	1906	"
Witton, Witton & Co.	"	1838	"

Wonder Pianoforte Co.	Established ——			London
Woods & Co., R. J.	"	——		"
Wright, W. A.	"	1879		"
Zender & Co.	"	——		"
Pohlmann & Sons, F.	"	1832		Halifax
Hartley & Sons, Stephen	"	1857		"
Shore, F.	"	——		"

PIANO SUPPLY MANUFACTURERS

Webster & Horsfall	Wire	——		Birmingham
Brooks, Limited	Keys and Actions	1810		London
Cassini, W. H.	Hammers	1878		"
Clark, R. W.	Keys	1871		"
Clark, John H., & Co.	Iron Frames	1734		"
Deighton, A.	Keys	1881		"
Finnimore Bros.	"	1880		"
Gibbs, B. A.	"	1895		"
Goddard, J. & J.	Felts and Hardware	1842		"
Homan & Sons	Strings	1853		"
Kilvert, J. Smith	Hammers	1860		"
Marshall, William, & Son	Materials	1841		"
Nott & Co.	Actions	1862		"
Paine & Sons, Thos.	Keys	1865		"
Sebright, T.	"	1852		"
Shenstone & Co.	"	1870		"
Vestey, R. F., & Son	"	1860		"
Wallis & Son	Materials	1848		"
Whitehead, R. R., & Bros.	Felts			"
Houghton, W. A.	Wire	——		Warrington
Naish	Felts	1859		Wilton

FRANCE

PIANO MANUFACTURERS

Aurand & Bohl	Established 1830			Lyon
Baruth, François Claude	"	——		"
Boudon, B.	"	——		"
Manufacture Marseillaise de Pianos.	"	1827		Marseilles
Klein, Gaston	"	——		Montreuil sous Bois
Klein, Henri	"	1879		" " "
Manufacture des Pianos Grillot	"	——		" " "
Staub, J.	"	1848		Nancy
Vuillemin-Didion	"	1846		Nantes
Rodolphe Fils & Debain réunies	"	——		Nogent sur Seine
Benard, Champ & Cie	"	1849		Paris
Blondel, Alphonse	"	1839		"
Bord, A.	"	1840		"
Bueher (Gauss Frères & Cie. Succrs.)	"	1848		"
Burgasser & Cie	"	1846		"
Carpentier. J.	"	——		"
Cocquet Fils, Leon	"	1865		"
Erard (Blondel & Cie. Succrs.)	"	1779		"
Focké Frères	"	1860		"

Frantz, J. B. (Mussard & Cie. Succrs.) Established 1852 ....Paris
Gaveau, I. G....................... " 1847 .... "
Gouttiere, Ed....................... " 1846 .... "
Guillot, A......................... " ——— .... "
Herz, Henri....................... " 1825 .... "
Herz, Neveu & Cie............... " 1863 .... "
Kriegelstein & Cie.............. " 1831 .... "
Leguerinais Frères............... " 1856 .... "
Leveque & Thersen............... " ——— .... "
Mustel & Cie..................... " 1855 .... "
Oury, Alphonse.................... " ——— .... "
Pleyel, Lyon & Cie................ " 1807 .... "
Pruvost, Henri................... " 1850 .... "
Pruvost Fils, E. Victor........... " ——— .... "
Ruch, J.......................... " ——— .... "
Schmitt, François................. " ——— .... "
Schotte Frères.................... " 1850 .... "
Laplanche-Deforge, C............. " 1796 ....Reims

PIANO SUPPLY MANUFACTURERS

Société Anonyme.................Wire.................——— ....Montbiliard
Gilbert ....Actions.............——— Montreuil sous Bois
Sommer ....Felt.................——— ....Mouzon
Voos, J. J........................ " ....——— .... "
Brees & Cie......................Actions.............——— ....Paris
Brou, Edouard....................Felt.................——— .... "
Delorme, F.......................Keys.................——— .... "
Deloye, Maurice.................. " ....1850 .... "
De Rohden, C....................Actions.............——— .... "
Fortin, Eugène...................Felt.................——— .... "
Gehrling & Cie...................Actions.............1842 .... "
Grillet, Père & Fils..............Keys.................——— .... "
Herrburger, J., Maison Schwander. Actions and Keys...... 1844 .... "
Kneip, Louis.....................Hammers.............1850 .... "
Lange, Julien....................Keys.................——— .... "
Levet, A.........................Hammers.............1869 .... "
Martin, L.........................Actions and Hammers..1895 .... "
Muller, E.........................Keys.................1835 .... "
Société Anonyme de Feutres français. Felts.................——— .... "
Truchot ....Hammers.............1848 .... "
Union ....Actions and Keys......——— ——
Rolle, Neveu & Succrs., E...........Felts.................——— ....St. Denis

SPAIN

PIANO MANUFACTURERS

Canto, J.........................Established ——— ....Barcelona
Charrier y Cia.................... " 1875 .... "
Chassaigne Frères................. " 1864 .... "
Estela, Vinda de Pedro........... " 1830 .... "
Estela y Compa., B.............. " ——— .... "
Guarro Hermanos.................. " 1860 .... "
Izabal, Louis..................... " 1860 .... "
Izabal, Paul...................... " ——— .... "
Prin, Mallard y Cia.............. " ——— .... "

Ribalta, Salvador................Established ——— ....Barcelona
Sociedad Franco-Hispano-Americana.   "   1898 ....   "
Vidal, J.........................   "   1879 ....   "
Montano, hijos de................   "   1838 ....Madrid
Piazza, Mauricio.................   "   ——— ....Sevilla
Ten y Cia., Rodrigo..............   "   1902 ....Valencia

PIANO SUPPLY MANUFACTURERS

Raynard, L......................Actions and Keys....1897 ....Barcelona

BELGIUM

PIANO MANUFACTURERS

Hainaut Frères...................Established 1840 ....Binche
Berden & Cie., François..........   "   1815 ....Brüssell
Bernard & Cie., A................   "   1898 ....   "
Günther, J.......................   "   1845 ....   "
Hanlet, A........................   "   1866 ....   "
Mahillon & Cie...................   "   ——— ....   "
Oor, J...........................   "   1850 ....   "
Oor, Lucien......................   "   1907 ....   "
Pley & Dahout....................   "   ———
Boone Fils.......................   "   1839 ....Gent
Gevaert, V.......................   "   1846 ....   "
Van Hyfte, B.....................   "   1835 ....   "
Van Hyfte Frères.................   "   1839 ....   "
Vits, Émile......................   "   1838 ....   "
Renson Frères....................   "   1857 ....Lüttich
Derdeyn Frères...................   "   1846 ....Roulers

NETHERLANDS

PIANO MANUFACTURERS

Allgäuer & Zoon, J. J............Established 1830 ....Amsterdam
Cuijpers, J. F...................   "   1832 ....Gravenhage
Rijken & Co., Ch. F..............   "   ——— ....   "
Mes, Antoine A. A. Az............   "   1874 ....Middelburg
Rijken & de Lange, Gebrs.........   "   1852 ....Rotterdam
Bocage, Ch.......................   "   ——— ....Schiedam
Leïjser & Zoon, N. S.............   "   1854 ....Zutfen

SWITZERLAND

PIANO MANUFACTURERS

Schmidt, A.......................Established 1830 ....Bern
Burger & Jacobi..................   "   1872 ....Biel
Pianofabrik Symphonia............   "   ....   "
Bieger & Co., J..................   "   1842 ....Rorschach
Ganter & Sohn, J.................   "   ——— ....Zürich
Hüni & Co........................   "   1860 ....   "
Rordorf & Co.....................   "   1847 ....   "
Suter, H.........................   "   1875 ....   "

SCANDINAVIA

PIANO MANUFACTURERS

DENMARK

Ehlert, J. H.	Established 1867		Kopenhagen
Felumb, Emil	" 1872		"
Geisler, A. H.	" 1876		"
Heidemann, H. P.	" ——		"
Hindsberg, H. T. P.	" 1853		"
Hornung & Möller	" 1827		"
Jensen, Sören	" 1893		"
Kofod & Co.	" ——		"
Landschultz, C.	" 1865		"
Larsen & Sön, J.	" 1855		"
Lendorf, Oscar	" ——		"
Mentzler, W.	" ——		"
Petersen & Sön, Herm. N.	" 1854		"
Schon, T. C.	" ——		"
Wedell & Aberg, C.	" 1881		"

SWEDEN

A. G. Ralins Piano Fabrik	" 1885		Amal
Pianofabriken Standard	" 1904		Arvika
Ostlind & Almquist	" 1888		"
Billbergs Piano-Fabrik	" 1868		Göteborg
Löfmark, J.	" 1903		"
Malmsjö, J. G.	" 1843		"
Hagdahl, J.	" ——		Karlskrona
Nyströms, J. P.	" 1865		Karlstad
Hansson, D.	" 1854		Lund
Ekström & Compis	" 1836		Malmö
Lofmark & Hagland	" 1899		"
Gustafson & Ljunquist	" ——		Norrköping
Bergquist & Nilsson	" ——		Stockholm
Engström & Johanesson	" ——		"
Franckel & Co., F.	" ——		"
Hoffmann, Aug.	" ——		"
Löfberg & Co.	" ——		"
Norbergs Pianofabrik	" ——		"
Pettersson, John	" 1889		"
Rapp, E.	" ——		"
Svahnquist, jun., C.	" 1899		"
Winkrantz, Fr.	" ——		"

NORWAY

Knudsen, Jacob	" 1896		Bergen
Hals, Brödrene	" 1847		Christiania

RUSSIA

PIANO MANUFACTURERS

Hellas, Osakeytiö	Established 1901		Helsingfors
Apollo	" 1899		Kalisch
Betting, Theodor	" 1887		"
Fibiger, Arnold	" 1878		"
Strobl, August	" ——		Kiew

Name	Established	Year	City
Koretzky, F. J.	Established	1887	Moskau
Uslall & Co., A.	"	1878	"
Rausch, M.	"	1856	Odessa
Schoen, Ad.	"	1843	"
Johannsohn, Th.	"	1855	Riga
Tresselt, J.	"	—	"
Weinberg, J.	"	—	
Becker, J.	"	1841	St. Petersburg
Diederichs, Gebr.	"	1810	" "
Hergens & Tönnoff	"	—	" "
Leppenberg, G.	"	1888	" "
Mayr, Hermann	"	1870	" "
Muhlbach, F.	"	—	" "
Offenbacher	"	1900	" "
Rathke, R.	"	1868	" "
Reinhard, W.	"	1874	" "
Rönisch, Carl	"	1898	" "
Schlesinger, S. L.	"	—	" "
Schmidt, P.	"	1880	" "
Schroeder, C. M.	"	1818	" "
Smidt & Wegener	"	1880	" "
Stein, J. J.	"	—	" "
Erikson, M.	"	—	Saratow
Kehrer, Hermann	"	1872	Tiflis
Kopp, Anton	"	1887	"
Angerhofer, F.	"	—	Warschau
Dütz, Anton	"	1873	"
Kerntopf & Sohn	"	—	"
Malicki, Julian	"	—	"
Nowicki, F. J.		—	"

AUSTRIA

PIANO MANUFACTURER

Name	Established	Year	City
Albert & Co., E. A.	Established	1868	Aussig
Rösler, G.	"	1878	B. Leipa
Protze & Co., Josef	"	1905	Georgswalde
Petrof, Anton	"	1864	Königgrätz
Warbinek, Rudolf A.	"	1906	Laibach
Baroitius, Karl J.	"	1898	Prag
Kopecky & Co.	"	—	"
Novák, V.	"	1901	"
Schnabel, Ludwig	"	—	"
Koch & Korselt	"	1891	Reichenberg
Proksch, A.	"	1864	"
Spira's Wwe., Carl	"	1892	"
Bremitz, Enrico	"	1874	Triest
Magrini e Figlio, L.	"	1870	"
Andreys, Anton	"	—	Wien
Baumann, Max	"	—	"
Belehradek, Johann	"	1870	"
Baumbach, Josef	"	1842	"
Berger, Ignaz	"	—	"
Bösendorfer, Ludwig	"	1828	"
Czapka's Sohn, Jacob	"	1842	"
Dörr, Karl	"	1817	"
Dörsam, Wilhelm	"	—	"
Ehrbar, Friedrich	"	1801	"

	Established		
Fritz, Sohn, J.	1805		Wien
Fuchs, jun., Franz	"	—	"
Gossl, Josef & Adolf	"	1854	"
Habler, Joh.	"	—	"
Hamburger, Carl	"	1874	"
Heitzmann, Otto	"	1839	"
Hnatay, Josef	"		"
Hofbauer, Gustav	"	1850	"
Hofmann, Friedrich	"	—	"
Hofmann, Karl	"	1876	"
Hölze & Heitzmann	"	1868	"
Horr, Moritz	"	—	"
Jirasek, Ferdinand	"		"
Karbach, Friedrich	"	1856	"
Klubal, Gottlieb	"	—	"
Kraus, Adolf	"	1898	"
Kubik, Josef	"	—	"
Lauberger & Gloss	"	1900	"
Littmann, Johann	"	1869	"
" Lyra "	"	1885	"
Maliwanck, Heinrich	"	—	"
Mayer, Eduard	"	—	"
Mayer, Wilhelm	"	—	"
Mayr, Franz	"	—	"
Nemetschke, Johann	"	—	"
Neuburger, Adolf	"	1890	"
Neumayer, Carl	"	—	"
Oeser, Franz	"	—	"
Oeser & Sohn, Vincent	"	—	"
Pallik & Stiasny	"	—	"
Parttart's Eidam, Alois	"	1868	"
Pawleck, jun., Josef	"	1894	"
Pokorny, A.	"	—	"
Reinhold, Robert F.	"	1890	"
Richter, Franz	"	—	"
Schaube, Wilh.	"	1870	"
Schmid, Heinrich	"	—	"
Schmid & Kunz, F.	"	1880	"
Schneider & Neffe, Josef	"	1839	"
Schweighofer's Söhne	"	1792	"
Skop, Josef	"	—	"
Stary, Johann	"	1892	"
Stelzhammer, Anton	"	1848	"
Stenzel & Schlemmer	"	1898	"
Stingl, Gebrüder	"	1887	"
Wasniczek, Ignaz	"	—	"
Windhofer Wwe. Rudolf	"	—	"
Wirth, Franz	"	1880	"
Wolck, Franz	"	1878	"
Zebrakowsky, Johann	"	—	"
Chmel & Son	"	1835	Budapest
Dehmal, Károly	"	1888	"
Eder, Anton Julius	"	1846	"
Havlicsek, Carl	"	1895	"
Heckenast, Gustav	"	1865	"

PIANO SUPPLY MANUFACTURERS

Gaiser, Emil	Hammers	1871	Wien
Karl, Jos.	Keys	1894	"

```
Kuda, Eberhard................... Hammers............ 1891 ............Wien
Littmann, jun., Paul............ Keys.................1887 ............  "
Miller's Sohn, Martin............ Wire.................1782 ............  "
Mraz, Franz..................... Keys.................1881 ............  "
Olbert, Franz...................   "   ................. ——  ............  "
Opletat, Alois..................   "   ................. ——  ............  "
Pichler, Johann.................   "   ................. ——  ............  "
Prohaska, Franz.................   "   ................. ——  ............  "
Schmidtmayr, Raymund...........   "   ................. ——  ............  "
```

JAPAN

PIANO MANUFACTURERS

```
Nippon Gakki Siezo Kabushiki Kwaisha...........................Hammamatsu
Nishikawa & Son....................................................Yokohama
```

UNITED STATES

PIANO MANUFACTURERS

CALIFORNIA
```
Pacific Piano Mfg. Co.............Established —— ....................Pasadena
Salyer-Baumeister Co.............      "      1907 .................Los Angeles
Behre, J., & Co..................      "           ...............San Francisco
Deitemeier Piano Co..............      "      1892 ...............  "       "
Fay, Robert......................      "      1880 ...............  "       "
Hornung, C. C...................      "      1880 ...............  "       "
Mauzy, Byron....................      "      1884 ...............  "       "
```

CONNECTICUT
```
Sterling Co., The.................Established 1866 ......................Derby
Huntington Piano Co.............      "      1894 ......................Shelton
Wilcox & White Co., The.........      "      1877 ....................Meriden
Mathushek Piano Co..............      "      1866 ..................New Haven
Shoninger, B., Co................      "      1850 .................  "      "
```

ILLINOIS
```
Johnson, Wm. A., Piano Co...,.....Established 1907 ..................Champaign
Bauer, Julius, & Co..............      "      1857 ....................Chicago
Bent, Geo. P., & Co.............      "      1870 ....................  "
Bush & Gerts Piano Co...........      "      1886 ....................  "
Cable Co., The...................      "      1880 ....................  "
Cable-Nelson Piano Co............      "      1903 ....................  "
Chickering Bros..................      "      1892 ....................  "
Clark, Melville, Piano Co.........      "      1900 ....................  "
Conover Piano Co................      "      1890 ....................  "
Concord Co., The................•...      "      1907 ....................  "
Decker Bros. Co..................      "      1907 ....................  "
Detmer, Henry...................      "      1885 ....................  "
Foley & Williams Mfg. Co.........      "      1870 ....................  "
Fuehr & Stemmer Piano Co........      "      1903 ....................  "
Kaiser, Adolph..................      "      1891 ....................  "
Kimball, W. W., Co..............      "      1854 ....................  "
```

King Piano Co.	Established 1903	Chicago
Lyon & Healy	" 1864	"
Marquette Piano Co.	" 1905	"
Maynard, R. K., Piano Co.	" 1905	"
Meyer, Franz.	" 1893	"
Nelson, H. P., Co.	" 1908	"
Newmann Bros. Co.	" 1880	"
Price & Teeple Piano Co.	" 1902	"
Reed & Sons Piano Co.	" 1842	"
Reichardt Piano Co.	"	"
Rothschild & Co.	"	"
Schaaf, Adam.	" 1873	"
Schaeffer Piano Co.	" 1873	"
Scherpe, B., & Co.	"	"
Schulz, M., Co.	" 1869	"
Seeburg, J. P., Piano Co.	" 1907	"
Singer Piano Co.	" 1894	"
Smith, Barnes & Strohber Piano Co.	" 1884	"
Starck, P. A., Piano Co.	"	"
Steger & Sons Piano Mfg. Co.	" 1879	"
Story & Clark Piano Co.	" 1869	"
Straube Piano Co.	" 1878	"
Weber & Sons.	"	"
Werner Piano Co.	" 1902	"
Hamilton Piano Co.	" 1889	Chicago Heights
Seybold Piano & Organ Co.	"	Elgin
Swan, S. N., Co.	" 1907	Freeport
Pizarro Piano Co.	" 1908	Joliet
Schiller Piano Co.	" 1893	Oregon
National Player Piano Co.	"	"
Standard Piano Player Co.	"	
Johnson, E. P., Piano Co.	" 1907	Ottawa
Western Cottage Piano & Organ Co.	" 1865	"
Haddorff Piano Co.	" 1902	Rockford
Nysewander Piano Co.	"	"
Schumann Piano Co.	"	"

INDIANA

Knight-Brinkerhoff Piano Co.	Established 1907	Brazil
Auto Grand Piano Co.	" 1905	Connersville
Packard Co., The	" 1871	Fort Wayne
Schaff Bros. Piano Co.	" 1866	Huntington
Cable, Hobart M., Co.	" 1900	Laporte
Krell-French Piano Co.	" 1898	New Castle
Chute & Butler.	" 1901	Peru
Starr Piano Co.	" 1872	Richmond
Tryber Piano Co.	" 1881	South Bend

IOWA

Bellevue Piano Mfg. Co.	Established 1906	Bellevue

KENTUCKY

Harvard Piano Co.	Established 1885	Dayton

MAINE

Hughes & Son Piano Mfg. Co.	Established 1866	Foxcroft

MARYLAND

Wm. Knabe & Co.	Established 1839	Baltimore
Chas. M. Stieff.	" 1842	"

MASSACHUSETTS

Bourne, Wm., & Son	Established 1846	Boston
Chickering & Sons	" 1823	"

Choralcelo Mfg. Co................Established ──		....................Boston
Emerson Piano Co..................	" 1849	.... "
Everett Piano Co...................	" 1883	.... "
Hallet & Davis Piano Co	" 1835	.... "
Hume Piano Co....................	" 1902	.... "
Ivers & Pond Piano Co............	" 1880	.... "
Jewett Piano Co...................	" 1899	.... "
Kraft, Theo. J., & Co..............	" 1903	.... "
Mason & Hamlin Co	" 1854	.... "
McPhail, A. M., Piano Co..........	" 1837	.... "
Miller, Henry F., & Sons Piano Co...	" 1863	.... "
National Piano Co.................	" 1911	.... "
Poole Piano Co....................	" 1893	.... "
Vose & Sons Piano Co.............	" 1851	....
Ackotist Player Piano Co..........	" 1906	..............Fall River
Cote Piano Mfg. Co...............	" 1890	.... " "
Gilbert Piano Co.................	" 1907	.... " "
Morrisette, Honoré, Co............	" ──	.... "
Trowbridge Piano Co..............	" 1888	..............Franklin
Webster Piano Co.................	" ──	..............Leominster

MICHIGAN

Grinnell Bros.....................Established 1882		.................Detroit
Farrand Co., The..................	" 1884	.... "
Brockmeier Piano Co..............	" 1908	.........Grand Rapids
Manville & Sons..................	" ──	.... " "
Bush & Lane Piano Co............	" 1901	..............Holland
Chase-Hackley Piano Co.	.. 1863	..............Muskegon
Germain Piano Co.................	.. 1895	..............Saginaw
Melin-Winkle Co..................	" 1909	...........South Haven

MINNESOTA

Schimmel & Co....................Established 1892		..............Faribault
Raudenbush, S. W., Co............	" 1883	...........St. Paul
Segerstrom Piano Mfg. Co..........	" 1900	...........Minneapolis
Wick, P. S., Co...................	" 1886	.........North St. Paul

NEW HAMPSHIRE

Prescott Piano Co...............Established 1869	..............Concord

NEW JERSEY

Delabar, Edw.....................Established ──		..............Newark
Lauter Co., The...................	" 1862	.... "
Winkler Piano Co.................	" 1875	..............Trenton
Alleger, H. W.....................	" 1869	..............Washington
Cornish Piano Co.................	" 1876	.... "
Florey Bros.......................	" 1909	.... "

NEW YORK

Boardman & Gray................Established 1837		..............Albany
Wegmann Piano Co...............	" 1882	..............Auburn
Brockport Piano Co...............	" 1893	..............Brockport
Smith, Freeborn G................	" 1848	..............Brooklyn
Wissner, O........................	" 1878	.... "
Chase & Baker Co.................	" 1900	..............Buffalo
Kurtzmann, C., & Co..............	" 1848	.... "
Ahlstrom Piano Co...............	" 1875	..............Jamestown
Aeolian Co., The..................	" 1887	..............New York
Aeolian-Weber Piano & Pianola Co..	" 1903	.... " "
American Piano Co...............	" 1909	.... " "
Amphion Co......................	" 1901	.... " "
Archer Piano Co..................	" 1906	.... " "
Autopiano Co., The..............	" 1903	.... " "

Name	Established	Location
Bacon Piano Co.	Established 1789	New York
Bailey Piano Mfg. Co.	" 1901	" "
Baumeister, H.	" 1894	" "
Bayer Piano Co.	" 1906	" "
Becker Bros.	" 1902	" "
Behning Piano Co.	" 1861	" "
Behr Bros. & Co.	" 1881	" "
Berry-Wood Piano Player Co.	" ———	" "
Biddle Piano Co.	" 1861	" "
Bjur Bros.	" 1887	" "
Boedicker's Sons, J. D.	" ———	" "
Bogart, Edwin B., & Co.	" 1899	" "
Bogart, W. F.	" ———	" "
Bollerman & Son	" 1880	" "
Brambach, Carl, & Son	" 1910	" "
Braumuller Piano Co.	" 1887	" "
Brunner & Co., C. A.	" ———	" "
Byrne, C. E., Piano Co.	" 1862	" "
Cable & Sons	" 1852	" "
Chilton Piano Co.	" ———	" "
Christman Sons	" ———	" "
Collins & Kindler	" 1910	" "
Connor, F.	" 1877	" "
Davenport & Treacy Piano Co.	" 1896	" "
Decker & Sons	" 1856	" "
De Rivas & Harris	" 1905	" "
Dobson, E. S., & Co.	" ———	" "
Doll, Jacob, & Sons	" 1871	" "
Dusinberre & Co.	" 1884	" "
Estey Piano Co.	" 1885	" "
Fischer, J. & C.	" 1845	" "
Frederick Piano Co.	" ———	" "
Furlong, A. B., Piano Co.	" 1910	" "
Gabler, Ernest, & Bro.	" 1854	" "
Greve, G. B.	" 1896	" "
Hardman, Peck & Co.	" 1842	" "
Haines, W. P., & Co.	" 1898	" "
Harrington, E. G., & Co.	" 1886	" "
Hasbrouck Piano Co.	" 1886	" "
Hazelton Bros.	" 1840	" "
Homer Piano Co.	" 1907	" "
Howard, R. S., Co.	" 1902	" "
Jacob Bros.	" 1878	" "
James & Holmstrom	" 1874	" "
Janssen, B. H.	" 1901	" "
Keller, Henry, & Sons	" 1892	" "
Kelso, S. R.	" ———	" "
Kelso & Co.	" 1891	" "
Kindler & Collins	" 1910	" "
Kirchhoff, Lawrence	" 1901	" "
Kohler & Campbell	" 1894	" "
Krakauer Bros.	" 1869	" "
Kranich & Bach	" 1864	" "
Kroeger Piano Co.	" 1852	" "
Laffargue Co., The	" 1896	" "
Lawson & Co.	" 1906	" "
Leckerling Piano Co.	" 1886	" "
Leins, E., Piano Co.	" 1889	" "
Lindeman, Henry & S. G.	" 1836	" "
Lindeman & Sons Piano Co.	" 1887	" "
Lockhardt Piano Co.	" 1892	" "

Name	Established	Year	Location
Lockwood Piano Co	Established	—	New York
Ludwig & Co	"	1889	" "
Macfarlane, John	"	1902	" "
Mansfield Piano Co	"	1906	" "
Marshall & Wendell Piano Co	"	—	" "
Mathushek & Son Piano Co	"	1871	" "
Mehlin, Paul G., & Sons	"	1889	" "
Metzke, O., & Son	"	—	" "
Milton Piano Co	"	1892	" "
Needham Piano Co	"	1846	" "
Newby & Evans	"	1882	" "
Ouvrier Bros	"	—	" "
Palmer Piano Co	"	1906	" "
Pease Piano Co	"	1844	" "
Peerless Piano Player Co	"	1889	" "
Peters, W. F., Co	"	1902	" "
Radle, F	"	1898	" "
Regal Piano & Player Co	"	—	" "
Rehbein Bros	"	—	" "
Ricca & Son	"	1891	" "
Rudolf Piano Co	"	1903	" "
Schencke Piano Co	"	—	" "
Schleicher, Geo., & Sons	"	1878	" "
Schubert Piano Co	"	1882	" "
Sohmer & Co	"	1872	" "
Solingen Piano Co	"	1910	" "
Stadie & Son	"	1899	" "
Steck, Geo., & Co	"	1857	" "
Steinway & Sons	"	1853	" "
Strich & Zeidler	"	1889	" "
Stroud Piano Co	"	1911	" "
Stultz Bros	"	1909	" "
Stultz & Bauer	"	1880	" "
Stultz & Co	"	1905	" "
Sturz Bros	"	1871	" "
Stuyvesant Piano Co	"	1881	" "
Technola Piano Co	"	—	" "
Telelectric Piano Player Co	"	1906	" "
Tonk, Wm., & Bro	"	1881	" "
Universal Piano Co	"	1908	" "
Valois & Williams	"	—	" "
Virgil Practice Clavier Co	"	1889	" "
Walters Piano Co	"	1899	" "
Warde Piano Co	"	1909	" "
Waters, Horace, & Co	"	1845	" "
Weber Piano Co	"	1851	" "
Weser Bros	"	1879	" "
Wheelock Piano Co	"	1877	" "
Wing & Son	"	1867	" "
Winter & Co	"	1900	" "
Wright Piano Co	"	—	" "
Wissner, Otto	"	1886	" "
Wuertz, O. W	"	1893	" "
Wurlitzer Mfg. Co., Rudolph	"	1856	North Tonawanda
Sporer, Carlson & Berry	"	1861	Owego
Armstrong Piano Co	"	—	Rochester
Brewster Piano Co	"	—	"
Cook Piano Co., J. B	"	—	"
Foster & Co	"	—	"
Gibbons & Stone	"	1821	"
Goetzmann & Co	"	1905	"

Haines Bros...............	Established ——	.... Rochester
Haines & Co...............	"	——	...............Milwaukee
Marshall & Wendell Piano Co......	"		.... "
Ropelt & Sons Piano Co...........	"	1901	.... "
Engelhardt, F., & Sons...........	"	1889	...............St. Johnsville
Vough Piano Co...................	"	1861	...............Waterloo
Huebner Piano Co................	"	——	...............Yonkers

OHIO

Baldwin, The, Co................	Established 1862	...............Cincinnati
Butler Bros. Piano Co............	"	1910	.... "
Church Co., The John...........	"	1859	.... "
Ebersole Piano Co.................	"	1910	.... "
Ellington Piano Co................	"	1890	.... "
Harvard Piano Co................	"	1885	.... "
Krell Piano Co., The.............	"	1889	.... "
Valley Gem Piano Co.............	"	1890	.... "
Wurlitzer, Rudolph, Co., The......	"	1856	.... "
Raymond Piano Co...............	"	1856	.... Cleveland
Columbus Piano Co..............	"	1904	...............Columbus
Chase, A. B., Co.................	"	1875	...............Norwalk

PENNSYLVANIA

Lehr, H., & Co..................	Established 1890	...............Easton
Kellmer Piano Co................	"	1883	...............Hazleton
Colby Piano Co..................	"	1859	...............Erie
Blasius & Sons..................	"	1855	...............Philadelphia
Cunningham Piano Co............	"	1891	.... "
Lester Piano Co.................	"	1888	.... "
Oeser Co., Fred, The.............	"	——	.... "
Painter & Ewing................	"	1893	.... "
Schomacker Piano Co............	"	1838	.... "
Bennett Piano Co., W. C..........	"	1900	...............Warren
Kleber, H., & Bro...............	"	1841	...............Pittsburg
Weaver Organ & Piano Co.........	"	1870	...............York
Van Dyke Piano Mfg. Co.........	"	1880	...............Scranton
Keller, Dunham Piano Co.........	"	1909	.... "

WISCONSIN

Conrad Piano Mfg. Co............	Established 1910	...............Milwaukee
Gram-Richtsteig Piano Co.........	"	1908	.... "
Kreiter Piano Co................	"	——	.... "
Waltham Piano Co...............	"	1885	.... "
Netzow, C. F., Mfg. Co..........	"	1885	.... "
Wilson Piano Co................	"	1909	.... "
Miller, S. W., Piano Co..........	"	1896	...............Sheboygan

PIANO SUPPLY MANUFACTURERS

CONNECTICUT

Pratt, Read & Co................	Keys and Actions......	1806	......Deep River
Comstock, Cheney & Co., The......	" " "	——	...............Essex
Universal Music Co..............	Music Rolls...........	1904	.........Meriden
Davenport, John, Co.............	Iron Frames..........	1868	.........Stamford
Blake & Johnson................	Hardware.............	1849	.......Waterbury

ILLINOIS

Gulbransen-Dickinson Co..........	Player Actions.........	1906	..........Chicago
Piano & Organ Supply Co.........	Actions and Keys......	1871	.... "
Schaff, John A.................	Strings...............	1889	.... "
Oregon Foundry & Machine Co.....	Iron Frames...........	1907	..........Oregon
Kurtz Action Co................	Actions...............	1903	.........Rockford

MASSACHUSETTS

Schwamb, Theo., Co.	Piano Cases	——	Arlington
American Felt Co.	Felts	1899	Boston
Faxon, Geo. H., Co.	Hardware	1850	"
Felters Co., The	Felts	1910	"
Frazier, Dan E.	Hammers	1860	Cambridge
Seaverns Piano Action Co.	Actions	1851	"
Standard Action Co.	"	1889	"
Tower, Sylvester, Co.	Keys and Actions	1854	"
Lockey, I. H., Piano Case Co.	Cases	1850	Leominster
Richardson Piano Case Co.	"	1891	"
Smith, F. G.	"	——	"
Wellington Piano Case Co.	"	1895	"
Tuner's Supply Co., The	Tools	1885	Somerville
Simplex Player Action Co.	Player Actions	1883	Worcester

NEW HAMPSHIRE

Parker & Young Co.	Soundboards	1857	Lisbon

NEW JERSEY

Abbott Piano Action Co.	Actions	1858	Fort Lee
American Musical Supply Co.	Supplies	1897	Jersey City
National Music String Co.	Strings	——	New Brunswick
Celluloid Piano Key Co.	Keys	1876	New York
Looschen Piano Case Co.	Cases	1885	Paterson

NEW YORK

Phelps, M. S., Mfg. Co.	"	1891	Brockport
Brown & Patterson	Iron Frames	1861	Brooklyn
Young. F. W. & Co.	Actions	1868	"
Wood & Brooks Co.	Actions and Keys	1901	Buffalo
Cheney, A. C., Piano Action Co.	Actions	1892	Castleton
Davis, I. E., Mfg. Co.	Cases	1903	Cortland
Breckwoldt, Julius, & Co.	Soundboards	1896	Dolgeville
Ramsey, Chas., Co.	Hardware	1897	Kingston
New York Pianoforte Key Co.	Keys	1890	Middletown
Grubb & Kosegarten Bros.	Actions	1837	Nassau
American Union String Co.	Strings	——	New York
Auto-Pneumatic Action Co.	Player Actions		" "
Connorized Music Co.	Music Rolls		" "
Courtade, Jos. N.	Cases	1872	" "
Erlandsen, J.	Tools	1861	" "
Goepel, C. F., & Co.	Hardware	1892	" "
Haas, Henry, & Son	"	1860	" "
House, C. W., & Sons	Felts	1902	" "
Kapp, Robt. L., Co.	Hammers	1910	" "
Koch, Rud. C.	Strings	1858	" "
Mapes, Stephen S.	"		" "
N. Y. Co-operative Piano String Co.	"	1892	" "
New York Piano Hardware Co.	Hardware	1907	" "
Pfriemer, Charles	Hammers	1870	" "
Tingue, Brown & Co.	Felts	1901	" "
Ramacciotti, F.	Strings	1867	" "
Schirmer, Charles	Hardware	1866	" "
Schmidt, David H., & Co.	Hammers	1856	" "
Schwander Action Co.	Actions	1845	" "
Staib-Abendschein Co.	"	1890	" "
Standard Pneumatic Action Co.	Player Actions	——	" "
Strauch Bros.	Actions	1867	" "
Wasle & Co.	"	1876	" "
Wessell, Nickel & Gross	"	1875	" "

Engelhardt, F., & Sons............Actions ....1889 .....St. Johnsville
OHIO
Fairbanks Co., The................Iron Frames...........1890 ....Springfield
Kelley, O. S., Co................... "   "   ....1890 .... "
Wickham Piano Plate Co........... "   "   ....1890 .... "
WISCONSIN
Billings Spring Brass Flange Co....Hardware..............—— ....Milwaukee

CANADA

PIANO MANUFACTURERS

NOVA SCOTIA
Willis Piano & Organ Co.........Established —— ....Stellarton

ONTARIO
Snyder & Co., Wm................Established —— ....Berlin
Dominion Piano & Organ Co......   "   1870 ....Bowmanville
Doherty & Co., W.................   "   1875 ....Clinton
Barclay, Glass & Co..............   "   ——   ....Dundas
Bell Piano & Organ Co............   "   1864 ....Guelph
Morris Piano Co..................   "   1892 ....Listowel
Wormwith & Co...................   "   ——   ....Kingston
William Sons, R. S...............   "   1849 ....London
Williams Piano Co................   "   ——   ....Oshawa
Martin Orme Piano Co............   "   ——   ....Ottawa
Blundall Piano Co................   "   ——   ....Toronto
Consolidated Crossin Piano Co.....   "   1908 .... "
Gourlay, Winter & Leeming.......   "   ——   .... "
Heintzmann & Co.................   "   1850 .... "
Heintzmann Co., Gerhard..........   "   ——   .... "
Mason & Risch Piano Co..........   "   1871 .... "
Mendelssohn Piano Co............   "   1885 .... "
Newcombe Piano Co...............   "   ——   .... "
Nordheimer Piano & Music Co.....   "   ——   .... "
Owen & Son, R. S................   "   ——   .... "
Stanley, Frank...................   "   ——   .... "
Palmer Piano Co..................   "   ——   ....Uxbridge
Uxbridge Piano & Organ Co........   "   ——   .... "
Karn Co., D. W..................   "   ——   ....Woodstock
Thomas Organ & Piano Co., The....   "   1832 .... "

QUEBEC
Craig Piano Co..................Established —— ....Montreal
Laffargue Piano Co., The..........   "   ——   .... "
Pratte, A........................   "   ——   .... "
Shaw & Co., J. W................   "   ——   .... "
Willis & Co......................   "   ——   .... "
Lesage & Fils...................   "   ——   ....St. Therese de Blainsville
Senecal & Quidoz................   "   ——   .... "   "   "   "

PIANO SUPPLY MANUFACTURERS
ONTARIO
Barthelmes & Co., A. A............Actions................—— ....Toronto
Best & Co., D. M................Hammers..............—— .... "
Bohne & Co......................   "   ....—— .... "
Canada Piano Action & Key Co.....Actions and Keys......—— .... "
Coates, A. E....................Strings................—— .... "
Higel Co., Otto..................Actions and Keys......—— .... "
Kerr, A.........................Actions................—— .... "
Loose, Jos. M...................Keys..................—— .... "
Toronto Piano String Mfg. Co......Strings................—— .... "

INDEX

GENERAL INDEX

469

INDEX OF NAMES